God, Honor, Fatherland

A PHOTO HISTORY OF PANZERGRENADIER
DIVISION GROSSDEUTSCHLAND
ON THE EASTERN FRONT 1942-1944

God, Honor, Fatherland
First Published April 1997
by
RZM Imports, Inc.
One Pomperaug Office Park, Suite 102
Southbury, CT 06488 USA
Tel. 203-264-0774
Fax 203-264-4967
e-mail: rzmimport@aol.com
http://www.rzm.com

Book Production Team
Photo Research by Remy Spezzano
Text Research by Thomas McGuirl
Layout and Design by Patrick Stansell
Photo editing by Remy Spezzano and Patrick Stansell
Text edited by Jeffery Hufnagel and Bruce Culver
Cover photo colorized by Vincent Wai, Alpha Image, Inc.

Photograph Credits
Bundesarchiv, Koblenz, ECPA, Traditionsgemeinschaft Panzer-Korps
"GD" und "Brandenburg"-Verbände, Heinrich Gerbener, Diddo S. Diddens,
Joachim Burchardi, Hans-Karl Richter, Hans Röger, Otto-Friedrich Emminghaus,
Franz Thomas and Kurt Schwarz

ISBN 0-9657584-0-0

T A B L E   O F   C O N T E N T S

F O R E W O R D

More than fifty years after the end of the Second World War, a commemorative history is being published in English designed to preserve the legacy of loyalty and courage of our fallen GD comrades who came from every German state and district. I was thus glad to comply with the authors' and publisher's request to assist them in the compilation of the present volume.

Since the American authors expressed to me their wish to produce, with the assistance of still living GD comrades, a faithful picture of our old division's service in Russia, I became convinced that a very good basis for cooperation had been established.

During my 14 years as an officer of the Bundeswehr from 1956-1970, I had frequent opportunity, both on and off-duty, to experience very good relationships with American and British servicemen and women of all ranks. I grew to appreciate their professionalism and great sense of fairness and I cherish the many lasting friendships which were formed during our service together in the NATO alliance.

As a former platoon leader, company commander and battalion commander in Pz.Gren.Rgt. GD, who as a frontline officer was fortunate enough to survive the conflict, I wish this volume the greatest possible readership and success. German-American cooperation in this instance has succeeded in preserving for posterity the memory of the achievements depicted in this book.

The authors' purpose in giving the names and ranks of as many soldiers as possible was above all intended to show their families and comrades that the individuals who had loyally fulfilled their duty in accordance with our motto "God, Honor, Fatherland" will not be forgotten.

Heinrich Gerbener
Oberstleutnant der Bundeswehr a.D.

A C K N O W L E D G E M E N T S

A book such as "God, Honor, Fatherland" is vastly more than the collective efforts of the two named authors. Many dozens of veterans, archivists, collectors, and friends gave unstintingly and ceaselessly of their time, their memories and their resources to help make this work the best possible book on the subject of Grossdeutschland at war in the East. Without the help of any one of them this book would be much the poorer and to all of them listed below the authors offer a heartfelt thanks.

Yet one individual performed services which by their scope, importance, and duration merit a more detailed expression of gratitude. From the moment the authors contacted him in the early summer of 1995 with what they felt were some routine but important questions, Oberstleutnant a.D. Heinrich Gerbener displayed an astounding enthusiasm for our project and an equally amazing capacity to enthuse and inspire everyone around him. This professional soldier, whose career spanned the 100,000-man Reichsheer of 1932 to the Bundeswehr of the 1970s, possessed an awesome fund of personal experience on all of Grossdeutschland's incarnations and readily shared his experiences and knowledge with us. Furthermore, he quickly became our liaison to the rest of the Division's veterans, persuading men who had hardly spoken of their army life to take part in this history. Whether he was poring through his own large collection of photos and documents, phoning his fellow veterans or taking upon himself a host of other tasks, "Hed" Gerbener became the indispensable man in this story. We soon learned the truth of his wartime motto "Mok Wi!" (Machen Wirs = We'll do it!) Thanks to you, Hed, we have done it!

The authors also wish to express their deep appreciation to their longtime collaborator Stephanie Force. Among a host of tasks, Stephanie typed the manuscript and applied her fluency in German to manage the constant flow of correspondence to and from Germany upon which this project was vitally dependent.

Grossdeutschland Veterans
Major i.G.a.D. Helmut Beck-Broichsitter
Major d.BW a.D. Kurt Bensinger
Horst Beskow
Rittmeister a.D. Horst Bethmann
Hauptmann a.D. Joachim Burchardi
Hans Büttner
Hauptmann a.D. Diddo Diddens
Gerhard Dürre
Oberstleutnant d.BW a.D. Ottfried Emminghaus
Oberst d.BW a.D. Peter Frantz
Hauptmann a.D. Harald Fuchs
Oberleutnant a.D. Ernst Günther Haarhaus
Eugen Hartmann
Brigadegeneral d.BW a.D. Karl Hoffmann
Dr. Med. Reinhard Immel
Oberleutnant a.D. Bruno Kliche
Major d.R. a.D. Gerhard Konopka
Ernst Laudahn
Brigadegeneral d.BW Hansgeorg Model
Paul Orth
Helmut Ortlepp
Klaus Putzmann
Eberhard Rahn
Oberleutnant a.D. Hans-Karl Richter
Hauptmann d.BW a.D. Hans Röger
Oberst a.D. Hugo Schimmel
Paul Schmid
Werner Schulze
Karl Schwappacher
Oberleutnant a.D. Kurt Schwarz

Oberleutnant a.D. Wilhelm Seelmann-Eggebert
Major i.G. a.D. Helmuth Spaeter
Fritz Uhlendorf
Oberstleutnant a.D. Eberhard Wackernagel
Brigadegeneral d.BW a.D. Rudolf Wätjen
Anton Weiss
Walter Wiese
Major a.D. Walter von Wietersheim
Oberst a.D. Heinz Wittchow von Brese-Winniary
Prof. Dr. Klaus Wollenweber

Others
Paul Ackerman
LTC. John R. Angolia USA Retired
Roger James Bender
Rhonda L. Bigford
Brigadegeneral d.BW a.D. Eberhard von Block
Magdalena Blümert, Deutsche Dienststelle (WAST)
Michael Dürre, Deutsche Dienststelle (WAST)
Frau Ruth Fabich
Joseph Garabrant
Doris Lenck
Oberst d.BW a.D. Friedrich Müller-Rochholz
Karl Rekkers
Hans-Günther Scholtz and staff of the Berliner Zinnfiguren/Preussisches Bücherkabinett
Major a.D. Konrad Staidl
Oberst d.BW a.D. Rolf Stoves
Richard Warfield, Warfield/Eastern Front Books
Mary Wentzke
Oberfeldwebel (BW) Thomas Westhoff

PANZERGRENADIER DIVISION GROSSDEUTSCHLAND

While conducting research in Europe for another book project, we by chance discovered a long forgotten selection of several hundred rare photographs depicting the Panzergrenadier Division Grossdeutschland on the Eastern Front. The photographs were dated roughly from April 1942 through September 1944. All the shots were taken by the divisional Kriegsberichters (War Correspondents); GD was unique in that it was one of the few divisions to possess its own organic propaganda platoon. This resulted in a much more interesting variety of photos due to the fact that unit Kriegsberichters were "on the spot" to record events as opposed to simply happening by as was so often the case with other units.

Until now most of the photos found had previously gone unnoticed and few had ever been published before. Although over half a century old, we were amazed to learn that almost all of the original negatives remained in storage and in excellent condition. This new find demanded that some type of photo book be produced. Though some of the photographs discovered had been published before, many have been either repeatedly miscaptioned or misidentified.

Several Grossdeutschland pictorial histories already exist in both German and English. These books were for the most part assembled by veterans of the division in the form of yearbooks for their wartime comrades. These depict GD in a very general manner and common to all of them is a minimum of text. In many cases photographs purporting to show GD in action are in fact depicting other units. We were determined to redress these inaccuracies within this volume.

Over one year was spent collecting hundreds of photographs from both official government archives and surviving GD veterans. We then began the lengthy and sometimes arduous selection process. In many cases, it was necessary to eliminate a photo of superb quality when careful research determined it did not portray the Division. This was followed by the slow but necessary task of researching the text. This took another two years to accomplish. Our ultimate goal was to produce a publication on the GD division unlike any other previously attempted.

We realized that to accomplish this properly it would be necessary to obtain the support of the Grossdeutschland Veterans Organization. These men constitute the only living link to the Division's past. Their help would be essential to identify previously unknown individuals along with the exact place and time a photograph was taken. As our research continued we were surprised to learn that many of the soldiers who appear in the photos are indeed still alive. One can imagine the thrill of discovering a surviving veteran, then actually conversing with him and receiving details regarding the events that took place in a particular photo! Most of the surviving veterans that we had the opportunity to work with soon became our constant and enthusiastic supporters.

The scope of this volume was determined by the number of quality photographs which we finally collected. Every attempt has been made to document the Division's various sub-units as thoroughly as possible. The subchapter text sections function as introductions to the photo-essays and in some cases the available photos determined their size. For example, you'll see that Operation "Zitadelle," the greatest clash of armor in history, has a relatively short description. While in no way intending to minimize its crucial significance, we possessed only one suitable photograph whose provenance was beyond doubt and therefore chose to have a brief coverage of this battle rather than relying on suspect or mediocre photographs. From September 1944 onwards, reliable photographs, comparable in quality to those in this volume, do not exist and thus the decision was made to end this volume when Grossdeutschland returned to East Prussia and was enlarged into a Panzerkorps.

It has been our intention from the very start of this project to present the reader with an intimate and up close look at the men and material who made up this great division. We hope that after reading this publication you will come away with a better understanding and appreciation of the men who made up Panzergrenadier Division Grossdeutschland, one of Germany's most celebrated military formations.

Thomas McGuirl & Remy Spezzano
Southbury, Connecticut
March, 1997

Facing page: Oberfeldwebel Georg Guschmann, the veteran commander of a Sd.Kfz. 251 command halftrack during the fighting around Targul Frumos, April-May 1944. He is an experienced NCO who wears the Infanterie-Sturmabzeichen and the Nahkampfspange (Close Combat Clasp) on his reed-green drill blouse.

The German states, especially Prussia, had traditionally maintained guards units varying in size from small detachments, like the Bavarian Hartschiers and electoral Brandenburg's Trabanten Garde, to the later Prussian Gardekorps, which was an army in its own right. In addition to its original role of being the reigning monarch's bodyguard, the Prussian Gardekorps also served as a "Mustertruppe"- the ideal in training and discipline for the whole Prussian (and later) Imperial Army. This role dated back to the reign of King Friedrich Wilhelm I who saw his "dear blue children" of the Potsdam Giant Grenadiers as the school of his army. They drilled incessantly and tested each new evolution of tactics on the parade ground in Potsdam. His son Friedrich II, the Great, replaced this regiment with his own 15. Regiment, whose 1st Battalion, known as the Bataillon Garde, became the model for all future guardsmen.

Prussia's war with Napoleon I in 1806, with the humiliating double defeats at Jena and Auerstadt and the uncontested surrenders of powerful, well-garrisoned fortresses, led Friedrich Wilhelm III to purge his army ruthlessly of all the regiments and officers who had so sadly lacked fighting spirit. These badly needed and long overdue reforms saw the old Fridrician/Prussian army, which Napoleon had destroyed so easily, transformed into a modern force much better suited to the new style of warfare preached by the Prussian reformers Scharnhorst, Gneisenau, Clausewitz and other like-minded soldiers and citizens. The old Guards Regiment disappeared to be replaced by a new Footguards Regiment — an amalgamation of several regiments who had fought honorably in the Winter campaign in East Prussia in 1807 and in the defense of Silesia. A new Mustertruppe, the Normal-Infanterie-Bataillon, was raised and soon attained Guards status. A new army, largely free from the dead hand of the past and motivated for the first time by a deep patriotism, fought in the War of Liberation from 1813 to 1815. Many units which fought bravely in this campaign were admitted to the Gardekorps and others were raised in the following years and decades. Among these was the Gardeschützenbataillon from the new Prussian province of Neuchatel in Switzerland. This battalion influenced the dress of the future Grossdeutschland Regiment.

By 1817 the Prussian Guards had grown into a miniature army within the Army and included all of its own branches and services. Commanded by the very best graduates of the cadet schools, and continuing a personal union to the ruling house, it served as the custodian of Prussia's military past. The great majority of army commanders and members of the General Staff had served in the Guards by the outbreak of the Great War.

Developments in the other German States generally followed broadly similar patterns. The Lutheran North Germans had closely copied the Prussian model since the era of Frederick the Great. The Western and Southern kingdoms later adopted the Prussian system but retained many of their own institutions up until the end of the Empire in 1918. The former Confederation of the Rhine States had been organized in Napoleon's time with their own miniature versions of "la Garde Imperiale" and kept these traditions in the post-unification Federal Army, commanded by the King of Prussia in his capacity as German Emperor.

The Prussian Gardekorps and the other state guards formations went to war in the great "Ausmarsch" of 1914 for four years of unparalleled fighting and sacrifice in every theater of the war. While 1. Garde-Infanterie-Division was greatly responsible for the victory at Tarnopol in 1917, the other Guards units were no less distinguished. The Garde-Füsiliere was heavily engaged on the Somme and the Garde Pioniere undertook daring and effective siege warfare at Verdun. By war's end all Guards units had suffered staggering casualties,

particularly among the pre-war professionals, but kept their morale and cohesion and were welcomed at the Brandenburg Gate as "undefeated heroes" by President Ebert.

The chaos of the immediate post-war period affected the Army as a whole, but in this confusion the various Guards units preserved their unity to a considerable degree. A key provision of the Versailles Peace Treaty which Germany was forced to sign required the demobilization of the wartime Army. Its replacement was to be a 100,000-man Army devoid of any means of aggressive war, a gendarmerie barely sufficient to keep order within the country's shrunken borders, with no tanks or aircraft.

The new Army was unlike any that had gone before it in German history. Its officers committed themselves for 25 years service while the NCOs and other ranks signed on for 12 years. Early release from service was obtainable only in exceptional circumstances as no body of reserves, as in the Krümper System of 1812, was to be allowed. The Krümper System had been a clever way to increase the number of trained cadres by demobilizing older, more experienced men and replacing them with selected trainees. This maintained the limit on the number of troops while training more than the allowable number of men. The demobilized troops formed an effective reserve force that could be brought into service easily. The Army High Command, under Generaloberst Hans von Seeckt, turned these highly unfavorable conditions to its advantage by packing the Army with many more NCOs than would otherwise be normal and by extensive cross-training of all personnel. By these and many other means they created the cadre of an expanded army — though not enough for the enormous expansion begun by Adolf Hitler after he came to power in 1933.

Along with the other regiments and corps of the "Old Army," the Guards were disbanded in 1919. Many individual guardsmen stayed on in the service and their regimental traditions were preserved by the so-called "Traditionsträgerkompanien" (Tradition-keeping companies) in each Reichsheer regiment. In this way continuity with the Old Army was kept by the transitional Reichswehr until the Army could expand to its proper size. One example of how this system worked shows its application in the 100,000 man Army. 1. Kompanie of 9. (Potsdam) Infanterie-Regiment carried the traditions of the former 1. Garde-Regiment zu Fuss, carrying the latter's colors on ceremonial occasions. The soldiers in this company were all six-footers and were constantly reminded of the great historic burden of tradition that they bore.

With the coming to power of Adolf Hitler's Nazi regime, Germany formally renounced the terms of the Treaty of Versailles and began an open plan of rearmament. The Army staff had prepared a plan to enlarge the army itself to some 21 divisions, but these plans were abandoned in the face of Hitler's insistence on an army of almost 50 divisions. Hitler was obsessed by numbers and did not consider or care that the quality of the troops could not possibly be maintained. Further, the German industrial base was not nearly large enough to supply all the vehicles and equipment that would be required. Many officers and men feared the effects of diluting the well-trained divisions of the Reichsheer to serve as cadres for so many new units. Their fears were justified, and many Reichsheer veterans, including many commanding officers, felt that the army of 1939 was considerably inferior to the army of 1935.

It was the usual practice of the German Army to recruit a unit from a specific area of Germany in order to foster unit pride and a sense of common origin. In most communiques and dispatches, the territorial name of each division or regiment was used along with the unit number, i.e., the Württemberg 10. Panzerdivision. In wartime orders or communiques, only the territorial designation was used for security reasons. GD was unique in not having a territorial designation.

Wachregiment and Kommando der Wachtruppe 1919-1934

With the Prussian Gardekorps no longer in existence, the Army Command and the national government were faced with the problem of finding a body of soldiers available for ceremonial duties to represent the honors and traditions of the Army and the Republic. The Wachregiment was formed in the spring of 1921 for ceremonial purposes in the capital. This designation was changed on June 24, 1921 to Kommando der Wachtruppe. The Guard Troop was formed from seven infantry companies, corresponding to the Army's seven infantry divisions, detached from their parent units on three-month rotations. A machine gun company and occasionally a mounted artillery battery rounded out the Guard Troop.

Soldiers of the Guard Troop were deeply conscious of the responsibility with which they were entrusted. Hauptmann Ernst Lang, then a Schütze in 11./13 I.R., which did duty as 5./Wachtruppe, recalled standing guard one evening, in the company classroom, over the old Prussian-German regimental colors which had been deposited there from the Berlin Arsenal (Zeughaus) for the next day's commemoration of the founding of the Empire on January 18, 1871. As he stood guard over the much-worn colors a steady stream of soldiers of all ranks came into the room to gaze awestruck at the relics. The

parade before Field Marshal von Hindenburg was carried out with a conscious attempt to be seen as the Army's best soldiers. Their reward was to be told by the Field Marshal that "This company stands very well." They all realized that he didn't solely refer to their posture. Lang further recalled the dramatic effect the parade had on the spectators: "Soldiers and citizens belonged together!"

Wachtruppe Berlin and Wachregiment Berlin

As of the autumn of 1936, the Wachtruppe Berlin consisted of a Headquarters (Stabs) Company, eight Rifle (Schützen) companies, a Communications Platoon and two Music Corps. The rapid expansion of the Army, together with the evermore pressing demand for ceremonial duties, caused the Commander-in-Chief of the Army, Generaloberst Werner Freiherr von Fritsch, to order every unit in the Army to send their best-drilled soldiers to Berlin for duty with the Wachregiment. In addition, these men were to be above the average height for soldiers. The cadre of the Wachregiment Berlin was composed of the Regimental Headquarters, all company commanders, the Regimental Sergeant-Major (Hauptfeldwebel) and Communications Sergeant. The balance of the Regiment's officers and NCOs rotated yearly on a 50% basis: half in the spring and half in the autumn. The enlisted men were rotated every six months. In addition to the prestige of belonging to the Army's premier representational unit, each soldier bore a gothic "W" on his shoulder straps or shoulder boards and received 1 Groschen (a silver penny) added to his daily pay as Kommandiertengeld (temporary duty pay).

On June 12, 1939, by order of the Commander-in-Chief of the Army, Generaloberst Walter von Brauchitsch, the Wachregiment Berlin changed its name to Infanterieregiment Grossdeutschland, the name it would carry thereafter and pass on to all the units of the future Panzerkorps Grossdeutschland.

Infanterielehrregiment

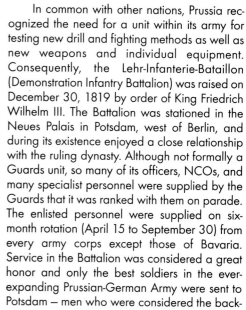

In common with other nations, Prussia recognized the need for a unit within its army for testing new drill and fighting methods as well as new weapons and individual equipment. Consequently, the Lehr-Infanterie-Bataillon (Demonstration Infantry Battalion) was raised on December 30, 1819 by order of King Friedrich Wilhelm III. The Battalion was stationed in the Neues Palais in Potsdam, west of Berlin, and during its existence enjoyed a close relationship with the ruling dynasty. Although not formally a Guards unit, so many of its officers, NCOs, and many specialist personnel were supplied by the Guards that it was ranked with them on parade. The enlisted personnel were supplied on six-month rotation (April 15 to September 30) from every army corps except those of Bavaria. Service in the Battalion was considered a great honor and only the best soldiers in the ever-expanding Prussian-German Army were sent to Potsdam — men who were considered the backbone of their parent regiments and candidates for NCO rank. Throughout its existence, the Lehr-Infanterie-Bataillon fulfilled its mission of setting the standard of training throughout the far-flung corps of the Prussian-German Army.

During the 19th century, the Battalion had been routinely disbanded during general mobilizations in periods of national tension or at the outbreak of war, such as in 1848, 1864, 1866, and 1870. However, in 1914 it was reinforced by two additional battalions of four companies each from the Unteroffizierschule (NCO School) Potsdam and the Infanterie-Schiessschule (School of Musketry) Spandau, and entered service as the Lehr-Infanterie-Regiment. Together with the Garde-Füsilier-Regiment, the Lehr-Infanterie-Regiment formed the 6. Garde-Infanterie-Brigade within the 3. Garde-Infanterie-Division. As a component of this elite division, the Regiment saw continuous service on both the Eastern and Western fronts until the Armistice on November 11, 1918 and won an outstanding reputation as absolutely reliable assault troops, purchased at the cost of the lives of 5,567 officers, NCOs, and men. Through four terrible years of war, the Lehr-Infanterie-Regiment upheld the honor and reputation of its parent battalion and of the Gardekorps. With the demobilization of the war-time army in 1919, the history of this century-old formation came to an end.

The 100,000-man Reichsheer of the Weimar Republic (1918-1933) was an elite "Lehrtruppe" in its own right, and had no need for a specialist demonstration battalion. However, it did establish a "Lehr und Versuchskommando für Infanteriewaffen" (Demonstration and Trial Unit for Infantry Weapons) at Döberitz, south of Berlin. Döberitz, with its 31 square miles of rolling meadows, hills, and woodlands, was an ideal training ground and had been used for training generations of Prussian soldiers, going back to the great maneuvers preceding the Seven Years War. Döberitz was purchased by the German government in 1895 and turned over to the military for its exclusive use. In October 1934, the Lehr und Versuchskommando formed the basis for a new infantry battalion to be stationed in Döberitz. At the same time, the Infanterieschule (Infantry School) Döberitz was established as a training school for infantry officers. The Lehrtruppe (the battalion's unofficial designation) was assigned to the school for instructional purposes and all of the school's units came under the authority of the Infantry Inspectorate in the OKH (Oberkommando des Heeres — Army High Command). As in the previous century, new weapons, tactics, and techniques were tested and evaluated under field conditions. At this time the men of the battalion wore uniforms similar to those of the rest of the infantry except they had no regimental number on their shoulder straps. This led to mocking accusations that they were a "sham unit" because they did not have a regimental number. With universal conscription in 1935, the Battalion received a Gothic "L" on its shoulder straps.

The Battalion was renamed the Infanterie-Lehrbataillon and simultaneously stopped enlisting recruits, instead drawing its manpower from specially selected infantrymen who had completed their initial service and had enlisted for longer periods of time than the normal conscripts. The OKH published special manuals for the Battalion, and potential candidates had to be at least 5'8" tall, have no arrest record, and have a good level of general education. The Battalion also furnished the cadre, NCOs, several machine gun battalions, and various other units for the new Infanterieschule at Potsdam. In October 1936, the five-company Battalion (one MG, one infantry gun, and three rifle companies) was joined by a second battalion. This fully motorized battalion consisted of a headquarters company and four line companies — 6.(PzJäger), 7.(2cm Fla), 8.(MG), and 9.(IG, with an integral mounted infantry platoon).

One year later, a regimental headquarters and a third battalion were added to what then became the Infanterielehrregiment. The former II Bataillon (mot.) was renumbered as III/I.L.R., and the new II/I.L.R. was motorized to train the so-called "Schnelle Truppen" (Fast Troops, the progenitors of the future Panzergrenadiers). RHQ and three companies were quartered in the Olympic Village built for the 1936 Berlin Games. These picturesque quarters immediately gave the site its reputation as "the most beautiful barracks in the world." The bulk of the Regiment was housed in various outbuildings and local farms, etc. When not cleaning their weapons and equipment, the soldiers enjoyed the various sports facilities, including the heated Olympic indoor swimming pool. All these specially selected soldiers had the unusual privilege of bunking two to a room in considerable comfort.

During the years of rapid army expansion and modernization (1935-1939), the Regiment and the Infantry School were commanded by the one-armed Great War veteran Oberst Hans-Valentin Hube, an outstanding soldier and a demanding superior who required the utmost from himself and his subordinates.

Hube was a superb tactician who wrote the standard training manual, "Der Infanterist" (The Infantryman). At this time, the Regiment was continually engaged in trying out Oberst Hube's latest tactical innovations, as well as those of other theoreticians such as Heinz Guderian and Hermann Hoth. When not involved in preparations for mobile combined-arms operations, the Regiment put on displays for visiting German and foreign military delegations and members of the German government, as well as representatives of the Nazi Party and its various organizations.

The outbreak of war on September 1, 1939 found the Regiment in the middle of its normal training cycle. The I.L.R. was rapidly reorganized for wartime requirements. Oberstleutnant Eugen Garski, a tough and popular East Prussian from Posen, took over I/I.L.R., II/I.L.R. was commanded by another East Prussian, Major Klaus Müller-Bulow, and III/I.L.R. was the responsibility of Oberstleutnant "Onkel" ("Uncle") Otto Köhler. Much to its chagrin, the Regiment saw no action in Poland, but Oberst Hube saw to it that a special detachment — Sturmbataillon (Assault Battalion) Garski — was raised from RHQ, 1., 3., and 4. Companies, as well as a company from an independent Sturmpionier (Assault Engineer) Battalion, and sent at once to the Saarbrücken sector of the Western Front where it remained from September 1 to October 10, 1939. With little actual fighting taking place, the Battalion continued its regimen of training. The Regiment itself supplied instructors and specialists for the newly raised I.R.(mot.) Grossdeutschland, whose previous role as Wachregiment Berlin had been confined to largely ceremonial duties. After its service on the Western Front, the Infanterie-Sturm-Lehrbataillon was recalled to Döberitz. Immediately upon returning to the Olympic Village, Oberstleutnant Garski was told that his battalion was to join I.R.(mot.) GD as its II Bataillon, effective October 1, 1939. Very soon after this, the I.L.R. provided nearly all the manpower for IV(Schwere — Heavy)/I.R. GD as well. Each soldier of the new I.R.(mot.) GD was issued a white (actually very light gray) cloth strip to be worn over the base of each shoulder strap/board as a sign of his membership in the German Army's premier infantry regiment.

During the rest of the Second World War, the Infanterielehrregiment continued to perform its mission of testing tactics and equipment, and giving potential officers their first opportunity to command troops during exercises. It went briefly into active service during the German counterattack at Anzio in February 1944, but its close association with Grossdeutschland ended when it turned over half its manpower to the regiment in October 1939, and its wartime record is not important to our story. However, it is impossible to overestimate the contribution of the Infanterielehrregiment to the wartime achievements of the Grossdeutschland Division, for those achievements would not have been possible without the presence of hundreds of officers, NCOs, and enlisted men who had learned and refined their skills on the training grounds at Döberitz.

Infanterieregiment Grossdeutschland
June 1939-June 1940

When the Heeres-Verordnungsblatt (Army Order of the Day) of July 1, 1939 ordered, effective June 12, that the Wachregiment Berlin was to be known as Infanterieregiment Grossdeutschland, a new era in German military history began. The very name Grossdeutschland (Greater Germany) implied that for the first time a guards regiment would be made up of soldiers from all over Germany, rather than from one region only.

The newly-raised I.R. Grossdeutschland took no part in the Polish Campaign of September 1939. Leaving 100 men behind in the historic Rathenowerstrasse Kaserne to form the Wachkompanie Berlin, I.R. GD entrained for the troop training grounds at Grafenwöhr, Bavaria. At Grafenwöhr, under Oberstleutnant Wilhelm-Hunert von Stockhausen, Grossdeutschland trained as a fully motorized infantry regiment — which at this time was rare in the German Army — prior to their transfer to the Western Front on November 6, 1939. During this month, Infanterie-Ersatz Bataillon (mot.) 99 was organized in Brandenburg. From January 1940, it formed the first replacement and training battalion for Grossdeutschland. Meanwhile, in October 1939, nearly half the strength of the Infanterie-Lehrregiment from the Infantry School at Döberitz, some 1,000 men, had been transferred to I.R. Grossdeutschland. While I.R. GD took no part in the Polish campaign, a contingent taken from the unit helped form the Führerbegleitkommando, later Führerbegleitbataillon (FBB) to accompany Adolf Hitler's headquarters in the field. An airlanding mission for I.R. GD had been planned by the OKH but the speed of the army's advance on the ground and the Regiment's incomplete training cancelled this mission.

Toward the end of its training period at Grafenwöhr on October 25, 1939, the Regiment adopted the formation sign it would carry on every front for the rest of the war — the white Stahlhelm (steel helmet). On November 11, 1939, I.R. Grossdeutschland was assigned to General Heinz Guderian's XIX Armeekorps in the Westerwald area. Four days later Sturmpionierbataillon 43 was attached to the Regiment, giving a total strength of over 4,000 men.

At the end of January 1940, I.R. GD was stationed in the area around Montabaur in the Central Mosel region of the Rhineland with the Regimental Headquarters located in Zell. On April 4, six Sturmgeschütz IIIs of the newly-raised independent Sturmgeschütz-Batterie 640 were assigned to the Regiment. Devised by then-Colonel Erich von Manstein to fulfill and expand the role of the First World War infantry-escort batteries, the Sturmgeschütz later was withdrawn from its original function as an infantry support weapon to take on what had been thought to be the secondary role of tank destroyer. In this role it achieved tremendous success, and Grossdeutschland soldiers were among the most successful crews.

On May 10, 1940, I.R. Grossdeutschland, with artillery and engineers of the Württemberg 10. Panzerdivision in support, moved through Luxembourg into the Belgian Ardennes as part of General von Manstein's offensive. Simultaneously, some 400 men of Oberstleutnant Eugen Garski's III/I.R. GD took off in Fieseler Storch aircraft from Bitburg and Deckendorf airfields to be airlanded at Nives and Witry. After some preliminary skirmishes, the main body of the Regiment, under Oberstleutnant Gerhard Graf von Schwerin, crossed the Meuse at Sedan on May 13. At this point the Regiment came temporarily under command of the Thuringian 1. Panzerdivision. Following some hesitant French tank attacks at Chemery and Bulson, the Regiment had a very rough time contesting a large-scale attack of the 3. Division Cuirassé and the 3. Division Legere Mechanique at Stonne from May 15-17. At the end of the first day's fighting the situation was critical. Grossdeutschland had to abandon Stonne. The French, however, failed to press their advantage and the Germans quickly recaptured Stonne.

Oberleutnant Helmut Beck-Broichsitter's 14.(Pz. Jäger)/I.R. GD held off a large-scale attack of the 3. Division Legere Mechanique and destroyed 83 of their tanks, a feat which earned Beck-Broichsitter the Ritterkreuz (Knight's Cross) on September 4, 1940. Oberfeldwebel Hans Hindelang of the same company also earned the Ritterkreuz for his platoon's destruction of 57 enemy tanks.

After a two-day lull, I.R. GD drove towards St. Omer, being engaged with the BEF (British Expeditionary Force) at Arras between May 22-23. The successful evacuation of the BEF from Dunkirk has been ascribed to Hermann Göring's boasting that the Luftwaffe alone was capable of securing the victory, the boggy condition of the ground, as well as the exhaustion of the Panzer spearheads.

On June 4, I.R. Grossdeutschland was moved to the German bridgehead at Amiens on the Somme opposite the Weygand Line. This line was a very skillfully organized checkerboard defensive system built around fortified villages with strong, mutually supporting artillery positions. Its fatal flaw, however, was the absence of a mobile armored reserve. Any German breakthrough would lead to a collapse of the whole line.

The German attack began on June 5, and after some initially severe fighting in which the French fought very well, the Weygand Line was breached the following day. In what became a triumphal procession, GD reached Lyons, the second city of France, on June 19.

The French Campaign had been a brilliant vindication of the Regiment's training, leadership and equipment. Although by not yet the "Lifeguards Regiment of the German People" that German propaganda and its own record would make it, Grossdeutschland was an elite motorized infantry regiment in an army which had all too few of these.

Infanterieregiment Grossdeutschland
June 1940 - June 1941

The fall of France and the end of the western campaign in 1940 seemed a tremendous vindication of the risky Blitzkrieg concept and Adolf Hitler's leadership. Only a few perceptive observers within Germany saw the danger inherent in leaving the British Empire still in the war while the Führer's attention was inexorably drawn to the east. Fewer still saw that the Wehrmacht was structured for short, intense campaigns and not for a struggle likely to last for years with demands on Germany far beyond her means. With Germany unable to cross the Channel and eliminate her last rival in western Europe, continuation of hostilities would inevitably mean war on a global scale.

During the remainder of 1940, Grossdeutschland underwent several reorganizations which brought it up to brigade strength. The 17.-20. Kompanien (Kradschützen, Pionier, Nachrichten and Fla) were formed within the new V/GD and the Regimental Transport Officer (Nachschubführer 400) commanded four transport Kolonnen and a vehicle repair platoon (Kfz. Werkstattzug). The most significant addition to the Regiment was Artillerieabteilung 400 with its three motorized batteries of leichte Feldhaubitze 18 10.5cm howitzers, which joined the Regiment on September 5, 1940. Back home, Infanterie-Ersatzbattalion 99 became Infanterie-Ersatzregiment (mot.) Grossdeutschland.

During the summer in Alsace the Regiment's elite status had been recognized on August 24 by issuing green cuff titles bearing the regimental title in gothic script. This was soon altered on October 7 to a black woven cuff title with somewhat different lettering. The cuff title was to become the distinguishing mark of elite formations. Cuff titles of various patterns would be awarded to a number of units in the course of the Second World War, but in strictly limited numbers, and they retained their elite status.

Grossdeutschland spent the first three months of 1941 resting and reorganizing in the Belfort area. A second logistics battalion was added to the Regiment at this time. The quiet was broken abruptly when anti-German officers of the Yugoslav Army overthrew the Regent Prince Paul, whose government had just signed an alliance with the Axis Powers. With Italy facing defeat in Greece, Adolf Hitler decided to end this threat to the southern flank of the future Eastern Front. Units earmarked for the invasion of the Soviet Union were hastily redeployed to overwhelm the ill-prepared Yugoslav Army as well. The campaign which followed against the hastily-mobilized enemy had relatively little serious fighting.

The Regiment entrained for Vienna on April 5, reaching the Austrian capital five days later. From Vienna it proceeded to Arad and Temesvar, where it formed part of Generalleutnant Georg-Hans Reinhardt's XXXXI Armeekorps (mot.). From Temesvar Grossdeutschland crossed the Yugoslav frontier, pursuing the retreating enemy as far as Pancevo on the Danube. I/GD took part in the occupation of Belgrade, heavily bombed on the opening day of hostilities in the aptly named Operation "Punishment". In Belgrade, Oberleutnant Maximillian Fabich of 3./GD and his men captured Radio Belgrade and reopened it as "Soldatensender Belgrad". While in command of the Division's Panzerfüsilierregiment GD, Oberstleutnant Fabich earned one of Grossdeutschland's last Ritterkreuze on May 8, 1945.

After a month spent on occupation duty, Grossdeutschland moved by rail via Budapest and Pressburg (Bratislava) to Freudenstadt-Troppau in Upper Silesia on May 17. By mid-June the Regiment was near Zelechow, southeast of Warsaw, as part of the reserve of General Heinz Guderian's Panzergruppe 2. Here the Regiment waited for what turned out to be the largest offensive of the war: Barbarossa, the invasion of Soviet Russia.

In the two years since the Regiment was raised on June 12, 1939, Grossdeutschland had evolved into a powerful brigade containing all the various elements needed to function as an independent unit available for a variety of tasks. Two years of active service, especially the French Campaign with its hard fighting and 1,108 casualties, had welded men detached from their parent regiments into a battle-tested brigade, conscious of their elite status and proud of the reputation they were building with the Army and the public. Well-armed and commanded by proven leaders and veteran NCOs, Grossdeutschland was ready for the next campaign.

Infanterieregiment (mot.)
Grossdeutschland June - December 1941

On June 21, 1941, a year after the French surrender at Compeigne, an order of the day was read out to the "Soldiers of the Eastern Front." The 3 1/2 million German soldiers who had been gathering on the Reich's eastern boundaries now learned the purpose of their deployment in the east. The assembled troops heard their commanders tell them that 160 Soviet divisions were gathered on the German and allied frontiers and that for months Soviet patrols had violated German territory. This could only mean preparations for a Russian invasion of Germany at a time when she was engaged in a war on several fronts with Great Britain. The Führer resolved with his allies to wage war on the Soviet Union, the world enemy, to preserve European civilization and culture and to create the necessary conditions for a final end to the war. The address concluded with a prayer that "the Almighty help us all in this struggle." The soldiers listened in stunned silence and then began their last minute preparations for the next morning's fighting.

Early on the morning of June 22, 1941, Artillerieabteilung 400, IV (Heavy)/I.R.(mot.) GD and 16.(StuG) Kompanie advanced across the Bug River at Janow, Poland, in support of the Thüringian 7. Pz.Div. The bulk of I.R.(mot.) GD advanced across the Soviet frontier six days later on June 28, 1941, north of the fortress of Brest-Litovsk (taken by Stu.Pi.Btl. 43 in September, 1939 and handed over to the Soviets as part of the Hitler-Stalin Pact). GD reached Minsk, the capital of White Russia (present day Belarus), on July 6 after taking an important part in containing the break-out attempt of Soviet units surrounded to the west of the city. From July 7-10, GD advanced over the Berezina River, against stubborn but uncoordinated Soviet resistance, to reach the Dnieper River. During this important phase of the early battles, GD came under the operational command of the Württemberg 10. Pz.Div. During this time, the men of GD got a foretaste of the inhuman brutality of the war to come on the Eastern Front. Oberleutnant "Maxe" Fabich, Kompaniechef of 3./I.R.(mot.) GD recorded how a sudden Soviet counterattack overran his lines in early July. When the positions were retaken a short time later, he found five of his men, including his Kompanietruppführer, mutilated and murdered. "Everyone now knew," he wrote, "what it meant to fall into Russian hands."

Between July 11-16, 1941, the heavily-reinforced Regiment attacked across the Dnieper — 18.(Pionier) Kompanie and the K-Bridge columns were especially important and fought against desperate Soviet resistance to consolidate the bridgehead and push on to the east. Again seeing wounded comrades brutally killed by the Soviets, the advancing grenadiers took no prisoners. From July 16-20, the Regiment, in XXXXVI Pz.Korps reserve, advanced as far as Mstislavl near Yelnya. The Regiment's main task at this time was to keep open 10. Pz.Div.'s main route of advance while simultaneously holding and securing the main Smolensk-Roslavl highway. The desperate fighting of the next two weeks saw the entire Regiment engaged against masses of enemy troops, with terrible losses on both sides before the enemy withdrew, leaving the hotly-contested crossing of Vaskovo in GD's hands. Oberleutnant Karl Hänert of 4./I.R.(mot.) GD was awarded the Ritterkreuz on August 23, 1941 for his exemplary courage and skill in holding off strong enemy pressure on the Regiment's flank at Yelnya between July 21-26. On August 6, 1941, GD was relieved by Generalmajor Walter Behschnitt's Main-Franconian 15. Infantriedivision, hastily transferred from occupation duty in La Rochelle, France.

After resting for a few days in the Dankovo-Vaskovo area, GD was back in the line west of Yelnya on August 9, where it remained until relieved by the Palatine-Bavarian I.R. 463 (263. I.D.) on the 18th. On August 10, Oberst Wilhelm-Hunold von Stockhausen turned over command of the Regiment to Oberst Walther Hoernlein, who began a two and a half year association with GD.

On September 1, I.R.(mot.) GD left the Yelnya area, moving south to take part in the greatest encirclement battle in history at Kiev, capital of the Ukraine. Its "Mot. Marsch" took it south by way of Roslavl, Lukaviza and Starodub, crossing the Desna at Novgorod-Seversk and securing a bridgehead. From September 5-8, GD moved toward Glukhov to secure the highway which was the main supply road to the east. Initially there was very little contact with the enemy and reconnaissance patrols were largely unopposed. Between September 9-13, GD attacked across the Seym River at Putivl, led by a Kampfgruppe (Battlegroup) commanded by Oberstleutnant Bandelow of IV/I.R.(mot.) GD. On September 14, GD moved to cut the Kiev-Kursk-Moscow railroad line and then turned west to roll up Soviet positions west of the Seym. The attacks continued through the 15th, taking Shilkova. On September 16, GD reached its final objective, Konotop, notable for having electric lights. On September 20, the Regiment attacked Belpoye against very stubborn resistance, reaching the Klimovka rail yards on the 22nd. Everything now depended on holding the line along the small Viry River east of Romny against repeated heavy Soviet counterattacks. The Regiment remained there until October 3.

Between October 4-10, GD moved to the area around Roslavl. The Regiment was not involved in the opening engagements of the great double encirclement battles of Vyazma and Bryansk, but on October 11, went to Karachev to bivouac north of the city. GD was then drawn into bitter fighting in the woods north of Karachev against Soviet troops attempting to escape the large pocket in which they were trapped. Both sides fought ferociously and GD's losses were very high. GD spent the period between October 17-21 resting and refitting in Orel.

On October 22-23, the Regiment moved to its new assembly area northeast of Mtsensk through thick autumn mud which slowed its travel to a crawl. GD's mission was to take a series of heights outside the town which had stalled the German advance. With the Berlin-Brandenburg 3. Pz.Div. and good air support from Stukas, GD advanced between the railroad lines and the main road against the well-fortified northeastern heights, which the Regiment took quickly in close combat. On October 29, GD advanced as far as Tula, fighting numerous engagements along the way. The entire month of November 1941 saw steadily worsening conditions for the fighting around Tula and Yefremov. On November 3, I/I.R.(mot.) GD reported only eight officers, 56 NCOs and 303 men fit for duty. Other battalions were in little better shape. November passed with a series of small engagements, worsening cold and generally miserable conditions.

On December 1, GD took part in 2. Pz.Armee's renewed attempt to capture Tula from the north and envelope its defenses to the east. At this time, during the assault on Ryazan and Kashira, 17.(Kradschtz.)/I.R.(mot.) GD suffered its "Black Day" when Soviet troops infiltrated its inadequately guarded bivouac and wiped out nearly the entire company. Oberst Hoernlein was compelled to take the drastic step of stripping the company of its cherished cuff-titles until it could redeem itself. By December 6, the record cold had stopped the insufficiently clothed and supplied German troops in their tracks. The next day General Zhukov threw dozens of fresh, winter-hardened Siberian divisions at the exhausted, frozen Germans on the Moscow Front — throwing them back and precipitating panic at the front and a crisis at Führer HQ. Hitler's insistence that retreat would quickly turn to rout and that holding out in place was the only viable course of action proved correct and the Eastern Front held.

Until the end of February 1942, GD engaged in battling both the Soviet offensives and the effects of the worst winter in living memory. The Regiment fought off a series of attacks to the north of Orel in the vicinity of Bolkhov where it remained until the end of the year, fighting on the Oka River and north of Bolkhov. By this point Hoernlein's crack Regiment had been split up among three other German infantry divisions. One bright spot in this catalogue of disasters (and disasters barely averted) was the brilliant counterattack by 17.(Kradschtz.) Kompanie on December 27, which drove the Soviets back across the Oka River and regained for the company its right to wear the regimental cuff-title.

GD's casualties as of January 6, 1942 (i.e. from the start of the Invasion of the Soviet Union) were: Officers: killed in action, 36; wounded, 89; missing, 0. NCOs: killed in action, 129; wounded 377; missing, 4. Enlisted Men: killed in action, 735; wounded 2,590; missing 110. This total of 4,070 casualties was more than the full strength of the heavily reinforced Regiment on June 22, 1941. A brilliant reputation had been won at a terrible cost in lives.

Between New Year's Day 1942 and January 19, GD was in action in a series of "Igel" (Hedgehog) positions on the Oka River between Orel and Belev. The end of January 1942 found the remains of the Regiment resisting continuous enemy breakthrough attempts and chasing partisans in the forests near Gorodok. On February 1, 1942, II/I.R.(mot.) GD was disbanded and its few remaining personnel dispersed as reinforcements among the other battalions. Between February 10-18, GD fought a series of costly engagements to clear the Bolkhov-Yagodnaya railway. These losses forced Oberst Hoernlein to combine I and III/I.R.(mot.) GD into one weak battalion. Bataillon GD was nevertheless still considered capable of remaining in the over-extended German lines and was ordered to retake Kosovka and Chuchlovo on February 20. The attack succeeded and after the new positions were consolidated, GD was withdrawn to rebuild the two disbanded battalions.

1942

DIVISIONAL HQ

The divisional commander presided over the entire division, assisted closely by his adjutant. The divisional commander's chief partner was his Ia, the Chief-of-Operations, who was a trained general staff officer. The Ia was responsible for advising the divisional commander and for translating the commander's orders into workable military plans. In this he was assisted by his chief aide, the O1. The Ib, the II Generalstabsoffizier, was responsible for all matters relating to supply and administration in the Division. This officer was assisted by the O2. This vital component of Divisional HQ directed the commander of the light columns and Divisional supply trains, the Provost Marshall and his Feldgendarmerietrupp (Military Police), and the Divisional Feldpost detachment, as well as being responsible for dealing with supplies for the Divisional engineers and communications. Intelligence work, both the obtaining and debriefing of POWs as well as radio intercept work, was under the jurisdiction of the Ic assisted by his O3. The Id was responsible for overseeing training within the Division, especially in the Field Training Battalion GD.

The IIa, the Adjutant, handled day-to-day administrative tasks. The IIIa was chief of the Feldjustizamt GD, the legal branch of Divisional HQ, and was responsible for courts-martial, civilian property, rights of enemy civilians, and other legal matters. The vitally important areas of supplies, clothing, pay, medical and dental care of the Division was the responsibility of the IVa who headed the Intendantur. The soldier's spiritual needs were tended to by the Va, the chief chaplain. In GD's case, the soldiers did not have permanently assigned chaplains, but were provided with such services on an as-needed basis by Corps level support. Extremely competent officers were appointed to supervise matters of motor vehicles, spare parts, fuel, clothing, weapons and equipment. Finally, the War Correspondent's Platoon was responsible for recruitment literature and propaganda.

In the field, this large HQ staff was divided into two working groups. The Tactical Group (Führungsabteilung) was composed of the Ia and Ic. This Tactical Group also included the Artillery Regimental Commander who functioned as Artillerieführer GD and advised the Divisional Commander and Ia on artillery matters and the Engineer Battalion Commander (Pionierführer GD) and the Signals Battalion Commander (Nachrichtenführer GD), who acted in the same manner as did the commander of Pz. Jäger-Abt. GD who oversaw all anti-tank elements in the Division. The final member of the tactical group was the officer in technical charge of the divisional motor transport.

The Supply Group (Quartiermeister-Abteilung) was the other, equally important, working group. This was composed of the Ib's department carrying out the roles outlined above plus the entire IVa's department.

Inevitably, in any division there is always some tension between staff and line units, with the troops often feeling that HQ is either unaware of their situation or indifferent to it when issuing orders. GD was especially fortunate since, when it was raised in 1942 nearly from scratch, it was able to select many officers with prior front line combat experience to fill staff billets. This was further reinforced by a continuing policy of regular transfers between HQ and the combat elements of the Division. GD's initial organization presented the Divisional Staff with the huge problem of coordinating and managing units, largely made up of inexperienced personnel who had never previously served together, under officers who were strangers to them. Nevertheless, the Division performed very creditably during the summer fighting and by the end of the Rzhev fighting had begun to settle down to a well-ordered routine. By 1943, GD's staff was successfully coping with one crisis after another as the Division was suddenly shifted from one disaster to the next without pause.

Left: Der Kompanieschreiber (Company clerk) attempted to deal with an inescapable part of military life, der Papierkrieg (Paper war), which threatened to sink many commanders. Divisional HQ consisted of 32 officers and 143 NCOs and men handling all the administrative and communications duties of the 18,000 man division which included enough men, heavy weapons, and vehicles to make two normal divisions. In addition, there was an eight-man map reproduction section and a fully mechanized 219-man Stabsquartier (HQ Company) to guard Divisional HQ. When reorganized as an SPW-equipped Begleit (escort) Kompanie, however, it often formed part of one of the Panzerkampfgruppen (armored battlegroups).

Below right: Lt. Siegfried Otto, the young platoon commander of 1. Zug (1st Platoon) of 3./Kradschtz.Btl. GD, plays a round of skat with Lt. Christian Thurau (center) and an NCO. German officers and men were no longer divided by rigid barriers of caste and education. The First World War had seen the beginnings of a closer relationship between officers and men and the Reichsheer, though still commanded predominantly by people of the titled and propertied classes, made a continuing effort to bring all ranks closer together. In the egalitarian-minded Third Reich, the mass army raised since 1935 was more than ever led by men who represented the same broad spectrum as German society itself. Officers, especially company and platoon commanders, lived among their soldiers, ate with them and shared all their privations. By 1942, these dedicated frontline junior officers where known to the troops as "Landser mit Schulterstücke" (ordinary soldiers with shoulder boards).

Facing page: Generalmajor Walter Hoernlein (right) presents several of his subordinate officers to Generaloberst Hermann Hoth at the camp at Faetsch, June 1942. At the left is Major Kurt Gehrke of I/I.R.(mot.) GD. To Gehrke's right is Hauptmann Otto-Ernst Remer, of IV/I.R.(mot.) GD 1. Partially visible to Remer's left is Oberleutnant Rene de L'homme de Courbiere of 7./I.R.(mot.) GD 1. Olt. de Courbiere was a descendant of a famous general from the War of 1806, who refused to surrender his garrison fortress to Napoleon's forces and was later honored with the title "King of Graudenz."

Generalmajor Walter Hoernlein

Generalmajor Walter "Papa" Hoernlein was the Division's first commander, assuming command of I.R.(mot.) GD from Oberst Wilhelm-Hunold von Stockhausen on August 10, 1941. He was a North German born on January 2, 1893 in Blüthen, East Prussia, and was appointed a Fähnrich on January 27, 1912 after attending the Hauptkadettenanstalt as a cadet. He was appointed a Leutnant in the 4. West Prussian Infanterie Regiment Nr. 140 on June 16, 1913. A First World War veteran taken over into the postwar Reichsheer, Major Hoernlein took command of the first battalion of the Hamburg I.R. 69 on April 1,1936, and was promoted to Oberstleutnant one year later. While commanding I.R. 80 of the Württemberg 34. Infanteriedivision, Hoernlein was awarded the Ritterkreuz on July 30, 1941. Generalmajor Hoernlein led GD as a motorized regiment, then from April 1942 as a motorized division, and then later, Panzergrenadier division. In recognition of Grossdeutschland's crucial role in the defensive battles around Kharkov in February 1943, Generalleutnant Hoernlein became the 213th soldier of the Wehrmacht to be awarded the Eichenlaub (Oakleaves) on March 15, 1943. On January 27, 1944, Hoernlein handed over command of GD to Generalleutnant Hasso von Manteuffel and received a simultaneous promotion to General der Infanterie. As can be seen in this and other photographs, General Hoernlein established the custom of GD's commanders wearing the GD cyphers on the general's pattern shoulderboards.

Walter Hoernlein was the type of fighting general who would stand out in any army. Helmuth Spaeter remembers him as a "gaunt North German who could judge by the crook of his finger whether someone was special or whether nothing was possible with him." The

well-bred Ia Cord von Hobe marvelled at the General's rough-hewn manner but had a very good working relationship with him and a large degree of mutual affection. General Hoernlein was devoted to GD and Major Heinrich Gerbener rememberd vividly the General telling him in the rawest manner possible that he bitterly resented his division having to stumble from one crisis to another during the Rhzev fighting. One rumor current in GD at the time attributed General Hoernlein's dismissal in January 1944 to an angry telex he sent to the Führerhauptquartier, which demanded to know whether GD were the only Germans left on the Eastern Front.

Left: The unit armorer cleans small arms in front of the 1st Platoon commander's tent of 2./Kradschtz.Btl. GD. All German small arms made use of the standard Model 1934 weapons cleaning kit which contained a pull-through chain, bore brush, oiling brush, oil-can, and a cleaning implement for the receiver, as well as a number of cleaning patches. The sign on the cut sapling indicates the platoon commander, 1st Platoon, 3rd Company, of the motorcycle (Kradschützen) battalion, along with the Divisional white helmet.

Right: While the co-driver of a Sd.Kfz. 10 one-ton light prime mover of 5.(Pz. Jäger)/Kradschtz.Btl. GD does some paperwork, a crewmate repairs an ammunition box for their PaK 38's Pz.Gr. 39 anti-tank rounds. 5. Schwadron's 5cm PaKs gave the Kradschützen sufficient anti-tank fire-power to extricate themselves quickly from any enemy heavy armored cars or even tanks the armored car or SPW patrols might meet.

Kradschützen relax by their mounts during a pause in the preparations for Fall Blau. Although designated as a motorcycle rifle battalion, only two companies (3. and 4.) were even partially equipped with motorcycles and sidecars — the remainder of these companies rode in light VW Kübelwagens.

L O G I S T I C S

Grossdeutschland was a community of some 20,000 officers and men who required food, fuel, clothing, shelter, medical and dental care, law and order much the same as a normal civilian community. The German Army made strenuous efforts to keep the administrative "tail" of each fighting division as low as possible a proportion to the combat "teeth" as efficiency demanded – 40% "tail" to 60% "teeth" in GD's case. Moreover, all the rear echelon personnel were trained soldiers and when the need arose, such as at Rzhev, on the Dnieper and in Romania, were ruthlessly "combed out" to fill gaps in the combat units. Grossdeutschland's support personnel were therefore no "Etappenhengste" ("Base Stallions" or "Garrisontroopers") but their primary mission remained the smooth functioning of the Division at all levels and at all times.

Grossdeutschland received its supplies from Germany via the existing Russian railroad network. From Germany, supplies went to large army railheads such as Smolensk, Orel and Kharkov where they were picked up by army supply columns for transportation to army supply dumps and parks. GD's organic supply columns received rations, fuel, ammunition and clothing at the army-level supply dumps while equipment was accepted at the army-level parks. The divisional supply columns then trucked the rations, fuel, ammunition, clothing and the like to the Ausgabestelle (distribution points) while equipment went to the Division's Sammelstelle (collecting points). Once at these locations, the supplies were turned over to individual battalion supply columns and thence transported to battalion or company supply points where the supplies were then issued to the troops. This was the general method of supply throughout the Russian campaign. Variations existed whereby the Division itself would establish a railhead to receive and distribute supplies as well as road networks for directly supplying the Division from the divisional railhead. Some figures should suffice to give an idea of the magnitude of the task of the supply services of the German Army. The daily average in pounds of food, fuel, clothing and ammunition. required by a frontline solder in Russia by mid-war was calculated to be: 5-10 lbs. in periods of inactivity (rare in GD's case); 15-20 lbs. during mopping-up operations; 20-25 lbs. in normal defensive fighting; and 25-50 lbs. during heavy defensive fighting and the same amount during offensive operations.

Members of Feldbäckereikompanie (Field Bakery Company) GD put freshly-kneaded loaves of Kommissbrot into one of the company's large bake ovens. Kommissbrot was the basis of all German military rations.

Above: A baker proudly displays some of his handiwork. Under the best of conditions, GD's field bakery company was capable of baking between 15,000-19,000 loaves of bread daily.

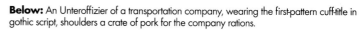

Below: An Unteroffizier of a transportation company, wearing the first-pattern cuff-title in gothic script, shoulders a crate of pork for the company rations.

Above: An infantry NCO carefully checks off supplies being unloaded off three-ton trucks from one of the Division's transportation companies at a rations distribution point. From here, the rations would be moved on by trucks of the individual battalion supply columns for issue to the troops. Incoming flour would normally go from here to the field bakery company while livestock would be sent on to the field butchery platoons for dressing.

Below: Hauptmann Kaufmann, Ib (2.GSO), chief supply officer on the Divisional staff, May 1942. Kaufmann came from the Panzertruppe and well appreciated the supply needs of a motorized formation such as GD.

R A T I O N S

The German High Command and the political leadership were determined that the German Army would not experience a recurrence of the situation which occurred in 1917-1918 when the troops at the front were subsisting on half their daily caloric requirements and the civilian population on less than that. When the war took an unfavorable turn in 1918 and the world-wide influenza pandemic ravaged Germany, the troops lost both the will and the ability to fight on. The collapse of German military resistance brought with it a complete collapse of the apparatus of government and a period of unparalleled chaos. Thus, in a future war, German troops would never be exposed to such risks to their health and fighting power.

Front-line divisions fighting in the Soviet Union such as Grossdeutschland were given the highest ration priority — Verpflegungssatz I (Ration I). The daily ration was the amount of food eaten by one soldier per day. This was divided into three meals with the mid-day meal, the dinner meal, constituting one-half, the evening meal one third and the next day's breakfast one-sixth of the total daily issue. Ration I consisted of fresh, dried, canned and other preserved meats, potatoes and vegetables prepared by the field kitchen units. This most often took the form of stews and soups with large portions of army bread. Cheeses, butter, eggs and, on occasion, fish supplemented those meals and a variety of spices and sugar were also available. Coffee and tea were the most common beverages. Beer and other spirits as well as tobacco were also provided. Seven cigarettes were issued per day to fighting troops in Category I, though soldiers could purchase their own cigarettes from canteens and from unit stores. Depending on availability, climate and medical advice, substitutions could be made within this category. Thus, 60 grams of dried vegetables might be issued in place of 400 grams of salted vegetables. In all cases, the famous Kommissbrot, at 700 grams, formed the foundation

of the Landser's front-line diet, with fresh fruit and vegetables adding another 250 grams, potatoes at 320 grams and fresh meat at 136 grams. Together with the other items, Category I came to a respectable 3.74 lbs. per man per day.

Troops in transit were issued with the Marschverpflegung (March Ration) which was eaten cold and required no preparation. Also eaten by front-line troops, who often combined the march ration with other food and cooked their own meals, it was issued by unit mess personnel on a day by day or meal by meal basis. The march ration consisted of bread, cold cuts, wurst with cheese, spreadable honey or fat, jams, ersatz coffee and/or tea, sugar and cigarettes. There was no attempt at a standard packaging of the contents — the individual items being either canned, wrapped in paper or packed in cardboard.

For emergency use in combat, to be eaten only at the express order of the unit commander, the Eiserne Portion (Iron Ration) was issued in either full or half portions and was often the only food available in combat. The ration, mostly canned, consisted of Zwieback biscuits, meat conserves, preserved vegetables, ersatz coffee, sugar and salt. A Halbeiserne Portion (Half Iron Ration) contained just the Zwieback and the canned meat. By 1943 the Grosskampfpäckchen (Large Combat Package) and the Nahkampfpäckchen (Close Combat Package), consisting of Zwieback, chocolate, fruit bars and cigarettes, began to be issued on a limited basis to front-line troops.

Field kitchen personnel performed miracles of culinary achievement and carried out their duties under sometimes dreadful conditions, having often to take up arms themselves to defend their positions or serve in alarm units during enemy breakthroughs. The Essenholer (Ration Bearers) of the fighting companies, who had to carry heavy canisters of hot food or coffee strapped to their backs, frequently over great distances and in full view of the enemy, were greatly appreciated by the front-line troops.

Right: "Der Küchenbulle" (Chief Cook) and his "Küchenfeen" ("Kitchen Fairies," cook's assistants) prepare hot soup. While much of their food came from Germany and the occupied countries, Grossdeutschland's logistics personnel purchased, requisitioned or captured outright large amounts of foodstuffs in the Soviet Union. On one occasion, during the advance to Voronezh, a Soviet supply dump containing over one million eggs was captured. For weeks thereafter, the Division's cooks had to devote themselves to finding fresh ways of serving eggs.

Below: Cookhouse personnel, May 1942, in front of a field tent assembled from "Zeltbahn" shelter quarters, a common practice.

Facing page: The Feldwebel in charge of one of the butchery platoons of the Fleischereikompanie (Butchery Company) inspects beef prior to dressing. The Division's butchery personnel could process 40 beef cattle (40,000 meat rations), 80 pigs (20,000 meat rations) and 240 sheep (19,000 meat rations) per day. From here the processed rations went to either of two types of field kitchens — known to the soldiers as "Gulaschkanonen" ("Goulash Guns"), the larger of which could feed 125 to 225 men and a smaller type which could supply 60 to 125 men.

J U L Y   1 9 4 2

In the weeks preceding the great summer offensive of 1942, Grossdeutschland was visited and inspected by a great many high ranking commanders at its camp at Fatesch. One of the most important visitors was Generaloberst Hermann Hoth, commanding general of 4.Panzerarmee, of which GD formed a key component. Generaloberst Hoth had been awarded the Ritterkreuz on October 27, 1939 for his leadership of XV Armeekorps in Poland. His corps distinguished itself again in France in 1940 and in Barbarossa his Panzergruppe was instrumental in winning the huge encirclement battles at Minsk in July 1941 and at Vyazma-Bryansk in October, the former victory earning Hoth the Eichenlaub on July 17, 1941. Generaloberst Hoth commanded 4.Pz.Armee in Fall Blau, racing eastward towards the Don and Volga and then southwards towards the Caucasus. One of Germany's most skilled Panzer commanders, Hoth carried out Manstein's brilliant counterattack in March 1943 and his Panzer army would shoulder the major responsibility for achieving success at Kursk.

Right: MG 34 light machinegunners of the 10./I.R.(mot.) GD 1 demonstate their proficiency with their weapon for their guests. The MG 34 in its light machine gun mode weighed 26 1/2 lbs. and was capable of a practical rate of fire of 120 7.92mm rounds per minute. GD was much more generously supplied with the MG 34 than any other combat formation of the German Army. Here the weapon is being loaded with 50-round metallic-link belts of ammunition, several of which could be connected together.

Below: Generaloberst Hoth (left) and Generalmajor Hoernlein tour the well laid-out encampment of the 10./I.R.(mot.) GD 1 with Hauptmann Eberhard Wackernagel as their guide.

Left: Men of one of the Division's six machine gun companies (one for each of its six infantry battalions) ready their s.MG 34 heavy machine guns for firing practice. Each of their companies' three MG platoons had four s.MG in two sections. The organic mortar platoon possessed six sections of one 8cm GrW 34 apiece. The MG 34 was the world's first general purpose machine gun. In its heavy machine gun mode the weapon weighed 42 pounds with its Model 34 tripod. The gun was operated by short recoil, assisted by the muzzle blast, and had a Solothurn-type breech mechanism. The standard 7.92mm rounds were fed by 50 round, non-disintegrating metal link belts. Made to exact tolerances by pre-war milling and boring, the MG 34 was prone to jamming in less than perfect conditions. Barrel changing was theoretically easy but in practice was a nightmare when the gun overheated. The s.MG 34 had a practical rate of fire of 300 rpm and a maximum effective range of 2,000 to 2,500 yards using the ZF34 telescopic sight. The MG 34, unlike the later MG 42, was a selective fire weapon; the top part of the trigger firing semi-automatic while the lower part fired full-automatic. The telescopic sight was used with the Dreifuss 34 tripod for aiming the gun in either direct or indirect fire. The two pads visible on the front leg of the tripod rested up against the gun bearer's back when the mount was folded and carried by means of slings.

Above: Generaloberst Hoth chats with a veteran Gefreiter of the 10./I.R.(mot.) GD 1 half-track-drawn 5cm PaK 38 anti-tank gun platoon.

Right: Generaloberst Hoth takes leave of General Hoernlein before boarding his Fieseler Storch liaison aircraft.

ARMORED CAR TACTICS

actical reconnaissance was carried out in stages, dependent on both the available cover in the terrain and on the road network itself. The closer the reconnaissance unit approached the enemy, the shorter the patrol limits. Roads were used as long as possible and different routes were chosen for the advance and the return. Most patrols did not venture more than 25 miles ahead of the reconnaissance battalion's main body. The battalion functioned as a reserve for the various patrols and as a Meldekopf (advanced message center). The composition of the patrols was usually dependent on the mission and the situation — armored cars, halftracks and motorcycle-sidecars being used together or separately in various combinations. Motorcyclists were used to fill in gaps and thicken the reconnaissance net. Kradschützenbataillon GD, in keeping with standard German doctrine — which was quite flexible in practice — rarely operated more than a day's march ahead of the main body, and covered an area roughly six miles wide.

Armored car patrols were usually composed of two Sd.Kfz. 222s and one Sd.Kfz. 232 (or two Sd.Kfz. 231s and one Sd.Kfz. 232).

When necessary, an artillery forward observer would accompany the patrol to call in quick covering fire. Nothing was allowed to interfere with carrying out the reconnaissance mission. Contact with the enemy was to be avoided if at all possible. If contact was inevitable, extra support in the form of assault guns, engineers from the organic Pionierzug, and even tanks could be attached to the patrol. Armored car patrols were never to split up, though distances between vehicles of 200-300 yards were allowed.

The troops were instructed to never rely too much on aerial reconnaissance or to neglect ground reconnaissance. The Soviets were masters of camouflage and concealment and rarely betrayed their positions to reconnaissance aircraft. On July 5, 1942, the day before Voronezh fell, reconnaissance aircraft reported that Voronezh was free of enemy troops. This was confirmed by Major von Hobe, Division Ia (Chief of Operations). The strong patrols sent forward by Divisional HQ ran right into well-concealed enemy machine gun and mortar positions and suffered heavy casualties. Had proper ground reconnaissance been done, this would not have happened.

Facing page: Sd.Kfz. 222 four-wheeled armored cars of 1./ Kradschützen-Btl. GD are eased off flat cars at the railroad yards at Orel, May 1942. The reconnaissance battalion had two platoons of these very efficient vehicles. Having only short-range FuG. Spr.Ger. A radios, the Sd.Kfz. 222's role was to accompany the Sd.Kfz. 232 radio command armored cars on reconnaissance missions and engage enemy reconnaisance vehicles. The Sd.Kfz. 222 was a modified version of the Sd.Kfz. 221, featuring a large, fully rotating turret which mounted one 2cm KwK 30 or 38 and one 7.92mm MG 34 machine gun. The 5.25-ton vehicle's basic design essentially added an armored body onto the standard four-wheeled heavy passenger car chassis. The vehicle had a rear-mounted Horch 3.5-liter V8 engine, independent coil-spring suspension, four-wheel drive, and four-wheel steering. The transmission had six gears, 5 forward and 1 reverse. The Sd.Kfz. 222 had a top speed of 53 mph and a range of 186 miles. The crew consisted of three men — driver, radioman/gunner, and vehicle commander. Later versions used the improved s.Pkw. 1 type V chassis with hydraulic brakes and a 3.8-liter engine. The 8mm armor gave adequate protection against small-arms fire but the vehicle relied on its speed to escape from anything heavier it encountered. The "Uhu" (owl) painted on the side of the vehicle was an unofficial sign of the Kradschützenbataillon.

Above: Newly-arrived from Germany, Sd.Kfz. 232 radio command armored cars of 1./Kradschützen-Btl. GD, seen at the marshalling yards at Orel, May 1942.

Left: Crewmembers of a Sd.Kfz. 232 remove the tarpaulins from their vehicle after unloading. Armored car crews were the only other personnel other than tank crews specifically authorized to wear the black woolen Panzer field uniform.

Above: Kübelwagens and other medium and light trucks of 3./Kradschützen-Btl. GD move out from the railroad yards at Orel. The individual vehicle number is painted on each vehicle as are white distance markers which made travel by night somewhat safer.

Left and facing page, above: The Divisional HQ Company had an armored car detachment, and this Sd.Kfz. 232 (8 rad) armored radio car displays the black outline on the top border of the white Stalhelm divisional insignia. Their primary mission was to gather information on enemy forces while avoiding serious combat engagements. When retreating from a superior enemy force, the normal practice was to fire smoke grenades for cover, then reverse from their position, keeping the heavier front armor to the enemy and traversing the turret to engage any pursuing units.

Below: The Sd.Kfz. 233 was developed in late 1942 to provide a self-propelled mount for the 7.5cm KwK 37 L/24 howitzer, and was one of a number of vehicles adapted to carry this versatile support weapon. The vehicle had a crew of three, and was issued to armored car companies in the reconnaissance battalion.

PANZERSTURMPIONIERBATAILLON GD

When raised in 1939, I.R.(mot.) GD had no organic engineers of its own except for its infantry pionier platoons. For operations in France in May 1940, Sturm-Pionier Btl. 43, lead by Oberstleutnant Mahler, was placed under GD's command and performed in an exemplary manner. On October 12, 1940, 18.(Pionier)/I.R.(mot.) GD was raised in Schlettstedt under Hauptmann Rudiger and consisted of three numbered platoons and a bridging platoon with K-Bridges. When I.D. (mot.) GD was constituted in April 1942 it was decided to use Sturm.Pi.Btl. 43, which had meanwhile fought very well at Sevastopol, as the core of the new Pi.Btl.(mot.) GD together with the old 18.(Pionier) Kompanie. The new battalion consisted of three motorized pionier companies, a K-Bridge column and a light pionier column. The first commander of the battalion was Major Karl Lorenz who had distinguished himself in the siege of Demyansk the previous winter. From the beginning the new battalion adopted the honorary title "Sturm-Pionier-Bataillon GD" (Assault Engineer Battalion GD).

The three numbered companies each had authorized strengths of 219 officers and men and were fully motorized and well armed with infantry weapons. Altogether, Major Lorenz's Battalion had 979 officers and men who were fully capable of carrying out missions independently or being integrated into armored spearheads. Infantry, Panzer and reconnaissance units also had their own organic engineer platoons (Regiments and Bataillonspioniere) of infantrymen, etc. who had received some basic engineer training and could carry out rudimentary engineer duties without overburdening the Engineer Battalion.

Upon its reorganization in 1943 as a Pz.Gr. Division, GD's engineer battalion officialy adopted the title "Pz.Pionierbataillon GD" — although the honorary title "Sturmpioniere" was retained in everyday use. At this point, 1. Kompanie was equipped with Sd.Kfz. 251/7 engineer halftrack SPWs which carried light bridging equipment. Battalion HQ was also mounted in Sd.Kfz. 251s.

German Army engineers prided themselves on being fighting troops and were frequently employed to defend the zone of obstacles or bridgeheads they created. Sturmpioniere, such as GD's, using special equipment, were also trained for infantry raiding parties to take part in attacks on fortified positions. By mid-war, with Germany on the defensive and desperately short of infantry, the Armored Engineer Battalion had become the Divisional commanders "iron reserve" to be committed only as a last, desperate measure when all other resources were exhausted.

GD's engineers were always in the forefront of action: building, repairing, destroying and fighting. Some of their greatest successes were bridging the Don at Voronezh, the Manytsch crossing, clearing the minefields at Kursk and building the bridges which enabled the Division and other German units to escape across the Dnieper. Besides Major Lorenz and Hauptmann Hans-Detlev Chrapkowski, many other Pioniere distinguished themselves on the battlefield, two of whom shall represent the rest. During the confused fighting which characterized the defensive battles in the Orel salient on August 9, 1943, Hauptmann Ernst-Albrecht Huckel's Sturmpionierkompanie broke into Staraya-Ryrkana and drove the enemy from the village while eliminating many enemy strong points in close combat. Hauptmann Hückel was awarded the Ritterkreuz on September 27, 1943. Oberleutnant Horst Warschnauer of 2./Sturmpionier Btl. GD was awarded the Ritterkreuz on December 12, 1942 for Operation "Max und Moritz" on September 22 of that year when his company stormed Chermassovo, destroying 120 bunkers in close combat in a 20-minute span using flamethrowers, satchel charges, spades, and knives. Without waiting for further orders, Warschnauer pursued the defeated Soviets for some distance beyond the town. In February 1945, by now commander of the Battalion, Hauptmann Warschnauer led his battalion in a counterattack west of Brandenburg, East Prussia to cover the retreat of the main body of the Division. Standing upright in his only available SPW and cheering his men on, Warschnauer led his unit and cleared the enemy from the heights overlooking the town, thereby accounting for 170 enemy dead. For this decisive action, Hauptmann Warschnauer became the 753rd recipient of the Eichenlaub on February 24, 1945.

Facing page: Hauptmann Hans-Detlev Chrapkowski, Oberst Lorenz's successor as commanding officer of Sturm-Pionier Btl.(mot.) GD and an enlisted helmsman cross a river in a wooden Sturmboot 39 assault boat. These light, keelless boats carried seven men in addition to their 2-man crews. Normally used in the initial stages of an assault crossing, the Sturmboot 39 was powered by a 12-horsepower, 4-cylinder outboard motor which drove a propeller through a 13-foot shaft contained in a tubular housing. The boat's maximum speed when fully loaded varied between 15 and 20 mph. Four men were required to carry the motor and eight to carry the boat. Boats could be nested in groups of three on special trailers for transport. The 27 assault boats formed the 3rd (Assault Boat) platoon of a Sturmpionierkompanie. The helmsman wears the Boat Pilot's Badge awarded to qualified engineers of motorboats on inland waters. The badge in this photograph has the peacetime version of the base cloth in bluish-dark green.

This page: Engineers of the Sturm-Pionier Btl. assemble the Brückengerät K ponton and trestle bridge. The Brückengerät K was the standard bridge carried by engineers in Panzer divisions. The pontons were of a standard three-section type. Bridges of two, three and four girders could be built, and the full girder length of 64 feet was normally used. The track-carrying load capacity and corresponding spans were: 4 girder, 48 foot span = 25 tons; 4 girder, 64 foot span = 21 tons; 2 girder, 32 foot span = 21 tons; 2 girder, 64 foot span = 10 tons. In practice these load tolerances were sufficient for all vehicles up to the Pz.Kpfw. IV and V but the superheavy Tiger I presented an unsolvable problem, for which even the heavy Brückengerät S and the Herbert Bridge were insufficient. The bridging column transported the K bridges, whose assembly was the responsibility of the engineers.

Major i.G. Peter Frantz

Major i.G. (later Oberst d.R.) Peter Frantz was born on July 24, 1917 in Leipzig. After passing his Abitur (school graduating examination which qualified the recipient for admission to university), Frantz joined the Saxon Artillerieregiment 4 in Dresden as a Fahnenjunker in October 1936. Fahnenjunker Frantz was promoted to FJ-Unteroffizier on September 1, 1937 and transferred to the Kriegsschule in Munich. After promotion to Fähnrich on March 1, 1938 and three months later to Oberfähnrich, Frantz was assigned to the Artillerieschule at Jüterbog, upon completion of which course he was commissioned as a Leutnant on September 1, 1938 in Pz. Artillerieregiment 74 of the Viennese 2.Pz.Div. Leutnant Frantz was assigned to 1.Batterie/Pz.A.R. 74 in Korneuburg, some 13 miles north of Vienna. Frantz's battery took part in the march into the Sudetenland in October 1938 and the following march helped to occupy the rump of Czechoslovakia which remained after the Munich Agreement.

Leutnant Frantz served as an orderly officer in RHQ Pz.A.R. 74 during the Polish Campaign of September 1939 and was decorated with the Iron Cross II Class. After returning to Vienna, he voluntarily transferred to the Artillery School at Jüterbog to help raise the German Army's first battery of assault guns, which became Batterie 640. In April 1940 the battery was attached to I.R.(mot.) GD on the Mosel where a short time later it was incorporated into GD as its 16.Kompanie. Peter Frantz remained with GD's assault guns until February 1944, holding successively the positions of platoon commander, battery commander and finally, battalion commander.

Leutnant Frantz was a platoon commander of 16.I.R.(mot.)GD in the French Campaign, winning the Iron Cross I Class and being promoted to Oberleutnant in August 1940. Frantz successfully led his platoon through the Balkan Campaign of April-May 1941 and the first six months of the invasion of the Soviet Union, being awarded a "Certificate of Recognition" by the Commander-in-Chief of the German Army on October 20, 1941 and the German Cross in Gold in December 1941. By March 1942 Oberleutnant Frantz commanded 16./I.R.(mot.) GD. Frantz's company, now styled 1.Batterie, was now part of the new StuG.Abt. GD commanded by the veteran Major Hans-Joachim Schepers. In May 1942 Frantz was presented the Ritterkreuz by his divisional commander, Walter Hoernlein, in recognition of his company's defensive successes in the winter battles around Tula. Simultaneously he was promoted to Hauptmann. Peter Frantz recalled that a color photograph which appeared a few months later in "Signal" magazine was the first news his parents had that he had been awarded the Ritterkreuz.

Hauptmann Frantz continued in command of 1.Batterie throughout the remainder of 1942, succeeding the late Hauptmann Helmuth Adam in command of the battalion on January 3, 1943. On April 14, 1943 Hauptmann Frantz was summoned to the Reich Chancellery in Berlin to personally receive the Eichenlaub to his Ritterkreuz from Adolf Hitler. Upon his return to the front, Frantz was feted by his battalion with a daylong celebration highlighted by a parade of the entire battalion. Hauptmann Frantz led StuG.Abt. GD throughout the Kursk Offensive and the long, bitter retreat to the Dniester and Bug Rivers. On January 17, 1944 Major Frantz was transferred to the Kriegsakademie for general staff training, being appointed Major im Generalstab the following August. In August 1944 Major i.G. Frantz was assigned as Quartiermeister of XXXX Pz.Korps and took part in all the Corps' actions back to the Elbe River. Major Frantz entered U.S. captivity in May 1945 and was shortly thereafter sent to a work camp in France because of his membership in the General Staff. In April 1946 Peter Frantz "discharged" himself and made his way back to his family, now settled in the Allgau.

Peter Frantz always led his battalion according to his motto "Erfolg geht vor Sicherheit" ("Success takes precedence over safety."). By this Frantz meant that cautiously handled, defensive minded tactics would never succeed against massive Soviet tank forces. Only ruthless, offensive-minded tactics, with a large element of calculated risk-taking based on the strengths of the vehicles and the skills of their crews could guarantee the Sturmgeschütz superiority on the battlefields of the Eastern Front.

Above: Newly decorated Oberleutnant Frantz wears an Iron Cross II Class around his neck in place of the actual Ritterkreuz. Often, as in Frantz's case, genuine Ritterkreuze were not on hand in the field and the award ceremony was conducted using the Iron Cross II Class in the field to preserve their award from

Left: Generalmajor Hoernlein decorates Oberleutnant Frantz with the Ritterkreuz on June 4, 1942 at the encampment at Faetsch. As was the German Army's custom, Oberleutnant Frantz wears a steel helmet for the investiture. Generalmajor Hoernlein's adjutant, Hauptmann Theo Bethke, stands behind Frantz to adjust the ribbon of the Ritterkreuz.

Below left: General Hoernlein, Oberleutnant Frantz and officers of StuG.Abt. GD inspect members of Frantz's 1. Batterie, drawn up as an Ehrenkompanie (Honor Company) within the hollow square formed by the entire Battalion. The Honor Company present arms with Kar 98k rifles issued to them for the occasion. Battalion Adjutant Oberleutnant Wilhelm Verch (second from the left) wears an adjutant's aiguilette on his right breast.

Below right: Oberleutnant Frantz presents the NCOs of his battery to their divisional commander. Behind Frantz is StuG.Abt. GD's first commander, Major Hans Joachim Schepers, and Hauptmann Bethke. Major Schepers had previously commanded StuG.Abt. 192 which supplied much of the manpower for the new StuG.Abt. GD. He assumed command of the new battalion in April 1942, leading it through the fighting on the Don. The strain of commanding his overtaxed battalion precipitated a physical and nervous collapse during the Rzhev fighting in September 1942, forcing him to hand over command of the battalion to Hauptmann Helmuth Adam and to take sick leave in Germany. From the far left, the first four NCOs are Unteroffiziers Donner, Handschuh, Bindseil, and Brauner.

Left: Oberleutnant Alfred Bruno Eduard Greim, commanding officer of II/I.R.(mot.) GD, shortly after the award of his Ritterkreuz on June 4, 1942. Greim, a Thuringian from Langensalza born on August 8, 1902, was one of the original members of GD, having served as commander of II/I.R.(mot.) GD since the French Campaign of 1940. Suspended from his right breast pocket button, Greim wears the most important medal of the Nazi Party, the Blutorden (Blood Order), which commemorated the abortive "Beer Hall Putsch" of November 9, 1923, in Munich. However, Greim was no party militant. Indeed, soldiers were prohibited both from membership in the Nazi Party or any of its organizations. Greim's Blood Order was authorized because he had been a young cadet at the Infantry School in Munich on November 9. The school commandant ordered the cadets out under arms to support the Putsch, which subsequently collapsed before the cadets could take part in the short-lived fighting. The Reichswehr command subsequently moved the school to Dresden and the cadets acquired an entirely undeserved notoriety as "Putschists" until calm returned some time later. When the Nazis came into power in 1933, they authorized a general issue of this most prestigious award to all serving or retired members of the Infantry School who participated in the events of November 9, 1923. This resulted in the bizarre situation of hundred of soldiers who had no connection with the party wearing a medal to which only a handful of genuine party faithful were entitled. Oberleutnant Greim's Ritterkreuz was awarded in recognition of his leadership of his battalion when it held its positions in the Kishkino area near Tula southwest of Moscow on December 13, 1941. Greim would later die of blood poisoning in the Reservelazarett Döberitz on May 19, 1943.

ARTILLERY ORGANIZATION AND TACTICS

When raised in May 1942, A.R.(mot.) GD consisted of three Abteilungen (battalion-sized "Detachments," a term used throughout the artillery and Panzer forces to designate those units) of three batteries each. The IV Abteilung was the regimental Flak battalion, but which almost from the beginning operated as an independent unit. Besides its Regimental HQ, the Regiment also was intended to include a battery of the powerful new Nebelwerfer multiple-rocket launchers but this latter battery did not appear until 1943, and its place within the Regiment was taken by the Observation Battery, consisting of a sound-ranging platoon, two flash-ranging platoons, a survey platoon, a warning platoon and two analysis platoons. Modules of the Observation Battery could be variously arranged to assist in locating enemy batteries, registering the regiment's guns, map-making, and in general providing the regimental commander (who also functioned as the Divisional Commander's artillery advisor) with a clear picture of the tactical situation. This highly sophisticated unit gave Divisional HQ very detailed information, but Russian artillery tactics were so predictable up to late 1942 that the Division's Ia recommended the unit be disbanded, as he felt it was too costly in manpower and vehicles.

GD's uniquely large size and composition meant that everything about it was on the grand scale. Artillerieregiment GD's organization thus mirrored the particular role for which the Division was intended to be used. GD, like other divisions, would assign an artillery battalion to each of its two infantry regiments. GD's infantry, however, was so well provided with its own organic firepower and mobility that the addition of an artillery battalion plus some additional tanks, assault guns, and engineers had the effect of turning each infantry regiment into a large mixed brigade or even a small division. Service in such a largely independent unit required that each of GD's first two battalions, rather than being "pure" 10.5cm howitzer units, had two (1., 2.; 4., 5.) "direct support" 10.5cm howitzer batteries plus one (3.; 6.) battery of 15cm howitzers — all drawn by halftrack prime movers. The absence of the third 10.5cm battery was more than made up by the infantry regiments' organic heavy weapons. Having 15cm howitzers in each artillery battalion provided the infantry with the range and striking power it did not itself have organically. The third Abteilung was a mixed heavy battalion of one (9.) 10cm gun and two (7., 8.) 15cm howitzer batteries, also towed by halftrack prime movers. This battalion was a "general support" unit and was used to create an artillery "Schwerpunkt" (Point of Main Effort) in offensive and defensive operations.

In common with the German Army as a whole, Grossdeutschland's artillery organization was much more flexible than any other army. Each battery was assigned a forward observer and each battalion a liaison officer. This flexibility allowed individual battalions or batteries to operate independently by setting up their own OPs and cooperating directly with other units. Battalions and batteries could be combined in various ways in order to use the weapons' technical characteristics to the greatest advantage and to fit the tactical circumstances without having to concern themselves with a rigid chain of command. Eventually this inherent flexibility meant that there was no need for permanently constituted mixed battalions because those could always be improvised. It was actually more difficult to suddenly assemble a battalion's worth of one type of gun on the same target. By late 1942, when thrown onto the defensive, A.R.(mot.) GD was faced with the almost daily requirement of massing 18 or even 36 guns of the same type and this superseded, temporarily at least, the occasional need to form two or more divisional-strength battle groups.

A.R.(mot.) GD performed extremely well in the Rzhev fighting from September to December 1942. Suggestions to rationalize its organization by doing away with both the "mixed" batteries and the observation battery came to nothing, but a IV Abteilung — with two (10. and 12.) batteries of towed 10.5cm howitzers and one (11.) battery of towed 15cm howitzers, together with the usual HQ battery in trucks and cars, was added in January 1943. The most important change followed in the spring of 1943 when I. Abteilung was reequipped as a Panzerhaubitze-Abteilung (Armored Howitzer Battalion) with a HQ battery in Pz.Kpfw. III observation tanks, two (1. and 2.) six-gun batteries of Wespe 10.5cm self-propelled howitzers and one (3.) six-gun battery of Hummel 15cm self-propelled howitzers, together with their organic ammunition vehicles on the same chassis. This remained Pz.A.R. GD's organization until the end of the war, and allowed for tremendous firepower and greater flexibility within both the armored battlegroups and in defensive fighting from prepared positions.

A.R. GD and Pz.A.R. GD were well-suited to support a division as large and mobile as Grossdeutschland. Individual battalions were allotted to the infantry regiments and, on occasion, massed for so-called Feuerschläge (Fire Strikes). In such cases the infantry's mortars and guns as well as the Flakabteilung's 8.8cm guns could be integrated into the fire plan as could the assault guns and assault howitzers. During the rapid maneuver battles of the summer of 1942, those tactics worked very well, particularly when Stuka strikes were added to the equation, and the only complaint heard from the artillery was that the infantry were often too hasty in calling for unnecessary box barrages.

Attacks were often preceded by mortars and artillery attempting to eliminate identified targets such as machine gun and mortar positions. For the attack itself, GD made every effort to prepare an exact fire plan. This initially proved difficult as motorized formations were not very well trained in such procedures. By mid-1942 the custom of attacking at dawn was being abandoned, as the Soviets were found to be fully alert at this hour and the Luftwaffe was very often unavailable. On the Eastern Front, moreover, the light was not favorable at this hour, as forces attacking to the east had the sun in their eyes.

The fireplan detailed which units would blind the enemy with smoke and which would use high explosives. A Feuerschlag of five minute duration included the infantry's heavy weapons and fell on previously identified targets while smoke shells blinded enemy observation posts and anti-tank gun positions. Offensive operations had previously been mostly a matter of tank thrusts supported by Stukas and other ground attack aircraft acting as long-range artillery. Artillery was largely decentralized and played a relatively minor role in offensive operations. GD with its completely mechanized guns suffered less than other divisions but even it had trouble massing sufficient guns and bringing up ammunition for sustained bombardments. By late 1942, with air superiority gone and the Panzers no longer able to equalize the overwhelming volume of fire the Soviets could bring down on any part of the front, a major change had to be made in GD's artillery methods, one that its basic structure made very difficult. From early 1943, with its four battalions — one of them a self-propelled Panzerhaubitze Abteilung, the so-called "Couleurabteilung" (Color Battalion) — Pz.A.R. GD, as was described in the armored battle group section, could carry out a large number of mobile support missions in local counter thrusts and counter strikes. However, in defensive operations, even with its large establishment of light and heavy howitzers and the longer-range 10cm K 18s of 9. Batterie, Pz.A.R. GD still had too few guns for the fronts it was assigned. The artillery could be strengthened on occasion by adding in the assault howitzers and the 8.8cm guns of the Flakabteilung but nothing was available to hit the depth of the enemy lines. After 1942 it became essential to organize the firing positions for the best anti-tank defense, and to include the artillery in the anti-tank plan. With a few exceptions, the decentralized nature of the Regiment's deployment remained in effect, and the Regiment had great difficulty in properly supporting the Division in crisis situations. This was admittedly counterbalanced by the fully mechanized nature of the Regiment, which allowed it to shift positions on short notice, and by the high quality of its observation battery.

Defensively, the Germans readopted the World War I tactic of holding the front lines with small numbers of troops who then withdrew unnoticed to the main line of resistance. When the Soviets had spent their fire on abandoned trenches and their troops and tanks were out in the open, GD's artillery would open up on them on carefully worked out fields of fire, isolating them from their support and cutting off their withdrawal. Another tactic found highly useful in both offensive and defensive operations was to fire a mixture of smoke and HE. This almost always resulted in panic among the enemy, especially in hilly or wooded terrain.

Panzer and motorized artillery in Pz.A.R. GD was utterly dependent on the quality of their radio equipment. By 1942 the existing equipment, though good, was found to be too weak. This need to have a radio whose range was double that of the maximum range of the guns was never fully met. In mechanized warfare, with all its fluidity, it was axiomatic that artillery radio and telephone operators could never be trained well enough. This was also true of the infantry, with whom the artillery were expected to cooperate. GD was fortunate in recognizing this need quite early and making provisions to lay in an adequate reserve of telephone and radio equipment, as well as telephone wire.

The lack of sufficient heavy, long-range guns — a decision at the root of German mobile doctrine as it evolved between the wars — made reliance on tactical air support in the form of Stuka divebombers and other ground-attack aircraft a vital component of mobile operations. Simultaneously with the first Stuka strikes right behind the enemy's main

line of resistance, ground attack aircraft attempted to suppress enemy batteries in the rear. Counter-battery fire, originally so important to the Germans (who invented the term in the First World War and refined it to a science), was largely neglected by them in World War II. German artillerymen felt counter-battery fire only made sense when they had a clearly identified target and sufficient guns available to suppress or destroy it. When GD's artillery was weak in numbers in relation to the target, the staff felt it was unproductive to split up the guns among many targets which were not clearly located. The Germans were strong believers in observed rather than predicted fire, another instance of rejecting their own experience which had proved so spectacularly successful in World War I. They felt that all fire should be controlled by forward observers and directed right onto the enemy front lines where their observers were to be found. Deprived thus of their observers, the enemy's guns would be much less effective. Once the first bombs had fallen, the infantry jumped off. This also signaled the beginning of the Feuerschlag. As soon as the first fire strike ended, the infantry, assisted by the artillery battalion assigned to them, used their heavy weapons to wear down targets as they appeared in the depth of the enemy positions. The remainder of the artillery, plus such heavy guns provided by Corps or Army HQ, remained in the hands of the artillery regimental commander in his capacity as Artillerieführer (Artillery Commander) GD and was used to build Feuerschwerpunkte (Fire Concentrations). The Stukas and ground attack aircraft continued to circle the battlefield after their last bombs had been dropped, as their presence often held the Soviets in their shelters and prevented them from intervening effectively at the critical phase of the battle.

Should the enemy counterattack, German doctrine as practiced by A.R. GD called for the tanks and assault guns to deal with this threat while the artillery moved on to targets farther in the rear. This then was the basic doctrine, very flexible in practice and subject to a great many variations according to any given situation, which served the German Army very well as long as it had air superiority and held the initiative.

Above: The crew of a Pz.Kpfw. IV Ausf. F2 observe the local terrain next to a Kfz. 15 mPkw. of 1. Batterie's HQ. Sitting behind the wheel of the Horch is Obergefreiter Schumann, while standing beside him are Batteriechef Oberleutnant Theermann (center, wearing a side cap) and Geschützstaffelführer Oberleutnant Burchardi (right). Standing in the rear are Wachmeister Powileit (left) and Unteroffizier Neumann of the B-Trupp (Observation Troop). At the left is one of the Sd.Kfz. 232 heavy armored cars which combined to make this Vorausabteilung (Advanced Unit) detachment a strong and balanced force.

Above: Beobachtungshalt: "Spitze hat Feindberührung" (Halt for Observation — the point unit has made contact with the enemy). Battery commander Oberleutnant Werner Theermann scans the horizon for Soviet activity while the crew of a Pz.Kpfw. IV Ausf. F savor fresh air. Divisional commander Hoernlein's Fieseler Storch liaison aircraft has just landed in the background.

Left: Batteriechef Theermann plays with the battery mascot while waiting for orders. Many German units of all types had animals as pets and unit mascots.

Facing page, top: Generalmajor Hoernlein (seated, center) and Ia Major Cord von Hobe (seated to the General's left) confer with subordinates during a brief halt in the race to the Lower Don. Hoernlein used both motor transport and his Fieseler Storch liaison aircraft to keep in touch with the operational units in his large command.

Facing page, bottom: GD and Luftwaffe personnel roll fuel drums from a Ju52/3m on the Don steppe. Keeping the Division supplied as it moved rapidly south in July 1942 was the joint responsibility of GD's logistics staff and Oberst Wilhelm Morzik's Luftwaffe Transport Command. Ju52s flew hundreds of sorties to deliver fuel, ammunition, and other supplies. The aircraft usually landed and took off from open fields along the march route.

Left: The Sd.Kfz. 11 3-ton Hanomag light prime mover of Nr. 1 gun of 1./A.R.(mot.) GD leads the battery south. Standing to the left is Oberleutnant Hans-Joachim Burchardi. Geschützführer (crew chief) Obergefreiter Posselt stands at the right rear. Seated, in the center of the photograph, is the vehicle's driver, Obergefreiter Eisler. The second vehicle in this column has an air recognition flag over its hood — a necessary precaution with Major Horst von Usedom's Vorausabteilung racing south and coming under the risk of being attacked by the Luftwaffe if not properly identified.

Left: While Oberleutnants Theermann and Burchardi scan the surrounding countryside, Nr. 1 gun is unlimbered. Only open firing positions were possible on the Don steppes.

Left: The unlimbered guns are now being lined up parallel to form a gun line.

Top: Oberleutnant Burchardi uses the standard Rundblickfernrohr (panoramic telescope) M 32K fitted to a tubular socket on the gun's sight bracket to lay the le.FH 18 directly. The M 32K was designed for both direct and indirect laying, and its complicated operation permitted accurate shooting up to the gun's maximum range of 13,200 yards. Direct laying was used when the gun was employed as an anti-tank weapon, firing either a hollow-charge AT round or a standard howitzer HE round.

Above left: 1./Pz.A.R.(mot.) GD, seen in firing position alongside the highway (rollbahn). Vehicles and Flak guns of Heeres Flakabteilung GD travel south on the road.

Above right: The shell case for the semi-fixed ammunition is passed to K3, the loader. Constant lifting and heaving 32.1 lb shells to maintain a steady rate of fire required considerable upper body strength, as well as rigorous training and practice for all crew members, especially K4 and K5, the Munitionskanoniere, who had to set the fuses on the shells. The le.FH 18 could fire HE, incendiary, illuminating, hollow-charge, and discarding sabot shells to a maximum range of 13,200 yards. An obdurator sealed the separate case and shell for loading.

Left: The round is away. The dust kicked up by the muzzle blast was the major problem in hiding artillery positions from the enemy.

V O R O N E Z H

hase one of Fall Blau was based on taking Voronezh, which sat astride both the Don and the Voronezh Rivers. The city, which served as a traffic junction for all north-south rail, road and river communications in Central Russia, from Moscow to the Black and Caspian Seas, was intended by German planners to function both as a pivot for the southward advance in phase two of Fall Blau and as a support base for the flanking cover to be provided by Generaloberst Maximilian Freiherr von Weichs' Heeresgruppe B.

The northern wing of the advance was spearheaded by Generaloberst Hermann Hoth's 4. Pz.Armee, the core of which was formed by General Werner Kempf's XXXXVIII Pz.Korps. Kempf's corps consisted of Generalmajor Bruno Ritter von Hauenschild's East Prussian 24. Pz.Division, newly raised from the old 1. Kavalleriedivision, in the center, with Generalmajor Siegfried Henrici's Westphalian 16 I.D.(mot.) on its right and I.D.(mot.) GD on its left. On June 28, 1942, the code word "Siegfried" was flashed to all units and the Corps jumped off. The Soviets, who after the disaster at Kharkov in May were dangerously thin on the ground, gave way quickly and the Tim River, east of Kursk, was quickly reached and crossed. By June 30, the Germans had covered half the distance to Voronezh. While the bulk of GD's two infantry regiments force-marched in terrible heat toward the next river, the Kshen, Kradschtz.Btl.(mot.) GD, under Major von Usedom, sped forward until rain and mud brought the advance to a temporary standstill on the 30th. When the advance resumed, the Soviets' rearguard fought stubbornly to cover the orderly retreat of their main body. On June 30, as GD approached the Kshen, General der Panzertruppen Leo Freiherr Geyr von Schweppenburg's XL Pz.Korps advanced eastwards from Volchansk, east of Kharkov, toward the Oskol. There it was to wheel northward to link up with Kempf's Corps at Stary Oskol in order to close the trap on the Soviets resisting 4. Pz.Armee. As GD had discovered, however, while the Soviet rear guards fought hard and tank counterattacks were made, the enemy's main body was withdrawing in good order towards the Don. The anticipated "Kesselschlacht" (Battle of Encirclement) was slipping away because the Soviets had finally learned to avoid fighting the well-trained Germans on their own terms.

Freiherr von Geyr realized faster than anyone else that the Soviets were not to be trapped in the pocket planned for them by OKH and requested permission to drive due east without delay. HQ 6. Armee,

however, insisted on closing the trap as planned. The trap was duly closed but proved empty — the Soviets succeeding in getting away with even their heavy weapons. A momentous decision, with the most fateful of consequences for Germany, was now taken in almost the most casual manner imaginable. Adolf Hitler realized intuitively that keeping to the plan of taking Voronezh might imperil Fall Blau, but chose to leave the decision to his theater commander, Generalfeldmarschall Fedor von Bock. Bock at first ordered Geyr to drive straight to the Don to cut off the Soviet's retreat on July 3. After rethinking his orders, Bock then reversed himself and ordered Geyr to turn northeast towards Voronezh. In this, Bock was influenced both by his desire to secure his left flank and by the events which brought XXXVIII Pz.Korps over the Don early in the evening of July 4. By 2000 hours that night, Oberleutnant Carl Ludwig Blumenthal of 7./I.R. GD 1 stormed the road bridge at Semiluki and established a bridgehead on the eastern bank. Soviet attempts to destroy the bridge at the last moment were frustrated by Unteroffizier Hempel, a section leader in 7. Kompanie, who waded beneath the bridge to remove the 120 lb explosive charge before it could be detonated. For his daring leadership, Oberleutnant Blumenthal was awarded the Ritterkreuz on September 18, 1942. Infantry of I.R.(mot.) GD 1 raced into the city, riding atop the Divisional assault guns to widen the bridgehead, getting as far as the railroad yards before being evicted by a spirited Soviet counterattack.

With this in mind, Bock's desire to go ahead and seize Voronezh by a coup de main before heading south along the great bend of the Don is understandable. His reasoning was undoubtedly influenced by his certainty that he had sufficient time to get his mechanized formations south quickly enough to cut off the Soviets' retreat across the Don in front of 6. Armee. This faulty appreciation of the situation led inexorably to the double disasters of Stalingrad and the retreat from the Caucasus six months later.

Hitler's attempts to get the attack redirected southward were thus frustrated, not only by Bock, but by the Soviets who realized what was at stake and hastily reinforced their troops in Voronezh. With Kempf's Corps fully committed in the street fighting in the city, only Geyr's XL Pz.Korps was free to begin the southward push on July 6. The Germans took Voronezh only after bitter street fighting and never succeeded in cutting the vital north-south railway line on the eastern bank of the Don. By this time, GD had been redeployed on the western bank of the Don and sent racing southward into the great bend of the Don towards Manytsch.

Left: Kradschützen move out while the crew of an Sd.Kfz. 250/3 leichter Funkpanzerwagen observe the enemy and report back to HQ from the shelter of an embankment. This ground to air communications vehicle, mounting a frame aerial, weighed 5.35 tons, had a four man crew and was furnished with FuG 7 and 8 radios to call in close-support aircraft. Note the partially obscured tactical sign for a reconnaissance company.

Below: Infantrymen accompanied by support weapons advance past blazing collective farm buildings near the Don. One man carries a "Flammenwerfer klein verbessert 40" (Model 40 small, improved manpack Flamethrower) which were supplied two per company in both of GD's infantry regiments. The Model 40 Flamethrower weighed 47 lbs. Its "Lifebuoy" tank contained just over two gallons of fuel and its range was up to 30 yards in ten one-second bursts.

Below right: Infantrymen look over the results of the Soviets' hasty retreat from a communal farm. Such devastation became a hallmark of the Russian Campaign almost from the first day of the war. The Germans later applied even more systematic destruction as they retreated from Russia two years later.

Facing page: Led by their company commander, Oberleutnant Carl Ludwig Blumenthal, 7./I.R.(mot.) GD 1 moves forward in extended order towards the Don and Voronezh, late June-early July, 1942. Blumenthal dresses much like his men in obedience to OKH orders that officers adopt the dress and equipment of their men when in the field. Two of the Schützen wear canvas belt support straps.

Below left: With a spotter perched atop a pile of recently cut grain, a 5cm PaK 38 anti-tank gun of a Panzerjägerkompanie engages Soviet armor outside Voronezh, where several energetic but poorly coordinated enemy tank attacks failed to deflect XXXXVIII Pz.Korps' thrust to the Don. The PaK 38 first entered service in 1938. A well designed and efficient gun, the PaK 38 featured a nearly 10-1/2 foot

monobloc barrel fitted with a muzzle brake. The breech mechanism was semi-automatic with a horizontal sliding block. The split-trail carriage was of conventional design and the sloping shield consisted of two 4 mm armor plates about one inch apart. The PaK 38 weighed just over one ton and had a muzzle velocity of 3,940 feet per second when firing the scarce tungsten-cored Pz.Gr. 40 A/P round. Normal muzzle velocity with the Pz.Gr. 39 A/P round was 2,740 feet per second, while HE was 1,800 feet per second. Projectile weights were: A/P, 4.56 lbs.; A/P 40, 2.025 lbs.; HE, 3.94 lbs. Firing the normal Pz.Gr. 39 A/P round, the PaK 38 could penetrate 2.2 inches of armor at a 30° angle of slope at 1,000 yards. Traverse was 65° and elevation was from -18° to +27° With its low silhouette and ease of operation, the PaK 38 gave good service until it encountered the well-armored Soviet KV I and T-34 tanks against which it was nearly ineffective at any range above 400 yards. By late 1943, GD had been fully rearmed with the 7.5cm PaK 40.

Above: A 2cm Flakvierling 38 on a Sd.Kfz.7/1 of 5./Heeresflakabteilung GD in action against ground targets at the edge of a wood during the advance down the Don, July 1942. The Sonderanhänger 46 trailer is attached to the halftrack and has white distance markers painted on the mudguards. The slung Kar 98k carried by the gunner in the center of the photograph shows that the Division had to deal with surprise attacks by Soviet stragglers who constantly raided the march routes of the armored battlegroups which the Division had assembled to race south ahead of the main body.

Below: Pz.Kpfw.IV Ausf. F2s of Stab/Pz.Truppe GD move down the road on the left bank of the Don while infantry march alongside. The Ausf. F2 was a result of Army Ordinance's need to upgun the armament of the Pz.Kpfw. IV, which had evolved from an infantry support tank mounting a low velocity, short-barreled 7.5cm KwK 37 L/24 gun to the Army's main battle tank. The space inside the turret and generally good layout of the vehicle made it possible to fit the longer barreled 7.5cm KwK 40 L/43. Although meant to be fitted in the planned Ausf. G, with the appearance of the Soviet T-34 and KV-1 tanks, and the inability of the KwK 37 to deal with this unanticipated threat, resulted in the new gun being installed in the Ausf. F. Some 87 rounds of Pz.Gr. 40 ammunition could be stored in the modified interior and the elevation mechanism was also altered. The longer barrel of the KwK 40 required the addition of a coil-spring counterbalance. Some complete Pz.Kpfw. IV Ausf. F2 units were formed and assigned to motorized infantry divisions such as GD, who equipped the HQ Platoon and one company with the Ausf. F2, but most went individually to Panzer units as replacements for losses. The new PzKpfw. IV Ausf. F2 gave the German Army a tank superior in range and hitting power to any possessed by the Soviets in the summer of 1942. The 200 built and converted Ausf. F2s allowed the Germans to bridge the gap between the decline of the Pz.Kpfw. III and the introduction of the Pz.Kpfw. IV Ausf. G. The Ausf. F2 is distinguishable from the later G by its single-baffle globular muzzle brake.

Above: Watched by officers of Panzertruppe GD, a Sturmgeschütz III Ausf. F of StuG. Abt. GD moves on a corduroy road along the Don. The Sturmgeschütz evolved from the infantry's need for organic support artillery to accompany it on the mobile offensive actions envisaged by Army planners in the 1920s and 30s. Every infantry division was to have a battery of these guns, but initial production was slow and the assault guns were formed into independent army-level battalions (later renamed brigades). A few privileged divisions like GD had organic StuG. III battalions which came to be seen as natural tank destroyers rather than the infantry support weapons they were designed to be. Crewed by artillerymen, the StuG. III was essentially a turretless Pz.Kpfw. III mounting initially a short 7.5cm StuK. 37 L/24 howitzer and later a long 7.5cm StuK. 40 L/43 or 48. All automotive specifications were as for the Pz.Kpfw. III. 44 rounds were authorized for stowage inside the vehicle, but in practice every inch of space was used to pack up to 95 rounds (Pz.Gr. 39/40 A/T plus HE for "soft" targets). The loader doubled as the radio operator of the FuG 15 or 16 for intra-battery transmissions. GD produced many Sturmgeschütz "aces" such as Major Peter Frantz, Hauptmann Hanns Magold, Hauptmann Diddo Diddens and Oberwachtmeister Wilhelm Wegner. The StuG. III in this photograph shows that both the area over the driver's roof and the right front extension roof have been filled in with a layer of concrete to improve the ballistic shape and afford better protection.

Below: The crew of a Krauss-Maffei eight-ton Sd.Kfz. 7/2 of 4./Heeresflakabt. GD use their 3.7cm Flak 36 against a ground target on the Lower Don. Having its own organic Flak battalion, GD was able to form Flak-Kampfgruppen (Mixed Anti-Aircraft Sections) built around at least two 8.8cm Flak guns, and two or three 2cm Flak 38s or 3.7cm Flak 36s. These mixed AA sections proved highly effective time and again during raids or in support of either defensive or offensive operations. The Heeresflakabteilung arose out of a need to provide Army Panzer divisions with their own organic Flak element, as cooperation with the Luftwaffe, who until 1942 had sole responsibility for anti-aircraft matters, was often difficult to achieve — inevitable in any case involving inter-service cooperation, but made worse by the special stature enjoyed within the Wehrmacht by the Luftwaffe.

STURMGESCHÜTZBRIGADE GD

I.R.(mot.) GD benefited from its elite status on April 4, 1940 in receiving Army Sturmgeschützbatterie 640, which then became 16.(StuG.)/I.R.(mot.) GD under Oberleutnant Freiherr von Egloffstein. One of the vehicle commanders of the six-gun battery was Leutnant Peter Frantz, a future commander of StuG.Abt. GD. These six StuG. III Ausf. Bs accompanied the Regiment through the French and Balkan campaigns and through the invasion of the Soviet Union. During this period the assault guns, with their low-velocity 7.5cm howitzers, functioned in the role for which they had been designed, as close-support weapons for the infantry. There was a noticeable tendency by late 1941 to employ them against Soviet armor.

In April 1942 I.R.(mot.) GD was upgraded to Division status, and the assault gun company became a full Sturmgeschützabteilung (battalion) having a Battalion HQ and three six-gun batteries with the new longer-barreled 7.5cm StuK. 40 gun. This reflected the StuG's changing role to that of a mobile tank destroyer. At this time the battalion battery and platoon commanders still were officially mounted in Demag Sd.Kfz. 250/3 observation halftracks. In practice, these commanders nearly always elected to lead their commands from the assault guns themselves rather than from the "sardine cans," as they called the observation vehicles. Each battery had a Sd.Kfz. 252 or 250/6 ammunition carrying halftrack as well.

The StuG.Abt. GD under Major Hans-Joachim Scheper's command gave a very good account of itself during the following year. During Fall Blau and the Rzhev and Kharkov fighting, the assault guns and the infantry they supported generally cooperated well. When the two infantry regiments (GD 1 and GD 2) were deployed side by side, the commanders found that attaching the assault gun battalion to one regiment and the tank battalion to the other was particularly effective. During small scale breakthroughs along the Don by Regimentsgruppen (regimental combat teams), the best method was to have the tanks pull the infantry forward while the assault guns pushed them from behind. At Rzhev the nature of the terrain prevented using tanks in this manner. Tank losses were consequently very high with little or no success to show for the losses. Assault guns did much better due to their low silhouette in hull-down observation positions. During the Rzhev fighting, StuG.Abt. GD knocked out about 150 Soviet tanks while losing four of its own vehicles. Pz.Truppe GD was much less successful, losing 30 tanks against only 100 Soviet tanks destroyed. A particularly useful method of countering Soviet tanks and bolstering infantry morale was to form mobile patrols of three to five tanks and/or assault guns just behind the main line of resistance. Over 100 Soviet tanks were destroyed in this manner in the Luchessa Valley at no cost to the Division.

By mid-war the Division's assault gun commanders, in common with the rest of the assault artillery, made their divisional commander aware that assault gunners were specialists who, when ordered to support infantry, should always be placed in charge of the operation. They were to complete their mission and withdraw as soon as possible. The infantry were ordered not to bunch up ("clinging like vines" or "building bunches of grapes" in the evocative original German) behind the assault guns. Assault guns drew fire like magnets and this would cause unnecessary casualties among the bunched-up troops. Moreover, the infantry could best protect the vulnerable assault guns from Soviet tank-hunting teams by deploying in extended order.

By 1944, Germany could no longer produce tanks in numbers sufficient to meet its enemies on anything near equal terms. Assault guns offered a reasonable alternative because of their mobility, low silhouette and powerful gun (upgraded now to a longer-barreled 7.5cm gun). Sturmgeschützbrigade GD, as it was now known, was primarily a tank-killer unit and had a large share of the 20,000 Soviet tanks reported destroyed by April 20, 1944 by the assault artillery. By this date the Brigade Commander and his battery and platoon commanders all served in StuG. IIIs. A total of 31 assault guns, an "Escort Battery" of accompanying infantry, and a truck-borne maintenance company rounded out the Brigade's strength. The 10.5cm Sturmhaubitze 42, issued in 1943, was organized either in a separate platoon per battery or in a separate battery within the battalion.

Right: A Gefreiter from the Kradschützen battalion in a denim fatigue jacket pauses to share a joke next to a GD StuG. III. This vehicle was used by Wachmeister Herbert "Mambo" Schmidt. The vehicle number "16" indicates 1st Batt., 6th StuG. in the battery. Of interest are the jerrycans filled with water (it was far too dangerous to store gasoline externally) marked with the vehicle number and the empty shell cases. Empty shell cases, unused or faulty ammunition, as well as packing cases were collected by the Division's logistics personnel and sent back to supply dumps to be returned to Germany and recycled for the raw-material starved German armaments industry.

Right and facing page: StuG. III crewmen relax with Kradschützen during a pause in the advance to Voronezh. In the photograph at left, a gunner assists an infantryman in removing his equipment, a common practice. In the next photograph the two soldiers chat, observed by a comrade who wears the Deutsches Reiterabzeichen (German Horsemen's Badge). Kradschtz.Btl. GD was organized into Schwadronen (squadrons) and most of its men had served with Krad or Kavallerieschützen squadrons before joining GD. They had originally enlisted or been conscripted into the cavalry. Peacetime cavalry training was long and thorough, and produced superb horsemen. The Horseman's Badge was instituted on April 9, 1930 by the German National Federation for the Breeding and Testing of Thoroughbreds with the objective of promoting the interest of German youth in every aspect of horsemanship. It was awarded in three classes: Bronze for success in horse racing; Silver for winning tournaments and displays; and Gilt for "outstanding achievements in the field of equestrian sport." During the Third Reich the Deutsches Reiterabzeichen was recognized as a national award and wearing it was permitted on the left breast of any uniform.

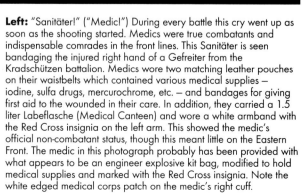

Left: "Sanitäter!" ("Medic!") During every battle this cry went up as soon as the shooting started. Medics were true combatants and indispensable comrades in the front lines. This Sanitäter is seen bandaging the injured right hand of a Gefreiter from the Kradschützen battalion. Medics wore two matching leather pouches on their waistbelts which contained various medical supplies — iodine, sulfa drugs, mercurochrome, etc. — and bandages for giving first aid to the wounded in their care. In addition, they carried a 1.5 liter Labeflasche (Medical Canteen) and wore a white armband with the Red Cross insignia on the left arm. This showed the medic's official non-combatant status, though this meant little on the Eastern Front. The medic in this photograph probably has been provided with what appears to be an engineer explosive kit bag, modified to hold medical supplies and marked with the Red Cross insignia. Note the white edged medical corps patch on the medic's right cuff.

Left: While a StuG. III Ausf. F. negotiates a railroad embankment, a soldier from a burial detail carries a wooden cross for the grave of a recently fallen comrade. Gefreiter Heinrich Krämer, born January 22, 1920, was killed in action on July 1, 1942 at Kautsuk on the northern approaches to Voronezh while serving with 6./I.R.(mot.) GD 1. After being temporarily interred near the battlefield, Gefreiter Krämer's remains were exhumed and reburied in the Soldatenfriedhof (Military Cemetery) some 21 miles southsouthwest of Kastornoye in the Ukraine. Wherever they fought, the German Army built attractive and well-maintained cemeteries to honor their dead.

Above: A Sd.Kfz. 132 Marder II of 1./Pz. Jäger/Abt. GD, vehicle No. 421, halts while its crew surveys the surrounding terrain. In spite of their high silhouette which made them difficult to conceal, Marder IIs gave very good service, provided their commanders and crews did not deceive themselves that Marders were anything other than stop-gap improvised tank destroyers. The Marder relied on the skill of its gunners using the powerful 7.62cm "Ratsch-Bumm" (Crash-Boom) gun to compensate for its thin armor and high profile. This vehicle appears to have been almost wholly oversprayed with sand-yellow paint, leaving only patches of the original "Panzer grey" basecoat remaining. This version of the Marder II was built on the chassis of the Pz.Kpfw. II Ausf. D or E, and later versions were converted from the Pz.Kpfw. II(F) Flammpanzer.

Left: This view shows perfectly the difference between the StuG. III Ausf. F and the Marder II in dimensions and crew protection. The light tank chassis was not capable of carrying more than a thin amount of armor, severely limiting crew safety. Also, the adaptation of existing light tank designs led to the higher, more vulnerable open design as seen here. The StuG. III provided much heavier armor protection and a low silhouette, which made concealment easier.

Above: Standing on a bridge repaired by Stu.Pi.Btl.(mot.) GD, gunners of a Luftwaffe Flak regiment gaze impassively at a group of just captured Soviet soldiers.

Below: An amused Flak officer, Leica 35mm camera in hand to record the scene, seems to be giving instructions to get a better shot as GD's Pioniers search the POWs for documents and hidden weapons. Ic (Intelligence) work tended to be largely overlooked during GD's rapid advance in Fall Blau. POWs were often held at unit level and used as labor troops for hours and even days, thus depriving the Division's intelligence officers of an opportunity to obtain timely information on enemy deployments, capabilities and intentions.

Generalmajor Hoernlein, accompanied by his aides, receives a first-hand situation report from the commander of Stu.Pi.Btl.(mot.) GD, Major Karl Lorenz, at the latter's command post. In the foreground are two radiomen using the Torn.Fu. d2 portable field radio. GD's engineers bridged the entire length of the advance into Voronezh. In the background a newsreel cameraman, accompanying the General on his tour of inspection, films the scene for "Die Wochenschau," the weekly cinema newsreel. At his side, acting as his assistant, is a HIWI (Hilfswilliger or ex-POW auxiliary).

Left: One of the most important artillery pieces in the German arsenal was the legendary 8.8cm Flak 18/36 dual-purpose gun. Designed as a medium anti-aircraft weapon, the "88" became one of the most effective, and feared, anti-tank weapons of World War II. Dug in behind an earthwork, this 8.8cm Flak 36 was set up to destroy enemy line positions and especially armored vehicles. Firing Pz.Gr. 39 A/P ammunition, the 8.8cm Flak 36 could penetrate 127mm of armor at 100 yards, 106mm at 1000 yards, and 88mm at 2000 yards.

This page above and below: Although the 8.8cm guns were usually fired when lowered from their wheeled carriages, they could be used from the travel position by locking the trailer brakes and extending the side stabilizer arms and support jacks, as seen here. This was not uncommon in situations in which there wasn't time to deploy the guns in the normal fashion. Another advantage was the guns could also be moved rapidly if required. The 8.8cm gun had excellent open sights for use against ground targets. This gun was from 1. Batterie of Flakartillerieregiment GD. Well aware of the GD photographer, this crew celebrates a successful engagement against the enemy.

Left: A fine close-up of squadron commander Oberleutnant Hans Klemme's Sd.Kfz. 250/3 radio command vehicle. Several jerrycans of fuel are strapped to the sides of the vehicle to extend its range. "Chef" denoted the unit commander and was often marked on the lead vehicle.

Left and below: Demag Sd.Kfz. 250s of 2./Kradschtz.Btl. GD advance through a Soviet farm village in columns of platoons. Their MG 34s are trained on the surrounding buildings to open fire instantly on parties of Soviet troops left behind to delay the German advance. Oberleutnant Klemme's Sd.Kfz. 250/3, on the right, displays the markings of 2. Schwadron, and the vehicle number "1."

Left: The vehicle commanders of two Sd.Kfz. 250 SPWs of 2./Kradschtz.Btl. GD scan the horizon for signs of enemy activity outside Voronezh, early June 1942. Both of these 5.38 ton vehicles mount s.MG 34 machine guns for sustained fire (an additional MG 34 was either stored on a rack in the vehicle or mounted aft for anti-aircraft protection). The main purpose of this basic vehicle in the 250 series was to transport the Halbgruppe (half section) of four men and their leader, who also served as the vehicle commander. Note the identifying number on the s.MG 34's optical sight.

Below: A Sd.Kfz. 250/10 le.SPW (3.7cm PaK) Zugführerwagen (platoon commander's vehicle). The Sd.Kfz. 250/10 was issued to each platoon commander of le.SPW platoons to provide heavy fire support. The crew consisted of four men – driver, gun/vehicle commander, gunner, and loader for the 3.7cm PaK 35/36, which featured a variety of gun shields. The weapon was not only useful for attacking known targets, but also for supporting the normal method of advancing, which was to have two or three groups of vehicles "leapfrog" through each other's positions, supporting each stage of the move. Carrying four men and 216 rounds of 3.7cm ammunition on board, space inside for stowage was at a premium and the crew members have stowed much of their gear on the outside of the vehicle.

This page: Major Horst von Usedom and some men of his Vorausabteilung observe the interrogation of a Soviet infantry officer. Many Soviet soldiers, particularly those in the technical branches, had studied German, the language of science and mathematics, and viewed the Germans, at least until 1941, as "Kulturnyi" (people of culture). The invasion of the Soviet Union soon changed their minds.

Above and below: Panzer crewmen and Kradschützen assemble to observe a Pz.Kpfw. IV demolish a farm building which a short time before had been a Soviet strongpoint. Training manuals warned in the strictest terms against employing tanks as bulldozers. The commander of this Pz.Kpfw. IV Ausf. F1 at least has turned his turret to 7 o'clock to avoid direct damage to his main gun or sights, but using a tank in this manner left it vulnerable to clogging the air intakes, ventilation system and vision ports with falling debris and dust.

Sd.Kfz. 251s of Stabsquartier (Div. HQ Co.)/I.D.(mot.) GD share a crowded road with Pz.Kpfw. IIIs and IVs of the Division's Panzertruppe. Pz.Kpfw. IIIs were found in the tank battalion's 2. and 3. Companies, which also had a number of the weaker Pz.Kpfw. IIs, largely relegated to reconnaissance duties. The Schützen in their SPWs were in the embryonic stages of becoming the "Hausinfanterie" (Personal Infantry) of the armored forces. This process took another two years to mature fully into the formidable Panzerkampfgruppen of the last year of the war. The crew of the Pz.Kpfw. IV in the foreground have covered the "Rommelkiste" ("Rommel Chest") storage bin on the rear of the turret with a shelter-quarter.

Pz.Kfw. IV Ausf. F2s of 1./Pz.Truppe GD advance towards Voronezh. For the first time since the invasion of the Soviet Union, German Panzer crews had a tank with sufficient armament to take on the T-34 and KV-I tanks of the Red Army. Pz.Truppe GD's unique marking system indicates that these tanks ("=1" and "=5") are the first and fifth tanks in 2. Zug (Platoon) of 1. Kompanie, the Pz.Kpfw. IV company of Pz.Truppe GD. Many of these marking systems were used only for a short time, or until the units were expanded or reorganized.

THE RACE TO THE LOWER DON

he march to the Lower Don began on July 8, 1942. GD was given top priority for the use of the road south. All other units had to make way for the Division with its huge train of over 2,500 motor vehicles of all types. The distances logged in each day's march were considerable — 75 miles on the first day alone. The columns often outraced their fuel supplies, a situation beyond the abilities of GD's logistical services to address, and the Luftwaffe had to intervene to drop barrels of fuel from JU-52s. This, however, only covered a fraction of the Division's needs; a motorized division required thousands of gallons of gasoline per day. While the armored spearhead moved forward rapidly and saw little sign of the retreating Soviets, the slower moving and frequently halted motorized units and supply echelons were less fortunate. Soviet stragglers and sometimes entire units retiring in good order constantly ran into and fought violently with the supply units, which were generally armed with nothing heavier than light machine guns. By mid-July the fuel situation had grown so critical that the divisional commander had to order that gasoline be siphoned from all the non-fighting vehicles in order to keep his thin

spearhead of AFVs moving at all. The very thin coverage of the line of advance positively invited counterattacks by the gradually stiffening Soviet forces. Only the speed of the attack helped to keep the enemy off-balance until the Division crossed the Lower Don on July 22. Although there had been some periods of hard fighting, the advance had been chiefly characterized by long marches in blazing heat and choking dust. The real heroes, on whom the whole burden of the advance fell, were the soldiers of the maintenance and supply echelons, doing their unheralded and unglamorous jobs superbly well in extremely trying conditions.

Spread: Standing in frustration at the head of the stalled column in his 1.5-ton Daimler-Benz 1500A troop carrier, the company commander of 1./G.R. GD waits for the road south to clear. The 1500A and its command car variant were built between 1941-1943 and had seating for 6 men plus the driver and passenger in the front seat. The vehicle number is painted on the right front mudguard.

Above: Grossdeutschland had over 2,600 motor vehicles of all types in 1942. Included in this large fleet were the trucks and cars of the 2 grenadier regiments, 2 communications companies and their supply column, 4 engineer companies also with a supply column, 18 other supply columns, 3 workshops, a field hospital, 2 medical companies, 3 ambulance platoons, a butchery, a bakery, a tire company, a spare-parts company, a field post office, the war correspondent platoon, the field replacement battalion and, to command and coordinate everything, the divisional HQ and a military police platoon. For the race to the Lower Don, the entire division was tied to one main road. The further along the Division moved, the further it was from its supply dumps and the more acute its logistical problems became. In this photograph a long column of 3-ton trucks, an Opel Blitz in the lead, move down the highway past a self-propelled 2cm Flak 38. The most important of the Wegweiser (sign posts) is that for the Ersatzteil-Staffel GD (Spare Parts Echelon GD).

Left: Holding a red/white folding traffic disc, a movement control officer keeps the traffic flowing smoothly. Soviet aircraft could hardly miss hitting targets on a road as crowded as this. Traffic control within GD's marching columns was largely effective due to well thought-out procedures. While moving at a normal pace, a fifty meter distance was maintained. This prevented unauthorized vehicles from getting into the columns and disrupting their order. Road sign erection squads of the Feldgendarmerietrupp GD were at the head of every column. Traffic control was the responsibility of a specially selected staff officer or military police officer from the divisional HQ. This officer was in constant contact with divisional HQ, and this allowed General Hoernlein to make changes in the order of march or to deal with changes in the tactical situation. River crossings were often dangerous and difficult, and in these situations, the military police whose duties were vital in allowing a smooth crossing, came under the command of Heeresflakabteilung GD whose batteries had to protect the crossing points.

Above: A Kfz. 69 6x4 Krupp "Boxer" of the infantry gun company from one of GD's infantry regiments tows a le.IG 18 on a dirt track which passes for a main road in Russia. The "Boxer," in many different variants, saw widespread service in the first half of the war. Equipped with an independent rear suspension and an air-cooled 4-cylinder opposed engine, the Boxer was very modern in concept but did not meet the Army's needs for a standard light truck.

Left: Moving two abreast, light Flak and men of G.R. GD 2 in their light passenger trucks halt to await new orders. The crew of the 2cm Flak 38 have added a shelter-quarter to the natural camouflage of their vehicle. Among the signposts is one for the 11. Kolonne of the divisional supply units.

Members of the Feldgendarmerietrupp (Military Police Troop) keep the endless columns flowing smoothly. The Feldgendarmes were organized in platoon strength and supplied with motorcycles and light passenger cars. Their armament consisted entirely of light weapons. As with all other units, GD's military police had been supplied by eligible members of the civilian Schutzpolizei whose insignia they wore on the left sleeve of their army uniforms. Apart from their Waffenfarbe (arm of service color) and cuff-title (worn on the left cuff), the Feldgendarmes were instantly recognizable by their Ringkragen (gorgets) on their chests — GD's unique version (worn by the bareheaded Feldgendarme in the photograph) featured the GD monogram on a piece of metal added to the gorget above the National Emblem. Feldgendarmes, known to the troops as "Kettehunde" ("Chained Dogs") because of the chains on which their gorgets were suspended, were responsible for a wide variety of tasks — the most critical being traffic control, collection of prisoners, and maintenance of order and discipline. All Feldgendarmes, with the exception of their officers and some drivers, were NCOs holding Army equivalent ranks of their civilian police ranks. Both BMW R75 and Zündapp KS750 motorcycles with side-cars are seen in this photograph. Note the MP 40 (without magazine) on the Zündapp.

Above: Kradmelder (dispatch riders) were the busiest and best informed soldiers in the German Army. Constantly traveling up and down the line of advance, they were the first to learn of any news and were quick to pass it along to the main body. This Kradmelder shows the wear and tear to which he and his mount were exposed. The sleeves of his field blouse have been carefully rolled up to expose his cuff title. He wears general purpose goggles which were provided with both clear and dark lenses.

Above: Looking for all the world like a party of quail hunters, complete with refreshments, soldiers from a motorized column try their luck against a passing Soviet aircraft. The soldiers' casual attitude and the new MG 42s sitting unused on the ground would suggest that the aircraft in question is a reconnaissance plane unlikely to do any immediate harm. The German Army had long held the idea that, for reasons of maintaining morale and fighting spirit, soldiers needed to participate actively in defending against air attacks. It was theoretically possible for rifle fire to damage or even destroy an enemy aircraft at ranges below 500 yards. Though this proved effective in only the rarest of cases, it could at least keep the enemy pilots at a more respectful distance. Contemporary German Army training manuals devoted considerable space to the subject, featuring elaborate charts, recommending a supine position, and carefully leading the target.

Left: Divisional Ia (Chief of Operations) Major i.G. Cord von Hobe interrogates a downed Soviet fighter pilot with the help of a Russian-speaking interpreter. In a paper prepared in 1943 for Generaloberst Guderian, Major von Hobe confessed that, during the rapid advance to Voronezh and south to the Don Bend, Grossdeutschland did not give sufficient importance to intelligence work or interrogation of POWs. This was complicated by the severe shortage of qualified interpreters at all levels.

Above: Generalmajor Hoernlein views enemy dispositions through a scissors periscope in company with Adjutant Hauptman Theo Bethke and O1 Oberleutnant Helmuth Spaeter, already highly decorated veterans in 1942.

Right: Generalmajor Hoernlein observes for himself the progress of his division in its baptism by fire on the Don Steppe. In the background heavily camouflaged 3-ton trucks return to the rear to pick up fresh supplies while 1./Pz.Truppe GD pauses to await further instructions. The metal command pennant (black, white, and red) was the standard divisional type. Pennants were fitted to most command vehicles used by senior officers.

Light trucks of the staff of 3. Batterie, II/A.R.(mot.) GD, a 15cm s.FH 18 heavy howitzer battery drawn by 8-ton halftrack prime movers, halt during the race to the Lower Don. Insufficient amounts of fuel turned the main body's advance into a series of quick dashes followed by halts of varying lengths. Feeder roads to the Rollbahn (Main Highway) were often particularly bad with many traffic jams, turning the Rollbahn into a Stehbahn (Stopway). Such congestion as this photograph plainly shows invited Soviet air attacks which in turn necessitated the strictest road march discipline.

Above: Generalmajor Hoernlein and Major i.G. Cord von Hobe observe the progress of the march from Hoernlein's Kfz. 15 Horch command car.

Right: While a Luftwaffe Unteroffizier of a Flak regiment shoulders his rifle and moves off, General Hoernlein scans the horizon. On the right mudguard is the standard general officer's pennant. Painted on the mudguard is the tire inflation marking, "3.5 atü" (51 psi). Hoernlein wears his favorite campaign uniform of a Model 35 officer's field blouse with colonel's shoulderboards and officer's collar patches. Of all his decorations earned in two world wars, General Hoernlein wears only his Ritterkreuz.

Kradschützen crouch behind a light truck of IV/I.R.(mot.) GD 1 to watch the shelling of some Soviet positions. IV/I.R.(mot.) GD 1 was the support battalion of the Regiment and contained the 16.(Fla.), 17.(Infantry Gun) and 18.(Pz. Jäger) companies.

Machine gunners (note the Model 34 barrel containers) watch a le.IG 18 of 17./I.R.(mot.) GD 1 shell Soviet positions. Allied armies had abandoned the development of infantry howitzers (to give these guns their actual role) but the Germans persevered and produced the le.IG 18. Although obsolescent in its design, the le.IG 18 gave German infantrymen a useful organic light artillery weapon for use on first contact with the enemy, or in situations where heavier support might not be appropriate or too slow in arriving.

Exhausted members of a forward observer detachment sleep in the baking afternoon heat of mid-July on the Don steppe.

Above: Generalmajor Hoernlein briefs Oberstleutnant Alfred Greim (left, wearing glasses), commander of II/I.R.(mot.) GD 1, while divisional artillery commander Oberst Georg Jauer looks on. German Army practice required that commanders personally issue orders for missions so that they would thus gain a first-hand impression of the situation at unit level. This was especially important in GD's case as General Hoernlein commanded a very large division which had only just recently been formed and whose officers and men had served together for only a short time prior to the start of the summer offensive. Oberst Jauer wears spiral puttees, which many old soldiers swore were just as practical and comfortable as the later high marching boots.

Left: The Orders group of I.R.(mot.) GD 1 during Fall Blau. Major Gehrke sits alongside his regimental commander, Oberst Otto Köhler, and other officers and NCOs. Born on August 11, 1897, in Essen in the Ruhr, Otto Köhler fought in the First World War and was a veteran of the 100,000 man Reichsheer. An old hand from Döberitz, Köhler distinguished himself in the French Campaign and led GD's "Vorausabteilung" — Kampfgruppe Köhler — on the race south to Mantysch. Awarded the German Cross in Gold on October 3, 1942 for his regiment's achievements in the September 1942 fighting in the Rzhev Salient, Köhler died when his Stabskompanie's command bunker at Chermassikovo was overrun on December 1, 1942. To the last moment Oberst Köhler remained on the telephone talking to Ia Cord von Hobe. Köhler was posthumously promoted to Generalmajor and interred in the Heldenfriedhof at Olenino.

Inset: Major Kurt Gehrke, CO of I/I.R.(mot.) GD 1 was one of the Division's most experienced combat leaders and received the Ritterkreuz for his battalion's holding out at Kusolevo in the Luchessa Valley, Rzhev Salient, in December 1942. In this photograph, taken on the Don in July 1942, Major Gehrke wears a somewhat eccentric campaign uniform — the most noteworthy items of which are the rebadged old style officer's field cap and the enlisted men's pattern National Emblem sewn above the right breast pocket of his field blouse. "Kiki" Gehrke left the Division in December 1942 to assume a 15-month assignment as commander of Wachbataillon GD in Berlin.

Above: Three men of 17.(IG)/I.R.(mot.) GD 1 pause during the advance to the Don, July 1942. In the center stands Feldwebel Karl Semper, Kompanietruppführer (Co. HQ Squad Leader). Semper, a native of Oberlunkwitz, near Chemnitz, was born on March 28, 1915. Before reporting for army duty in 1937, he worked in a factory producing women's stockings in his home town. Semper served in the IG platoon of the Infanterielehrregiment in Döberitz where he proved to be an exceptional marksman. The Kradmelder to Semper's right is 25 year-old Gefreiter Hermann Laubinger from Nürnberg. Behind the Feldwebel stands Unteroffizier Georg Holzhammer from Passau. Laubinger and Holzhammer survived the war while Semper died in action outside Balga, East Prussia, on March 18, 1945. In the background is a "Panjewagen" pressed into service by GD, and which the Wehrmacht found so invaluable on the Eastern Front.

Left: As befits a senior NCO, Feldwebel Semper carries a machine pistol – in this case an MP 38. Extremely well made and capable of a cyclic rate of fire of 500rpm, the MP 38 was a revolutionary weapon. Its single major deficiency was the safety mechanism, which locked the bolt only in the open position, causing numerous casualties as a result of accidental discharges. Note the absence of a muzzle nut on the weapon's barrel.

Right: A well-camouflaged SP 2cm Flak 38 of 5./He.Flakabteilung GD pauses during the advance on the Don steppe. An air recognition flag for friendly aircraft has been attached to the hood and the gun commander has stuck an M24 stick grenade in his belt. Light Flak units often were caught up in close quarter fighting when they overran Soviet positions and, on their totally exposed mounts, needed infantry weapons of their own to defend themselves. Foliage and other more extensive camouflage methods became increasingly necessary as the Allies gradually gained air superiority over the Luftwaffe.

Left: Hauptmann Otto Ernst Remer, CO of IV(Schwere-Heavy)/I.R.(mot.) GD 1 places himself in front of 17.(IG) Kompanie's gun line on the Upper Don. Hauptmann Remer still wore the insignia of an Oberleutnant at this time. Unit commanders in the German Army typically led from the most forward positions. This gave them the best information on the actual tactical situation.

Left: The crew of Generalmajor Hoernlein's Sd.Kfz. 251/6 Ausf. B Kommandopanzerwagen receive and transmit orders and information. This was a fully-equipped command-post vehicle whose eight-man crew used the FuG 11 and FuG Tr 100mw radios as well as the "Enigma" code machines (for higher HQs). Production of the 8.5-ton vehicle was terminated in 1943.

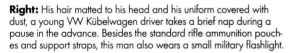

Right: His hair matted to his head and his uniform covered with dust, a young VW Kübelwagen driver takes a brief nap during a pause in the advance. Besides the standard rifle ammunition pouches and support straps, this man also wears a small military flashlight.

Above: With an officer blowing his whistle and raising his right hand, 16.(Fla)/I.R.(mot.) GD 1 prepares to engage an enemy force approaching from their left.

Below: Infantry gunners of 17.(IG)/I.R.(mot.) GD 1 ready their 15cm s.IG 33 for firing during the advance down the Don, July 1942. 17. Kompanie had one platoon of six of these powerful guns. They were as effective as tanks against bunkers and fortifications in both high and low-angle fire. The s.IG 33, a direct descendant of the infantry-accompanying guns of the First World War, fired an 84 lb HE shell to a maximum range of 5,140 yards. Having those powerful guns organic to its two infantry regiments meant that A.R.(mot.) GD did not have to be taken away from main artillery objectives and that the infantry regiments had their own artillery close fire-support. Also, should the need arise, the s.IGs could be integrated into the artillery regiment's fire plan.

Above: Infantrymen, one carrying a new MG 42 machine gun, come to attention as a regimental HQ vehicle passes them on the outskirts of a farming village on the Don steppe. Crewmen of a well camouflaged self-propelled 2cm Flak of 16.(Fla.)/I.R. GD 1 check their weapons in the background.

Below: A senior officer in one of Divisional HQ's Sd.Kfz. 251s (note the "Stabsquartier" pennant painted on the rear of the vehicle) issues orders to the crew of one of Pz.Truppe GD's Pz.Kpfw. IIs on the Don steppes.

Right: Infantrymen ride aboard a battery commander's StuG. III (note the "star" aerial) during Kampfgruppe Köhler's advance down the great bend of the Don, mid-July 1942. GD's two infantry regiments were totally truck-borne at this time and riding on tracked vehicles was the only available way to keep the infantry up with the Division's armored spearhead. The soldier at the left wears web gaiters and belt support straps together with a first-pattern cuff-title in Gothic script.

Below: Grenadiers of I.R.(mot.) GD 1, jammed together on Leutnant Konrad Schenk's Sturmgeschütz, 3./StuG.Abt. GD, hurry towards Voronezh. Most trucks were left behind and much of the infantry not taken along by the armored spearhead had some very hard marching ahead of them. The introduction of the SPW provided a major improvement in infantry transport.

Young grenadiers, fresh from the depot, and their experienced sergeant ride a StuG. III on the Don steppes, July 1942. Well before reaching the line of departure, the men would dismount and reform as foot infantry.

NON-COMMISSIONED OFFICERS

The German Army had for generations possessed the finest NCOs, but until the First World War these long-serving professional soldiers had been entrusted solely with training and disciplinary functions. Even the company and regimental sergeant-majors lost most of their authority when the Army was in the field. They merely transmitted their officers' orders and saw that they were carried out. This was a wasteful use of a reservoir of military talent and leadership potential. In the First World War, however, the high casualties among the officer corps and the revolution in infantry tactics brought far greater responsibility to the Army's NCOs, who rose magnificently to the occasion. The postwar Reichsheer institutionalized this new organization by assigning one platoon in each company to a senior NCO and formalizing their new responsibilities.

Being an elite unit and, from 1942, a division made up exclusively of Kriegsfreiwillige (war volunteers), Grossdeutschland was provided with the highest-caliber NCOs, who then formed the backbone of the Division. As officer casualties mounted, these men assumed ever greater responsibilities and many were given short-service wartime commissions as "Kriegsoffiziere" — men who were trusted to do their jobs competently but who were unlikely to be retained as officers after the war. This was no longer a matter of class-exclusivity but rather of the former NCOs' lack of the broad liberal and professional education required of a modern officer. Throughout World War II, German Army units had many fewer officers than the Allied armies. The Germans firmly believed that too few officers were better than too many of the wrong type of officer.

Right: The very model of a regimental sergeant-major, "Der Spiess" of G.R. GD 1. In peacetime, the Hauptfeldwebel was largely responsible for discipline, training, and administration in the garrison or cantonment. In World War II, for the first time, he became an invaluable member of the Regiment in the field. This "Hauptfeld" is a highly decorated veteran holding both grades of the Iron Cross, the General Assault Badge (Allgemeines-Sturmabzeichen) and has been wounded in action.

The Leutnant at the right is evidently a commissioned ex-NCO of very long service, as shown by his Weimar-era National Sports Badge, and of proven valor, as attested by his combat decorations — including the German Cross in Gold (Deutsche Kreuz in Gold) and the Wound Badge in Silver (for at least three wounds suffered). As both men wear the General Assault Badge rather than the Panzerkampfabzeichen, they are most probably members of Pz.Aufklärungsabteilung GD.

Major Horst von Usedom

Major Horst von Usedom, commander of Kradschützenbataillon GD, was a veteran cavalryman, one of whose ancestors had commanded a regiment of hussars bearing his name in 1806. Horst-Viktor von Usedom was born in Celle/Hannover, the heart of German horse country, on March 9, 1906. Major von Usedom was the reconnaissance battalion's first commander. He took over the Battalion on April 1, 1942 after a very successful command of Kradschützenbataillon 61 of the Silesian 11. Panzerdivision, where he had been awarded the Ritterkreuz on December 31, 1941, outside Moscow. Von Usedom went on sick leave and handed over command of Kradschtz.Btl. GD to Rittmeister Rudolf Watjen on July 29, 1942 after reaching Manytsch. After a month's convalescence Oberstleutnant von Usedom (from August 1, 1942) took over command of Pz.Gr.Rgt. 67 of the newly-raised Potsdam 26. Pz.Div., "die Meissen Soldaten." On March 28, 1945, while serving as commander of Pz.Brigade "Kurland," Oberst Horst von Usedom became the 809th recipient of the Eichenlaub. As commander of a battalion which had both an armored car (eight-wheel and four-wheel) squadron as well as Kradschützen in SPWs, Kübelwagens and on motorcycles, Von Usedom exercised his privilege of wearing both the standard service dress and the black Panzer field uniform. The battalion wore two different Waffenfarben (branch colors) — the armored car squadron wore Goldgelb (gold-yellow) while the Kradschützen wore Wiesengrün (meadow green). In the photo at right, the Major proudly poses with his pet cocker spaniel, who accompanied him throughout the campaign. A born cavalryman, von Usedom so impressed his own character on his battalion that the Kradschützen came to be known as the "Usedom Husaren" ("Usedom Hussars") in tribute both to their commander, his distinguished forebears, and the daredevil nature of their role in the Division. The reconnaissance battalion kept this nickname throughout the war.

Below: A bespectacled Wachmeister of Kradschützenbataillon GD at the head of a long column of reconnaissance vehicles waits for the traffic to clear during the advance to the Lower Don. Screens have been fitted to the top of the fighting compartment to keep out Soviet hand grenades and an MP 40 machine pistol is ready to use. The interesting and varied collection of vehicles in the background show the firepower and flexibility of the reconnaissance battalion to carry out a wide range of missions. Among the vehicles are a Pz.Kpfw. II, used now as a scouting vehicle, a couple of Demag Sd.Kfz. 250 SPWs, some light trucks, and an Sd.Kfz. 247/II. This vehicle, with its lesser cross-country ability, was based on the Horch heavy passenger car chassis. Armored units such as GD used it as transportation for senior commanders or staff officers. Note the large "star" aerial for the FuG 12 command radio.

Facing page: Two Funker, one wearing the Panzer field uniform with specialty patch on his sleeve, receive incoming messages on an FuG 12 radio used for controlling motorized formations. This radio was often mounted in the Demag Sd.Kfz. 250/3. Interestingly at this rather late date, the man in the Panzer uniform is still wearing the field grey "Schiffchen" field cap. The Gefreiter in the foreground operates a scissors periscope, standard-issue on these vehicles.

Above: Machine gunners assemble in a barnyard before moving off again. The gunner at the left carries two Model 41 machine gun ammunition boxes suspended from carbine hooks on a webbed mortar-carrying harness strap slung around his neck. Standing right center with his back to the camera is a soldier carrying a canvas engineer's explosive kit which held 3kg explosive charges. Contrary to published regulations, these soldiers in the field have arranged their personal equipment to suit their particular needs and comfort. The right-hand man in the photograph is resting his hand on the muzzle of a new MG 42 light machine gun — yet more evidence of Grossdeutschland's favored status, as the MG 42 had just then entered service and would not be generally available for over a year. 6. Armee in Stalingrad did not see the MG 42 until early 1943.

Below: While two of his fellow machine gunners prepare to drink, a gunner carrying the 42 lb. Lafette 34 tripod stands holding a P-38 automatic pistol. His gasmask container and shelter quarter have been rearranged to carry the tripod on its leather carrying straps. The Model 42 ammunition boxes in the background are attached to tripod carrying straps.

Above: Two Schützen of I.R. (mot.) GD 1 pause while heavy weapons engage dug-in Soviet troops along the Lower Don, July 1942. The classic silhouette of the German M-35 steel helmet is evident in this photograph. First designed in 1916 to protect troops from plunging fire in the trenches of the Western Front and lightened and slightly modified in 1935 with better internal fittings, it was already obsolescent on the eve of the Second World War. As early as the end of the Polish Campaign, the Heereswaffenamt (Army Ordnance Dept.) had, despite Hitler's orders to the contrary, begun preliminary research for a new steel helmet. The HWA eventually selected four types as worthy of further study and this number was subsequently reduced to two. The main reasons behind this research were both the dramatic increase in head wounds caused by flat-trajectory rounds penetrating the straight vertical crown of the M-35 helmet and the need to reduce manufacturing costs. Both prototypes were submitted for Hitler's inspection and were rejected undoubtedly much more for ideological than military reasons. The Führer remained convinced that the traditional helmet was bound up with the essence of the German soldier. Note that the Schütze in the foreground wears canvas webbing originally designed for troops in North Africa but widely issued throughout the Army due to leather shortages and has painted his helmet with a mixture of matte field grey paint and fine sand. He wears the first-pattern cuff-title on his right sleeve.

The squad gets ready to move out. The soldier at the right, resting his rifle on an ammunition box, has covered his helmet with mosquito netting. The swamps of the Lower Don Bend were a fertile breeding ground for disease-carrying mosquitoes and the overtaxed soldiers of GD at the spearhead could prove especially susceptible to disease.

Right: While a veteran MG 34 section leader (note the case for the ZF 34 optical sight on his left hip) contentedly puffs his pipe, a radio man awaits fresh instructions over his Tornister Funkgerät 02 portable field radio set. The Torn.Fu. 02 was one of the most widely used radios and was employed from regiment to battalion and from battalion to company level. The radio was furnished with a six-foot sectional rod antenna and had a four-mile range on radio-telephone and nine miles on continuous-wave. The Torn.Fu. 02 was powered by a two-volt storage battery and a 130 volt dry battery. The set came supplied with two headsets, a throat microphone, a hand microphone, and a morse code sender key. Each unit had its own radiomen who had received signals training and wore a shoulder patch showing a lightning bolt in their branch color (in this case, infantry white).

Left: An exhausted and nearly dehydrated young machine gunner, his collar-liner undone in the 100° heat, pauses during the advance. On his waistbelt is the Model 34 tool pouch for the MG 34 machine gun.

Feldwebel Semper and Unteroffizer Holzhammer watch through field glasses as men of 17.(IG)/I.R. (mot.) GD 1 use an MG 34 light machine gun from the shelter of their Sd.Kfz. 10 prime mover. In keeping with the Einheits (standard) principle, all support units were provided with sufficient light automatic infantry support weapons to enable them to defend themselves at close quarters. 17. Kompanie had four MG 34s.

Crew members of a s.IG 33 15cm heavy infantry gun — gun "C" in the six-gun company — watch as an infantry company advances in extended order to clear out some farm buildings. In addition to its usual role of infantry close-support fire and its secondary anti-tank role, plunging fire of the s.IG 33's HE rounds could clear paths through enemy minefields by blast-effect alone.

Above: Moving parallel to a skirmish line of infantry, a StuG. III Ausf. F takes up its firing position to engage enemy infantry. When using assault guns in support of infantry, several basic principles were established. First, as defensive weapons to be employed at the Schwerpunkt of an action, Sturmgeschütze were never to betray their presence prematurely by deploying in small actions. To maintain the element of tactical surprise, the guns went into position at night and camouflaged their assembly areas. Second, because their primary mission was the neutralization of the enemy's support weapons at close range, Sturmgeschütze were best employed in concentrated numbers. They were never to be employed singly and never against targets which the infantry themselves could eliminate on their own (something even GD's infantry asked them to do). Although employing Sturmgeschütze in small units negated their advantage to a degree, when this proved unavoidable they were to be used in pairs, covering each other by fire and movement. When supporting the infantry, Sturmgeschütze never led the attack; rather they advanced alongside or just behind the infantry. Immediately upon reaching the objective, the assault guns withdrew about one thousand yards behind the newly-taken position, leaving the infantry to consolidate the gains. This served both to rest the assault gun crews and keep them beyond immediate enemy fire, while freeing them for further missions. During infantry support missions, the infantry was tasked with protecting the assault guns during close combat where they were rather vulnerable to Soviet tank-hunting teams.

Right: A machine gun section with two MG 34s moves cross-country. The men carried their personal gear and equipment as they found most comfortable and practical. Again, despite regulations, most of these men have strapped their gas cape pouches to their gas mask canisters.

On August 1, 1942, I.D.(mot.) Grossdeutschland was pulled out of the line on the Manytsch River and went into OKH reserve. The previous month's fighting had not been too costly in casualties, though the wear and tear on the vehicles and equipment had been severe. The Division assembled at Shakhty on the north bank of the Donets between August 1-14. Meanwhile, the Canadians had staged their ill-fated and costly landing at the former resort city of Dieppe on the English Channel on August 14, and GFM Keitel saw imminent danger for the neglected German defenses in the West. As a result, he convinced Adolf Hitler to order the immediate transfer to France of the Leibstandarte SS "Adolf Hitler" and I.D.(mot.) GD. In the event, only the Leibstandarte made the journey. GD was still at its railheads at Smolensk when the situation on Heeresgruppe Mitte's (Army Group Center) front led to the cancellation of the transfer order.

Grossdeutschland had used the past few weeks to convalesce into a more effective fighting unit, a process which had barely begun when the Division was suddenly assigned to one of the most dangerous and exposed sectors on the central Eastern Front. The Rzhev salient had formed in the frontline as the Soviet winter counter-offensive of 1941-42 spent itself. At its farthest point eastward it reached the Volga barely 100 miles from Moscow, making it a natural springboard for a renewed German assault on the Soviet capital. In the same way, it also could serve the Soviet High Command, the Stavka, as a springboard for outflanking either Heeresgruppe Nord (North) or Mitte (Center). GD reached the Rzhev Salient on August 30, 1942, going into bivouac as a reserve for Generaloberst Walter Model's 9. Armee until September 9. Model's troops had held the salient throughout the winter, and the spring had seen a general cleaning-up of the lines. By the end of July, the Soviets had lost tens of thousands of troops trying to eliminate the salient. General Ivan Konev, the new Soviet sector commander, was determined to retake Rzhev, whatever the cost.

On August 31, the Soviets launched a massive attack from north of the salient, at the confluence of the Vasuga and Volga rivers, where they quickly established a bridgehead. Allowing the Soviets to consolidate a bridgehead was always fatal and Model wasted no time in committing I.D.(mot.) GD, now part of XXVII Armeekorps, against this threat on September 9. Behind a massive artillery "fire strike" which the Red Army evolved from World War One German practice, Soviet infantry advanced in dense waves on the German positions, which they swiftly overran. GD's counterattack started at dawn on September 10 and disappeared under a curtain of Soviet artillery fire and aerial attack. With the fate of 9. Armee and the salient in the balance the Grenadiers and Panzertruppe pressed forward, their losses rapidly approaching the unacceptable level. When the fighting ended on September 10, some units had lost 60% of their strength and the frontline had not been restored. Fortunately though, the Soviets' forward movement had at least been temporarily halted. The attack was resumed the next day with no more success and equally heavy losses. On September 12, the Soviets mounted a new attack which was thrown back with high losses. For the rest of the month, GD fought in conditions similar to Flanders in the First World War: in mud, rain, and general misery. On September 30, every man capable of shouldering a weapon was drafted from the rear echelon units to mount a counterattack to restore the line. The appalling carnage that resulted saw only a few hundred yards of ground recovered and GD in the process reduced to the strength of a very weak regiment.

By October 2, the fighting had quieted and Rzhev was held, thanks to the sacrifice of Grossdeutschland. The Division was withdrawn to Olenino until November 25 to lick its wounds, reorganize, and receive what replacements it could from the depots. With the onset of the "Rasputitsa" (season of bad roads) in November, Stavka exerted pressure simultaneously on the eastern and western sides of the salient. GD's front faced west and northwest in the Luchessa valley against two Soviet tanks corps, whose mission was to cut the main Byelo/Olenin road in support of other formations trying to cut Model's vital railroad link to the west. By December 1, with all but one of its infantry battalions in the line, Generaloberst Model committed II/G.R. GD to restore the positions which had been lost by the sudden collapse of the Westphalian 86 I.D. The battalion held its ground in a sea of Soviet armor and infantry until other GD units gradually joined it. With no food and soldiers living in flooded trenches, conditions rapidly degenerated but still the remnants of the Division hung on. The Panzerjägers' 5cm PaK 38s were useless except at point-blank range. The Division's infantry facing the armored onslaught of three Soviet divisions had to move out and stalk the enemy tanks with hand-held anti-tank mines and grenade bundle charges. Men such as Wilhelm Anding and Gerhard Konopka became legends within GD at this time. By the day's end, the infantry line finally broke and the Soviets surged forward toward the road. Unexpectedly, the Soviet assault slackened, giving GD time to take up new positions barely 1 1/2 miles from the road. Reinforcements arrived the next day to counterattack and maintain the Germans' grip on the Luchessa Valley. For the next three weeks, while some GD units took part in local counterattacks, others which had been nearly annihilated were withdrawn to rest and refit. The Divisional Cemetery at Shisderovo was already too full by this time and far worse was yet to come.

On December 2, while moving forward with the Pomeranian 12. Panzerdivision, the newly renamed Füsilierregiment GD was hit by the Soviets in thick fog and snow. The surviving members of the Division were too stunned by their recent experiences to celebrate Christmas. Five days later they joined 12. Pz.Div. for a renewed counterattack north of the Luchessa Valley to recapture the village of Merkoshy, vital as a proposed site of an anchor for the belt of fortifications designed to hold the salient. On January 9, the Division's bleeding came to an end as it passed again into OKH reserve.

The four months in the Rzhev Salient had been a terrible ordeal for Grossdeutschland, which culminated in the bloodbath in the Luchessa Valley in December. The Division had suffered particularly as a result of its being continually overextended. The cause of this can be fairly traced to both OKH and Model's 9. Armee staff overestimating the Division's capabilities, which they based on GD's large establishment and generous supply of weapons and equipment. They failed to realize that GD had never been given sufficient time to train as a full division and, with few breaks, had been in action continuously since June 1942. Being drawn piecemeal into a war of attrition, Grossdeutschland suffered a steady incidence of heavy casualties. Among the 12,000 officers and men reported lost in 1942, the majority — including two regimental commanders, Oberst Eugen Garski and Oberst Otto Köhler — fell at Rzhev. Of all Grossdeutschland's battles in the Second World War, Rzhev is the battle upon which the survivors look back with undiminished horror.

A Pz.Kpfw. IV Ausf. F of 1./Panzertruppe GD in the Rzhev salient, September 1942. The tank commander appears to be wearing a captured British blanket-lined leather jerkin, great numbers of which were captured from British supply dumps in France and Belgium in 1940. They made ideal motoring coats. The F version of the Pz.Kpfw. IV had much-improved armor but was still armed with the low-velocity 7.5cm KwK 37 L/24. Note the wider 40cm tracks made necessary by the 6% weight increase of the Ausf. F over the previous E model. Spare tracks were often hung on the front armor, to improve the vehicle's protection.

Pz.Kpfw. IV Ausf. F2s of 1./Pz.Truppe GD at Rzhev. The KwK 40 L/43 gun of the lead tank has a canvas cover fitted to its globular single-baffle muzzle brake to keep dust out of the bore during road marches. The recuperator housing differed from that on the previous Ausf. F. It was more angular in section and had a flat front plate held in place by four conical bolts. With the F2, GD's Panzer crews no longer had to close to dangerously short ranges to engage the less heavily armored sides or rear of Soviet tanks. These vehicles appear to have been sprayed with patches of Afrika Korps-pattern sand yellow paint over their dark grey base coats. Many vehicles intended for the war in Africa had to be sent to the Eastern Front to replace losses, and so sand yellow tanks were not uncommon.

Pz.Kpfw. IV Ausf. F1s of 1./Pz.Truppe GD, heavily garlanded with local foliage, halt in a field in the Rzhev salient and are given a quick check. Tank crewmen were cross-trained and quite capable of carrying out routine maintenance on their own.

Right: Crewmen of a Pz.Kpfw. IV Ausf. F1 lubricate one of the tank's eight bogie trucks. These used quarter elliptic leaf springs and required regular lubrication so they would not dry up and begin to rust. Once the reed-green denim work suit was issued to them in 1941, tank crewmen tended to wear it over the black special clothing, itself originally introduced as working dress. In summer, the denims were worn in place of the black clothing with only the side cap remaining of the Panzer uniform. In this manner, the black clothing became something akin to a dress uniform for Panzer soldiers.

Below: Major Hacke's Panzerjägerabteilung GD was the Division's partly self-propelled and partly halftrack-drawn anti-tank battalion. The battalion was composed of a Nachrichtenzug (communications platoon) in VW Kübelwagens, 1. Kompanie in Sd.Kfz. 132 Marder II 7.62cm self-propelled anti-tank guns on Pz.Kpfw. II Ausf. D chassis, and 2. and 3. Kompanien consisting of 5cm PaK 38 anti-tank guns towed by one-ton Sd.Kfz. 10 prime movers.

While observers keep a close watch on the horizon, a Spähtrupp (battle reconnaissance patrol) returns to the German lines near Chermassovo in the Rzhev salient, September 1942. Battle reconnaissance patrols were well-armed with machine pistols and grenades and consisted usually of a sergeant with 3-4 men. Their main mission was to obtain information on the location of enemy positions and minefields. Stosstrupps (combat patrols) were usually much stronger, as a rule consisting of 15 or 20 men in two equal sections, each commanded by a section leader (Gruppenführer) with the whole under the command of a senior NCO (Truppführer). The main mission of such patrols was bringing in prisoners of war for interrogation. Such patrols also tested the strength of enemy outposts and often attacked and held them until relieved. Other types of patrols were used to demolish enemy fieldworks and had infantry Pioniers attached for this purpose. In static line warfare like that at Rzhev, Grossdeutschland conducted aggressive patrolling to maintain fighting spirit, relieve the tedium of trench duty, keep the enemy off balance, and dominate the no-man's land between the lines. The Soviets were also actively reconnoitering and patrols frequently clashed between the main lines of resistance. GD produced one of the most skilled Stosstruppführers in Oberfeldwebel Herbert Dost of I.R. GD 2, whose combat patrols were a major factor in keeping the Soviet lines in a constant state of unease.

This page and overleaf: The strain of the past few hours evident in their expressions, the Spähtrupp reenters its trenches. Note the large supplies of ready ammunition for the s.MG 34 heavy machine guns and Kar 98k rifles. The patrol obviously ran into some trouble, as the bareheaded grenadier has a slight wound to his right arm. There was sufficient time in this sector to carefully sight in the heavy machine guns with well-established fields of inter-locking fire out to their maximum effective range of 2,500 yards.

A casualty is assisted to the rear. The Division repeatedly stressed that no more than two men were to bring back casualties, as more than this number weakened the unit's firepower. In basic training, soldiers spent much time doing rifle PT with one arm against just such a requirement. German soldiers never willingly abandoned casualties — especially members of elite divisions such as GD who could expect short shrift from the Soviets if captured. During the Rzhev fighting, lack of space often prevented GD from establishing main dressing stations. Instead, the wounded were sent on to medical units of divisions holding fixed positions. To help with the additional workload, GD attached medical teams to these divisions. GD HQ assigned medical teams with ambulances located near regimental command posts and medical officers were assigned to vehicle repair areas.

Above: Oberst Eugen Garski, regimental commander of I.R. GD 2 (from October 1, 1942, Füs.Rgt.GD), with men of one of his companies during an inspection of the lines around Shuprovo in the Rzhev salient, late September 1942. Oberst Garski was a veteran officer who had been awarded the Ritterkreuz on July 19, 1940 for his leadership of III/I.R.(mot.) GD during Unternehmen "Niwi." This was an air-landing operation to secure the villages of Traimont and Witry ahead of Heeresgruppe B's advance into Belgium at the outset of Fall Gelb (Case Yellow), the German invasion of Western Europe on May 10, 1940. Oberst Garski led I.R. GD 2 throughout the 1942 summer offensive and was killed in action on September 30, 1942, shortly after this photograph was taken. Oberst Garski was later promoted posthumously to Generalmajor.

Right: A Kompaniechef of I.R. GD 2 at Rzhev, September 1942. Active service conditions gradually altered the outward appearance of German soldiers, with practicality and comfort being the dominant goals. This officer wears enlisted men's Model 1911 cartridge pouches in an attempt to present a less conspicuous target for Soviet snipers. He wears a very well made shelter-quarter material camouflage jacket and has also used shelter-quarter cloth to cover his steel helmet. In addition, the officer has replaced his breeches and top boots with enlisted men's trousers and short lace-up boots and canvas gaiters.

Facing page, below: An Auto-Union Horch Kfz. 69 four-wheel drive medium car of I.R.(mot.) GD 2 in the Rzhev salient, September 1942. I.R.(mot.) GD 2 was mounted in these light 1-1/4 ton cross-country cars in contrast to I.R.(mot.) GD 1 which rode in 3-ton trucks. This Horch car had a chassis frame which consisted of two parallel side pieces and various cross pieces and brackets. The Horch V8 Type 901 water-cooled 3.5 liter gasoline engine produced 82 brake hp at 3,600 rpm and was mounted in the front. The wheels were independently sprung by two coil springs with double-action hydraulic shock absorbers. Spare wheels mounted on stub axles on either side of the chassis prevented bellying when driving over broken ground. The Kfz. 69 had two gasoline tanks. Its 18.7 gallon main tank was protected in the center of the chassis frame while the 10.8 gallon reserve tank was located in the rear of the vehicle. The vehicle also had two gear boxes. The main transmission had four forward speeds and one reverse, while the auxiliary gearbox gave two ratios: normal and cross-country. By 1941 Army Ordnance realized that the Einheits chassis took far too many man-hours of production and maintenance and had proved too heavy with limited payload capacity and production was terminated in 1943.

Above: An abandoned Soviet T34/76 tank amid the ruins of a town in GD's sector of the Rzhev salient, September 1942. Throughout September, the Division was hit by wave after wave of Soviet tank and infantry assaults supported by massed batteries of artillery, mortars and Katyusha multiple rocket launchers. With the Division's Panzerjägers' 5cm PaK 38 anti-tank guns useless at anything but point-blank range, GD had to rely more and more on its three 8.8cm Flak 18/36 batteries, whose capabilities and flexibility permitted Divisional HQ to shift them all over GD's tactical area of responsibility on short notice. Much of what made the T-34 so formidable is apparent in this photograph — the low silhouette, powerful gun, thick well-sloped armor and broad tracks, which gave vastly better ground traction than contemporary German armor.

Below: The crew of a bogged-down Sd.Kfz. 252 ammunition carrier wait for a captured T-34 to tow them and the crew of a staff car they had attempted to aid from the thick mud in the Rzhev salient, November 1942. This Sd.Kfz. 252 was assigned to 18.(Pz. Jäger)/G.R.(mot.) GD. The carrier was designed to transport 60 rounds of 7.5cm StuK 40 L/48 ammunition or 70 rounds of the shorter 7.5cm StuK 37 L/24 rounds. The Sd.Kfz. 252's fully enclosed armored body was distinguished by its steeply sloped rear armor, which was intended to reduce the vehicle's overall weight.

Kradschützen enjoy an alfresco meal during the mild early autumn weather. Soldiers in camp and in the field would form "Zeltkameradschaften" (literally, tent associations) whereby the members of a squad would club together and pool their rations and whatever else they could purchase or obtain from the countryside.

1943

P A N Z E R R E G I M E N T   G D

I.R.(mot.) GD, upon its upgrading to full divisional status, received its own organic tank component, a battalion-sized unit known as Panzertruppe GD. Commanded initially by Major Walter Pössl and afterwards by Oberst Hyazinth Graf Strachwitz von Gross-Zauche und Camminetz, Pz. Truppe GD was a conventionally organized battalion with a HQ platoon, three companies of tanks and a maintenance platoon in 3-ton trucks. Headquarters consisted of two Pz.Kpfw. IVs, together with Demag Sd.Kfz. 250 command vehicles and organic motorcycle dispatch riders and light cars. 1. Kompanie was a Pz.Kpfw. IV company with a company HQ consisting of two Pz.Kpfw. IVs and three platoons of five Pz.Kpfw. IVs apiece. Both the Pz.Kpfw. IV Ausf. F1 and F2 were on hand in time for the summer offensive of 1942. 2. and 3. Kompanien were similarly organized but with Pz.Kpfw. IIIs, by now with the 5cm KwK 39 L/60 long-barreled gun.

The Panzertruppe (also known as Pz.Abteilung GD) performed very satisfactorily during the summer offensive of 1942 where it led the advance and helped account for the destruction of nearly 300 Soviet tanks, but did less well in the Rzhev salient where it lost thirty tanks against only 100 Soviet tanks destroyed. This was largely the result of the tanks operating on poor terrain against strong enemy defenses. All the various counterattacks led by the Panzertruppe until December 1942 were unsuccessful despite heavy losses. By early winter the ground had hardened and the value of tanks increased again. Along with the Division's assault guns, the tanks remained either in groups of three as counterattack reserves or in ambush positions within the main line of resistance. Regular reliefs were organized and the nights were clear enough for the tanks to be driven safely, something not normally done as it usually led to chaos. There were standing patrols, which inhibited enemy attempts to penetrate the Division's lines, and helped sustain the infantry's morale. Positioned behind the main line of resistance during heavy fighting, when Soviet artillery had the rest of the Division's support weapons pinned down, the fully armored tanks took part in the fire fight by delivering indirect fire.

After the bloodbath in the Luchessa Valley where GD was almost annihilated, the newly-organized Panzerregiment GD was joined by a company of the new 56-ton Pz.Kpfw. VI Tiger I tanks. On February 2, 1943, II Abteilung was raised similar to the original Pz.Truppe GD (now known as I/Pz.Rgt. GD). Under the command of Graf Strachwitz, Panzerregiment GD performed exceptionally during both the defensive fighting around Kharkov and in Manstein's counter-offensive to recapture the city and drive towards Belgorod. Following the winter campaign, GD went into a well-deserved rest and refitting. On June 23, 1943, the Division was officially reconstituted as a Panzergrenadier division. As such, it had little in common with other Panzergrenadier divisions or, for that matter, Panzer divisions. While a normal Pz. Grenadier division had an organic Panzerabteilung, this was most often composed partially or wholly of assault guns. With its new establishment of a Stabs (HQ) Kompanie of 17 Pz.Kpfw. IVs and two Abteilungen, each with a HQ Co. and four tank companies (three in the company HQ; five per platoon) and its own organic company of Tiger tanks (two in the HQ platoon and three platoons with four Tigers each); Pz.Rgt. GD was far stronger than most "pure blooded" Panzer divisions on the Eastern Front at this time — the more so since the Eastern Front's Panzer divisions had each lost half their tank strength a year earlier to bring the attack divisions for Fall Blau up to strength, and could now field barely a battalion of 50-odd Pz.Kpfw. IIIs and IVs apiece. Only the three SS-Panzergrenadier divisions — LSSAH, Das Reich, and Totenkopf were as well favored as GD. In addition, GD was in the process of forming its own organic Tiger

battalion. This became III/Pz.Rgt. GD but did not join the Division until August 1943.

Again under Graf Strachwitz's inspired leadership, GD's Panzers spearheaded XXXVIII Pz.Korps' advance to Oboyan, destroying hundreds of Soviet tanks and AFVs before the failure of the SS Panzerkorps to break through to Belgorod spelled the end of Operation "Zitadelle." Pz.Rgt. GD was caught up in the hectic and costly attempts to contain and throw back an unending succession of Soviet attacks along the length of the front from Orel to Kharkov. This fighting so debilitated the Regiment that by the time it had been pushed back to the Dnieper on September 29, 1943, Panzerregiment GD had one tank remaining in action (III (Tiger)/Pz.Rgt. GD, which rejoined the Division on August 4, had ten Tigers in running condition). Rebuilt as far as OKH's resources allowed, the Regiment fell back across the Dnieper, the Bug, and over the Dniester into Romania by March 1944. On January 16, 1944, I/Pz.Rgt. GD left for the West to train on the new Panther tanks (GD had a brigade of the new Panthers attached to it for Zitadelle, where they proved a disappointment due to their being rushed into action before they were fully ready). Pz.Kpfw. IV now formed all of II/Pz.Rgt. GD. The first battalion's place in the Regiment's order of battle was taken for nearly the remainder of the year by I Abteilung (Panther) of the famous Potsdam Pz.Rgt. 26. I/Pz.Rgt. 26 was a 1944-model battalion with HQ Co. (two Panthers in the HQ section and three five-tank platoons, and four numbered companies similarly organized). Regimental HQ also was mounted in Panthers, with its personnel coming from both GD and Pz.Rgt. 26.

The fighting in Romania from April to June 1944 saw Pz.Rgt. GD engaged in constant maneuvering, with Soviet thrust followed by German counter thrust from Iasi on the frontier to Targul Frumos in the foothills of the Carpathians. At Iasi the Regiment had the nasty surprise of encountering the Soviet's massive new JS II superheavy tanks and watching as the Tigers' 8.8cm rounds bounced harmlessly off the Soviet tanks' armor. The Tigers had to close to dangerously short range to eliminate this new enemy. As before, the Regiment's greatly superior crew drill and their commander's skilled handing of the Regiment's sub-units prevailed over the sheer weight of numbers of the Soviets. By April 24, the Regiment had destroyed 150 Soviet tanks — 476 enemy tanks and AFVs being claimed by GD by May 2. After two months of intense combat the Regiment went into a well-earned rest before being ordered to retrieve the disaster which was overtaking Generaloberst Ferdinand Schörner's Heeresgruppe Nord (Army Group North) in the Baltic States.

Attacking practically straight from the railheads in East Prussia, the Regiment quickly recovered the key crossroads town of Vilkovishken in Lithuania before pressing on towards Stauliai (Schaulen) in the direction of Riga. After a series of bitter fights with greatly superior numbers, the Regiment fell back on the vital port city of Memel which it defended stubbornly, destroying 150 enemy tanks between October 9-11, before being evacuated to East Prussia in November 1944.

During October 1944 I(Panther)/Pz.Rgt. GD returned to the Eastern Front, serving under the command of the Westphalian 6. Pz.Div. in the defense of East Prussia before rejoining GD when it returned to Königsberg. The Regiment then formed the core of the newly raised Pz.Korps Grossdeutschland.

Oberst Strachwitz confers with Leutnant Rietsch, Battalion NO (Signals Officer) of II/Pz.Rgt. GD. Leutnant Rietsch wears the field-grey reversible to white camouflage winter suit. The radio antenna could be raised or lowered into the trough from inside the fighting compartment. The Pz.Kpfw. III Ausf. M was the last battle tank version of this series, but was nearly obsolete as a combat vehicle. The basket on the rear of the tank's cupola held signal flags.

KHARKOV, FEBRUARY-MARCH 1943

After five months of terrible bloodletting in the Rzhev Salient, culminating in the horrible Christmas battle of the Luchessa Valley, the numbed survivors of Infanterie-Division(mot.) Grossdeutschland were hastily withdrawn and built up to strength as much as OKH's limited resources permitted. With a large infusion of specially selected personnel from Generaloberst Model's 9. Armee, GD was sent south to the Kharkov area to fill the vacuum left by the collapse of Germany's allied armies and the surrender of 6. Armee in Stalingrad. Grossdeutschland found itself operating in a void as allied remnants streamed past them in total disorder with the Red Army close on their heels. A battalion of Grenadier-Rgt.(mot.) GD attempted to hold Belgorod, but was driven out after intense street fighting in the blazing town. By the evening of February 13, the Division had fallen back on Kharkov, which was in chaos as thousands of rear echelon troops and civilians tried to escape encirclement by the Soviets.

Military common sense dictated that the Germans evacuate the city as rapidly as possible and wait to mount a counterattack at the moment the Soviets overextended and exhausted themselves. Adolf Hitler, however, demanded that the city be held at all costs by SS-Obergruppenführer Paul Hausser's newly-arrived SS-Panzerkorps. Hausser, for his part, courageously chose to disobey the Führer and on the evening of February 15, covered by Major Peter Frantz's Sturmgeschütze and Major Otto-Ernst Remer's I(SPW)/G.R. GD, the SS broke out of the doomed city through a corridor barely a half-mile wide. The evacuation was bitterly contested by the Soviets who overran and annihilated a company of Grenadiers on February 18. A counterattack planned for the next day was cancelled in the face of overwhelming Soviet pressure. The front itself was in danger of collapse when a neighboring unit abandoned its positions.

Grossdeutschland was now withdrawn from the line to rest 30km south of Poltava until March 4. Here Panzerregiment GD received its II Abteilung as well as a company of the new 56-ton Tiger Is. A new IV Abteilung was added to A.R. GD and an SPW-equipped Divisional escort company joined Divisional HQ. The Soviets' advance had created a trap into which they continued to pour troops, and GFM Erich von Manstein now judged the moment was right to begin his counterattack. On March 7, the counterattack began. 4 Panzerarmee, with GD in the lead, moved forward in the direction of Belgorod after a short preliminary bombardment. Bogodukmov fell on March 11, and from March 14 to 15, a fierce tank battle raged near Borissovka. Graf Strachwitz's Panzers destroyed 48 Soviet tanks in one day as the enemy frantically attempted to halt the Germans. The newly-renamed Füsilierregiment GD scattered the Soviet infantry in its path, taking large numbers of prisoners. On March 19, Tomarovka fell and the next day 62 Soviet tanks and AFVs were destroyed by I/Pz.Rgt. GD and the Panzerjägers and Sturmgeschütze.

On reaching the Kharkov-Belgorod road, the Division was relieved and transferred to a rest area north of Poltava on March 23. Here it refitted as a Panzergrenadier division, the most powerful in the German Army. GD received new SPWs and increased the Panzerregiment with a full battalion of Tiger Is. OKW was generous in its rewards for GD. Generalleutnant Hoernlein and Major Frantz received the Eichenlaub, while the new commander of Panzerregiment GD, Oberst Graf Strachwitz, earned the Schwerter (Swords). Among many others, Majors Remer and Pössl earned the Ritterkreuz, as did Hauptmann Magold for his skillful intervention at Borissovka.

Divisional commander Generalleutnant Hoernlein visits a battalion headquarters during the operations around Kharkov, February 1943. The mouse grey, reversible-to-white, winter combat suit was in wide use, as was the newly-issued M43 visored field cap and a customized winter version of the same.

The shortage of sufficient SPWs and 4x4 trucks forced GD and most other units on the Eastern Front to use their tanks to transport infantry up to the line of departure and return them to the rear for rest and refitting. By late 1942, the Pz.Kpfw. III was at a disadvantage fighting better Russian tanks, and supplemental armor, like the spare track links seen here, was commonly used. It is interesting to note that this is the "Flammpanzer" flamethrower version. Designated F-1, it was identical in almost all aspects to the Panzer III Ausf. M. The 50mm main gun was replaced with a 14mm flame-throwing jet and an internal 2-stroke motor was installed to propel the burning oil. 1,000 liters was carried and this allowed for approximately seventy-five, 2 or 3 second bursts at a range of 35 meters. The F-1 always carried the additional 30mm armor on its mantlet and bow, but perhaps its most distinguishing characteristics were its large thick barrel and unusually long mantlet sight. Although an effective moral booster, the F-1s combat performance was poor and most were later re-converted to gun tanks.

A Sd.Kfz. 7/2 8-ton halftrack prime mover of HE Flakabteilung GD, with a Rheinmetall 3.7cm Flak 36 and its special ammunition trailer (Sd.Anhänger 56), moves up to support the counterattack to retake Kharkov and push the Soviets beyond Belgorod, March 1943. 4. Batterie of the Flakabteilung had four of these extremely versatile guns, which saw considerable use against ground targets. The 1.5-ton gun had an effective rate of fire of 120rpm and an effective range of 4800m. The 3.7cm Flak fired HE, AP and tracer ammunition.

Below: SPWs of Major Remer's I/G.R. (mot.) GD assemble for an attack north of Kharkov. Remer's men played a prominent role in Manstein's counterattack, as they were some of the few infantry able to keep pace with the rapid armor advances and fight from their vehicles. These dark-grey-finished SPWs have been only sketchily whitewashed, making them stand out starkly in the winter landscape.

Above and below: Grenadiers of Grenadierregiment GD mount up on a Sturmgeschütz III prior to moving out to continue the operations north of Kharkov. It was outside Borissovka that Hauptmann Magold's battery saved the spearhead of A.A. (mot.) GD from certain destruction by Soviet armor.

Left and above: The command tanks for II/Pz.Rgt. GD were Pz.Kpfw. III Ausf. M models. They are seen here at an assembly point with a Pz.Kpfw. IV Ausf. G of I/Pz.Rgt. GD along a snow covered road towards Kharkov, March 1943. The "star" command radio antennas were not visible from great distances, making the command vehicles far less noticeable on the battlefield. These vehicles are not camouflaged in white and unfortunately could be seen from miles away. Sudden snow storms or shortages of white paint were a serious problem during the winter months, since there was no foliage available to hide conspicuous vehicles.

A column of Pz.Kpfw. IV Ausf. Gs of Pz.Rgt. GD advance along a snow covered road towards Kharkov, March 1943. Note that the guns are pointed over the front corners of the hulls, a common tactic which placed all the tanks' armor at an angle to the enemy's tanks, increasing the armor's effectiveness.

Below: The Pz.Rgt. worked closely with the reconnaissance units responsible for battlefield scouting. The Sd.Kfz. 250/1 le.SPW and heavy motorcycles were indispensable for gathering the critical information needed to plan and guide German armored assaults.

This page: Grenadiers of a MG company board their 3-ton Opel Blitz trucks during the counterattack of March, 1943. Except for I(SPW) Bataillon, GD's grenadiers were road-bound in their unarmored trucks. The Opel Blitz, the primary transport of the motorized grenadiers, was powered by a water-cooled, straight-six OHV gasoline engine of 3.6 liters, generating 68HP. The truck was a 4x2 design driven by the rear wheels. One of the main drawbacks of the reversible-to-white winter combat suit is obvious in these photographs: the suit quickly became very dirty, losing its camouflage properties. It also absorbed water, quickly becoming very heavy and taking a long time to dry out. When worn in combat, the suit's weight considerably slowed down advancing troops, necessitating changes in artillery support firing plans.

Right: Spotters on the thatched roof of a peasant cottage relay information to a radioman of 9. Batterie, III/Artillerieregiment GD during the fighting around Belgorod, March 1943. 9./A.R. GD was a tractor-drawn 10cm Kanone 18 (field gun) battery. The German Army placed great stress on observable fire and organized observer parties on three levels: one team up forward with the front-line infantry, another team at the gunline, and a third team at regimental headquarters. As a motorized formation, GD relied heavily on radio communications and this Funker is using a Feldfunksprecher B short range radio normally used for company to battalion level transmissions. The Feldfu. B had a range of about one mile. The 30 lb radio had a 32" antenna, was battery-powered, and came furnished with headphones, and hand and throat microphones.

Below: A 7.5cm light infantry gun of 17./G.R.(mot.) GD in service during delaying operations around Belgorod. 17./G.R.(mot.) GD, the infantry gun company of the Regiment, had six of these light guns (known as the le.IG 18) as well as six of the heavy 15cm s.IG 33s. The le.IG 18, in development since 1927, was first issued to the Reichsheer in 1932. It was a direct descendant of the infantry-escort guns of the First World War and fulfilled the same mission in the Wehrmacht. The gun's design was unconventional in that when the loader operated the breech opening lever, the breech block remained fixed and the barrel, mounted in a cradle, was raised up to open the breech for loading. The gun (also known as an infantry howitzer) weighed 880 lbs and could be elevated to 73° and depressed to 10°. It fired a 12.2 lb HE shell (an AP shell was also provided) to a maximum rate of fire of 20rpm. In motorized and Panzer divisions, the gun had pneumatic tires and was drawn by a 1-ton halftrack prime mover. In this photograph the gunner is using the Rundblickfernrohr 16 panoramic sight to aim the gun while an assistant gunner steadies the box-type trail. Another crewman is getting more 7.5cm rounds from an ammunition box containing four HE rounds.

Left: The crew of a Rheinmetall-Borsig Granatwerfer 34 8cm mortar fire on the Soviets during the extremely fluid defensive operations between Belgorod and Kharkov. Various powder increments (visible on the base of the round held by the gunner at the left) were attached to the base of the mortar shells to increase their range. In extreme cold, the hot gas and powder residue from the muzzle blast often caused ice to form in the barrel, making it too small to insert new rounds. A stack of 3-round ammunition cases is piled along the wall of the cottage.

Below: An MG 34 light machine gunner of an infantry squad watches the horizon for Soviet activity. The alternating thaws and frosts caused the reversible to white winter combat suit to be very conspicuous on the snowless terrain. The MG 34, the world's first general purpose machine gun, was then in the process of being largely supplemented – although never completely replaced – by the more easily manufactured and faster-firing MG 42.

Above: Grenadiers examine the wreckage of an overrun Soviet outpost during the fighting around Belgorod. Among the abandoned weapons are two of the venerable 7.62mm PM Model 1910 Maxim machine guns on their wheeled carriages and a 45mm PTP obr. 1932c anti-tank gun, slightly modified longer-barreled variants of which remained in Soviet service until the end of the war.

Left: In the German Army the Company First Sergeant, der Kompaniefeldwebel, was known as "Die Mutter der Kompanie" — the company commander being "Der Vater der Kompanie." As in the traditional German household, "Mother" ran the day to day business of the family sternly and efficiently but with great care for his men. This freed the company commander to direct the tactical employment of his command. Here the first sergeant samples some hot food from an Unteroffizier in the cook house truck. The meals would not be issued until they had passed Der Spiess' inspection.

Below: Der Spiess, wearing the ribbon of the War Merit Cross in his button hole, distributes newspapers — here, "Fliegende Blätter" — to a group of soldiers warmly dressed in reversible to white winter combat suits and a variety of headgear, including M 34 and 42 side caps, fur pile caps and Der Spiess' customized M43 cap. Two soldiers have attached the Division's monogrammed shoulder straps to their right sleeves. Most units had their own papers — GD later had "Die Feuerwehr" (the "Fire Brigade") — and armies and army groups published their own papers and magazines such as Heeresgruppe Mitte's "Ostfront" and 3. Pz.Armee's "Die Panzerfaust". Although by no means a forum for free expression, these publications portrayed the war in a far more realistic manner than did the homefront propaganda organs.

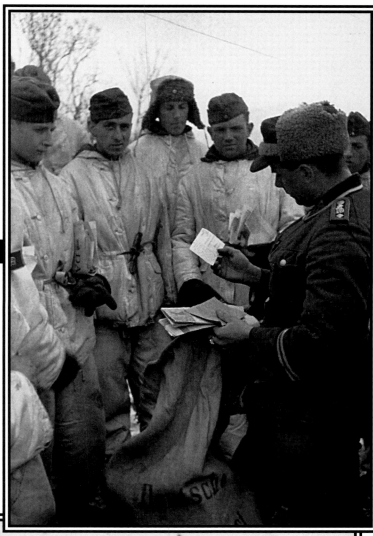

Right: Mail from home: Der Spiess distributes letters to the same, now anxious-looking, group of soldiers. By this point in the war, the troops at the front became increasingly more apprehensive for the safety of their families, especially those in industrial areas. Germany's cities were being successively levelled by the Anglo-American air forces' round-the-clock bombing offensive. For the first time in modern war, the telegram announcing the loss of a loved one was likely to travel in either direction. Due to the overstrained Russian railways and the huge demands of the armies for essential supplies, parcels from home were severely restricted.

Below: His "crime book" firmly in place, Der Spiess checks the serviceability of a soldier's Kar 98k. Based on the classic Gewehr 98, the Kar 98k, with its limited 5-round magazine and high-powered long range ammunition (effective range of 800m) was obsolete by the outbreak of the war. Even with their generous allotment of machine guns, the German soldiers quickly found themselves in danger of being buried in an avalanche of Soviet automatic rifle and submachine gun fire by 1942. These soldiers belong to a divisional rear area unit. Such units normally issued their men only one cartridge pouch, containing 9 5-round clips of 7.92mm ammunition, as seen on the soldier in the center of the photograph.

T A N K   M A I N T E N A N C E

In World War Two, combat tanks were as likely to be taken out of action for mechanical failures as from damage from enemy fire. The German Panzer divisions had a highly developed system for retrieving and repairing damaged or unserviceable vehicles of all types. In addition to repairing vehicles, the Werkstatt (Workshop) companies also had the task of recording failures and repairs and for maintaining sufficient supplies of spare parts and raw materials suitable for repairing or making new parts.

The first task in repairing disabled tanks was to retrieve them. This was a very dangerous task, as it often had to be done under enemy fire. German recovery crews were responsible for saving thousands of tanks and other vehicles that might otherwise have been captured or destroyed. For most of the War, the primary recovery vehicle was the Famo Sd.Kfz. 9 18-ton halftrack tractor. In addition, there were transport trailers and engineers' equipment (winches, snatchblocks, pulley arrays) to assist in pulling damaged tanks from rivers, gullies, soft ground, etc., to where they could be loaded onto a trailer or prepared for towing. It took two tractors to tow a Panther and three to tow a Tiger. Later, the Bergepanther recovery vehicle was issued and made it possible to retrieve many Panthers and Tigers that previously were given up.

Repairs to damaged vehicles covered everything that could happen on the battlefield. Damage to armor was filled by welding and trimmed by grinding. Damaged wheels, broken torsion bars, broken sights, hatches, shot-up vision ports — all were skillfully repaired or replaced. Vehicles too badly damaged for front unit repairs were generally stripped of whatever parts were needed to repair other vehicles. It was common to combine parts from damaged vehicles to return some of them to service. This on occasion resulted in "hybrid" tanks with features from different production models.

The workshop companies were equipped to make parts that could not be repaired and also added extra details requested by unit crews or commanders, such as stowage racks for jerrycans or extra supplies. Sections were devoted to repairing radios, engines, sights, guns, small arms, and suspensions. Portable generators and shop trucks allowed the workshop companies to set up wherever they were needed. Most maintenance was done outdoors, and a common sight was to see a crew working on their tank in the open. The driver was responsible for preventive maintenance and servicing, but the whole crew was called upon to assist when needed.

The recovery and repair of the heavier tanks, such as the Panther and Tiger, had their own specific problems. Both vehicles were notorious for mechanical breakdowns, and were also very difficult to recover. Fortunately, workshop crews were able to recover many of these heavier tanks and return them to service.

In action, a good workshop unit could keep a Panzer battalion or regiment at about 50% strength for extended periods of time. Any lulls in the fighting would be used to bring strength up as much as possible. German tank crews generally had a very high opinion of the workshop and recovery crews, and often worked with them to speed recovery and repairs.

A typical repair scene on the Eastern Front shows the normal conditions of outdoor maintenance. While the mechanic at the right works on the final drive, one of GD's numerous administrative officials, a Beamte (army civil servant) with the rank of Hauptmann, supervises. The steering brake for the right track has been uncovered for maintenance. It was essential to keep the brakes adjusted to avoid slipping or worse, grabbing, which could put excessive stress on the final drive units.

Left: The glacis plate hatches on the Pz.Kpfw. IV allowed mechanics to perform most service tasks without having to remove any of the drive train components. Oil and lubrication, brake adjustment, and other tasks could be done fairly easily. The Werkstatt Kompanie mechanics were a major reason many Panzer formations could maintain their tank strength at a useful level during prolonged action. Working day and night, they rebuilt damaged components and vehicles, cannibalizing those too badly damaged to be repaired. Often the crews worked alongside to complete the repairs.

Below left: The tank repair shops were an integral and extremely important part of every Panzer Division. By their nature and use in combat, armored vehicles were operated under heavy loads and great stresses were placed on their suspensions and power trains. Good drivers could extend the reliable service life without repairs, but sooner or later, almost all serviceable tanks ended up in the Werkstatt Kompanie shops. Here, mechanics repair the final drive assembly of a Pz.Kpfw. IV Ausf. G. Much field maintenance had to be done outside, but this crew has the luxury of working in a shop building. The Pz.Kpfw. IV was designed so that the transmission and final drives could be serviced and removed from the front through the glacis plate hatches.

Below right: One of the functions of the repair workshop units was to keep accurate records of all repairs made. In this way, faulty or weak designs could be identified and orders could be sent back to the Heereswaffenamt (Ordnance Department) and the manufacturer to improve the design or manufacturing process. Shortages of the proper high-strength alloy steels crippled many fine designs, yet manufacturers, steel producers, metallurgists, and front-line mechanics all worked together to bring vehicles and weapons to the highest state of readiness possible. Disassembled units, such as this final drive from a Pz.Kpfw. IV Ausf. G, were constantly inspected when taken apart to ensure that proper manufacturing standards were maintained. The Beamte on the left is Instandsetzungtruppführer (Maintenance Detachment commander) Eberle. He consults with Major Thiele, commander of II/Pz.Rgt. GD, March 1943, outside Kharkov.

Left: This Mercedes staff car was generally used to transport officers in areas outside the immediate front line. Though most German cars and trucks were fairly reliable, the tremendous number of different models caused strains on the logistics echelons who had to stock all the critical spare parts to keep the vehicles running. Mechanics were forced to work on dozens of different variants, particularly as the war progressed and more and more vehicles were impressed from civilians or captured sources. Here, Werkmeister Kuschke, a WWI veteran from Bavaria, supervises Obergefreiter Paul Orth. Orth had been Oberleutnant Heinrich Gerbener's driver in France in 1940.

Right: Because so much of the equipment and vehicles used by the Wehrmacht in World War Two was very simple and built of standard steels, much of the parts fabrication was essentially blacksmithing work. Unit workshops usually built much of their own field equipment, such as the forge at the right. The metalsmiths in a regimental or divisional workshop could rebuild most parts of a damaged vehicle. Here, the workers, in denim twill work uniforms, shape a replacement leaf for a truck spring. These shops could cut, shape, and even heat-treat metal. By cannibalizing damaged vehicles and components, other vehicles could often be restored to service quickly. Here, Ogefr. Paul Orth swings the hammer as Gefreiter Cramer holds the metal strip on the anvil.

Right: Although individual tank crews often were tasked to repaint their vehicles as required to comply with changes in camouflage, soft-skins were often painted in the shops. The spray equipment seen here was the ideal way to apply new camouflage schemes, though the white winter temporary paint was often brushed or mopped onto the vehicles. This Stoewer Kfz. 4 le.E.Pkw. is being repainted in overall dark grey. Overpainted markings would then be restored using stencils.

Above: Among the many procedures German mechanics had to perform was the repair of cracked castings, including transmission housings, manifolds, and even engine blocks as seen here. Shortages of vehicles and parts forced many shops to repair or rework many components that would have been scrapped under more favorable conditions. In the background is a 3-ton Opel "Blitz" shop truck. The repair shops had much of their equipment mounted in standard trucks so that the shops could be moved quickly to keep up with the unit's progress. Obergefreiter Werner Rohde carefully heats the block under the watchful eye of Gefreiter Mai.

Right: A young soldier eats some hot soup from his mess tin during a short break. The soldier wears the recently issued Model 43 Feldbluse with unpleated pockets to which he has attached the bluish-dark green badgecloth shoulderstraps and National Emblem of the Model 35 field blouse. His headgear is the short-lived Model 42 side cap, basically an unvisored mountain cap. Especially interesting is the non-standard, extra-wide Divisional cuff title.

Major der Reserve Gerhard Konopka

Gerhard Konopka was one of Grossdeutschland's most celebrated and highly-decorated soldiers. Born on March 27, 1911 in Tirschtiegel in the Meseritz District of Prussia east of the Oder River, Konopka attended the local schools before joining the Freiwilligenarbeitsdienst (Voluntary Labor Service) of the Weimar-era government in the early 1930s. When this became the Reichsarbeitsdienst (RAD) in 1934, Konopka remained on as part of its cadre and rose rapidly through its ranks, becoming an Arbeitsführer by 1939 (Work Leader, a rank equivalent to Major in the German Army). During his time in the RAD, Gerhard Konopka underwent voluntary military training with the Prussian Infanterieregiment 8 at its depot in Frankfurt an der Oder, emerging at first as Unteroffizier der Reserve and later being commissioned as Leutnant der Reserve.

Upon the outbreak of war in September 1939, Konopka rejoined his regiment, part of the Berlin-Brandenburg 3. Infanteriedivision (mot.), as a platoon commander. Leutnant Konopka spent the first two and a half years of the war with 3. I.D., seeing much action in all its campaigns and achieving a promotion to Oberleutnant d.R. In the spring of 1942, Oberleutnant Konopka transferred into the newly-expanded I.D.(mot.) GD as commander of I.R.(mot.) GD 1's Stabskompanie's Pionierzug (Regimental HQ Company's Engineer Platoon). Oberleutnant Konopka's Regimentspioniere distinguished themselves repeatedly during Fall Blau at the crossing of the Tim, the Upper Don at Voronezh and the Lower Don at Radzorskaya where Konopka's men hid in their rubber assault boats while Soviet POWs paddled them across the river. It was during the advance southwards that Gerhard Konopka was awarded the German Cross in Gold (the award itself taking place on December 9, 1942). At this time Konopka established his reputation as one of GD's premier "Panzerknackers" (Tank Busters), on one occasion knocking out two Soviet tanks in a single day. The basic engineer training and equipment of his platoon plus his previous experience in the RAD made Konopka especially qualified to undertake such dangerous work. Oberleutnant Konopka led his platoon throughout the murderous fighting in the Rzhev Salient from September to December 1942, destroying two more Soviet tanks and bringing his tally to four without being wounded in the process (he would, however, be wounded eight times in action, the last time quite seriously in August 1943). In late 1942, after the fighting in the

Luchessa Valley had abated, Oberleutnant Konopka was among several successful "Panzerknacker" summoned to Berlin to report personally to Propaganda Minister Dr. Paul Joseph Goebbels.

In August 1943, during the desperate and confused fighting in the Orel sector which followed the failure of Germany's Kursk offensive, Konopka assumed command of II/G.R.(mot.) GD. On August 3, 1943, Oberleutnant Konopka led his battalion in a successful attack on the "Yellow Heights" near Alissovo where the Soviets, supported by precisely registered artillery, were well dug in. Konopka's decisive exploitation of the situation, which resulted in the capture of this position together with the enemy guns, encouraged him to expand his attack the next day from this position. These actions, carried through in the face of fierce opposition, captured valuable ground and numerous enemy guns, though resulting in Oberleutnant Konopka being seriously wounded and evacuated to Germany. Konopka received the Ritterkreuz on September 10, 1943 while convalescing in the depot hospital at Cottbus. Simultaneously he was promoted to Hauptmann der Reserve. After convalescing, he returned to the front in October 1943, still in command of II/G.R.(mot.) GD. Shortly thereafter, he was once again wounded in the leg (his eighth and final wound) and was invalided home.

Gerhard Konopka saw no further action until March 1945 when Germany's situation had assumed its most catastrophic dimensions. As an Oberarbeitsführer (Oberstleutnant) Gerhard Konopka was recalled to active duty as Major d.R. and Höhererarbeitsführer (a position designating responsibility for RAD matters within the Armed Forces) and commander of RAD I.R. 1 of RAD I.D. "Friedrich-Ludwig Jahn," which was raised in Jüterbog (Wehrkreis III) around a cadre of the veteran Hessian 251. I.D. (Oberst Klein, later Oberst Weller). Initially short of anti-tank and communications personnel, the teenagers of this division did not lack fighting spirit and were assigned to General Walter Wenck's 12. Armee. RAD Division "Friedrich-Ludwig Jahn" was almost immediately involved in heavy fighting south of Berlin in the Jüterbog-Luckenwalde-Treuenbrietzen area. The young Arbeitsmänner led by their veteran Regimental Commander successfully engaged in the intense fighting near Lehnin and between Plauen and Genthin. The division then formed part of the force which assisted General Theodor Busse's 9. Armee to escape from encirclement on the Seelow Heights. After crossing the Elbe north of Ferchland, Gerhard Konopka and the remnants of his young regiment surrendered to the U.S. Army in May 1945.

PANZERNAHBEKÄMPFUNGSLEHRGANG (CLOSE-QUARTER TANK DESTRUCTION COURSE)

In order to provide its soldiers with the skills to give them a fighting chance against the waves of Soviet tanks then being thrown against them, GD's Divisional HQ organized a four-day training course in single-handed destruction of Soviet tanks at its camp at Akhtyrka in April 1943. The course — the first and only one held — brought several of the Division's most successful "Panzerknackers" ("Tank Busters") together under the leadership of the commander of 1./G.R.(mot.) GD, Oberleutnant Gerhard Konopka. Thirty-five to forty specially selected NCOs were chosen to take part in the course which was held out-doors. The entire purpose of the course, according to Konopka, was "to explain to the participants where they would find the weak spots on Soviet tanks and how and by what means they could be destroyed in close combat. The knowledge gained was meant to be disseminated downwards to the individual companies and this was successfully accomplished. I explained to the participants in great detail how I had achieved this without being wounded

in the process. Simply saying that when nearing such an armored monster, everything depended on rapid but well thought-out action and always approaching from the tank's 'dead angle,' hardly covered just what this really involved."

After lectures from Oberleutnant Konopka and other experts in front of display boards detailing the weak points of Soviet tanks and instructions on various hand-held anti-tank weaponry, the participants moved on to a live demonstration of what they had just learned. Konopka further recalled that "as the finale of the course, an exercise was conducted using high explosive and incendiary charges, Teller mines, hollow-charge weapons and Molotov cocktails against five Soviet tanks, meant to represent a Soviet "Panzerrudel" ("Tank Pack," their typical tactic) towed on long cables by 18-ton halftrack prime movers at roughly 50-60 meters distance. All the tanks were successfully put out of action. This demonstration, held in the presence of high-ranking generals, found great approval as it had been staged in as realistic a manner as possible."

Above: On the table in front of Oberleutnant Konopka are several weapons either designed for or having an additional anti-tank applicability. At the left rear, behind the Model 42 Teller Mine, is a hollow-charge sticky grenade which functioned as both an anti-tank and as a demolition grenade. The hollow-charge was contained in the tapering steel body of the grenade. The grenade attached to the surface of the target by means of a flat, sticky pad, covered by a press-on lid with a small handle, at the nose. Attached to the base of the grenade was a tapering fuse adapter terminating in a socket which was threaded to receive the igniter (this socket was sealed in transit by a black plastic plug). The detonator and igniter assembly were similar to that on the Model 39 egg grenade and had a 7 1/2 second delay. The "sticky-grenade" was widely used before the Panzerfaust made such close proximity to the target no longer necessary. Interestingly, the Germans were so concerned with the enemy using this type of weapon on their own tanks that they began to coat their tanks' vulnerable surfaces with "Zimmerit" anti-magnetic mine paste. To the right rear is a box containing four Blendkörper 2H smoke grenades.

Above: Oberleutnant Konopka teaching his very attentive students in the outdoor classroom. The display boards detail the "K.O. Punkte" (Knock Out Points, an example of the universality of this term by the mid-1940s) of various Soviet-made and Allied tanks used by the Red Army. In the background are a Pz.Kpfw. IV Ausf. F2 and a Soviet T-34/76 tank. On the table behind Oberleutnant Konopka are arranged various anti-tank devices such as a Molotov cocktail and several Model 24 stick hand grenades.

Right: A talented amateur artist applies the finishing touches to a life-size sketch illustrating the theme of the course.

Facing page, below: An instructor demonstrates one method of throwing a Model 42 Teller (Plate) Mine onto the engine deck of a T-34/76 tank. The user would approach the enemy tank, whereupon he would arm the mine, place it either under the tank's tread or at the base of the turret, and then race to a safe distance. German tactics involved separating oncoming Soviet tanks from their accompanying infantry and then sending out either individual "Panzerknackers" or parties of tank-busting teams, each man carrying two of the 18lb. mines. Their hazardous work was somewhat helped by the limited visibility from within the tanks and by the general confusion prevailing in such conditions.

Right: Standing in a hastily dug shallow one-man hole, an Unteroffizier prepares to throw a Blendkörper 2H smoke grenade. This grenade, shaped somewhat like an elongated light bulb, but made of thicker glass, contained 260 grams of Titanium Tetrachloride and gave off dense white smoke when it shattered against its target. Panzerknackers often improvised "Geballte Ladungen" (Bundle Charges) by taping six Model 24 hand grenade heads around a seventh complete stick grenade. This gave a consid-erable blast effect when wedged between the enemy tank's turret overhang and hull or wedged in the running gear. Using the bundle charge against all but light armor (much less common in 1943) only rarely resulted in success commensurate with the risks taken by the user.

Facing page, above: On March 14, 1943, the spearhead of Panzeraufklärungsabteilung GD was attacked on the flank, east of Borrisovka, by large numbers of Soviet tanks covering the disordered retreat of Soviet forces toward Belgorod. Intervening in this dangerous situation, I/Pz.Rgt. GD, under the leadership of Major Walter Pössl, destroyed 39 T-34s and thereby saved Pz.A.A. GD from almost certain destruction. For his battalion's decisive action, Major Pössl was awarded the Ritterkreuz on April 20, 1943. In this photo, Pössl receives the Ritterkreuz from his regimental commander, Oberst Hyazinth Graf Strachwitz on April 20, 1943. Divisional Adjutant Hauptmann Theo Bethke helps adjust the ribbon of the Ritterkreuz.

Facing page, below: Accompanied by Oberst Graf Strachwitz, Major Pössl passes in review his assembled battalion, drawn up in a hollow square. As was the German Army's custom, the enlisted men and NCOs stand at attention while the officers salute. Off-duty, all Ritterkreuzträgers, whatever their rank, were entitled to a salute from every member of the armed forces.

This page: The new Ritterkreuzträger proudly displays his award. It was customary in the Wehrmacht for Ritterkreuzträgers to wear their medal with the ribbon on the day of the award ceremony. Thereafter the cross was worn at the throat. Many Ritterkreuzträgers chose to preserve their medals from loss or damage by wearing a second, privately purchased Ritterkreuz or substituting the Iron Cross 2nd Class when in the field. Walter Pössl was born on September 16, 1909, in Vienna. A "Theresianer" (a graduate of the Maria-Theresien Military Academy at Wiener-Neustadt), Pössl transferred from the Austrian Bundesheer after the Anschluss of March 1938. Hauptmann Pössl joined Pz.Truppe GD in the spring of 1942 from Pz.Abt. 100 and led 1. Kompanie in the summer campaign on the Don before assuming command of the battalion, which he then led through the remainder of 1943. Major Pössl fell in action outside Warsaw, Poland, at the head of Pz.Rgt. 27 of the Hanoverian 19. Pz.Div. on September 25, 1944.

Generalleutnant Hyazinth Graf Strachwitz

Generalleutnant Hyazinth Graf Strachwitz von Gross-Zauche und Camminetz was born on 30 July 1893 on the family estate of Grossstein in upper Silesia. His Christian name had been bestowed on the first born son for over 700 years. Young Graf Strachwitz attended the Hauptkadettenanstalt at Gross Lichterfelde in Berlin and in 1912, as a Leutnant, joined the most senior and socially exclusive regiment in the Prussian Army, the Regiment Garde du Corps where he distinguished himself in numerous prewar sporting events. Early in World War One, during the advance to the Marne, Leutnant (since 1916 Oberleutnant) Graf Strachwitz was captured by the French during a long range reconnaissance and demolition patrol, remaining a prisoner of war despite numerous escape attempts, until after the Armistice.

Serving in the Garde-Kavallerie-Schützen-Division in the post-war chaos, Strachwitz helped organize the defense of his Silesian homeland from Polish incursions. After conditions stabilized Strachwitz left the Army to run his family's estate. During the 1930s, Graf Strachwitz took part in several exercises with the Silesian Reiterregiment 7 (Breslau) and the Thuringian Panzerregiment 2 (Eisenach). Major d.R. Strachwitz was awarded the Ritterkreuz on 25 August 1941 while commanding I/P.R. 2 in Russia (now in the Westphalian 16.Pz.Div.) and became the 144th soldier of the Wehrmacht to be awarded the Eichenlaub on November 13, 1942. With effect from January 1943, Oberst d.R. Graf Strachwitz assumed command of Pz.Rgt. GD. "Der Panzergraf" (The Panzer Count), as he was now universally known, led his regiment — often the core of an independent battlegroup far ahead of the main body — through the counterattack at Kharkov (earning the Swords on March 28, 1943), Operation "Zitadelle" and the retreat to the Dneiper.

Graf Strachwitz left GD in November 1943, officially on grounds of ill health. For some time tensions had existed between the Count and his equally strong-willed divisional commander, Generalleutnant Hoernlein. Many officers at Divisional HQ and in the Panzer Regiment felt that Strachwitz was forced to go because the Division was not big enough to include both of these domineering personalities. In any event, Strachwitz went on sick leave until early in the new year. In early January he was recalled to active duty, becoming a Generalmajor d.R. on April 1, 1944, and became the 11th soldier of the Wehrmacht to receive the Diamonds on April 15, 1944 while commanding a battlegroup on the Narva front.

During the late August 1944 attempt to reopen a land link to Heeresgruppe Nord in Courland, Panzergruppe Strachwitz accomplished the nearly impossible feat of capturing the city of Tukkum, Lithuania with only ten tanks. During a frontline inspection, Graf Strachwitz (who had already been wounded 13 times) was injured so severely in an accident that little hope was held out for his recovery. With his unconquerable will power, the Count was soon back on his feet and reporting back for active duty. Promoted to Generalleutnant on January 1, 1945, Graf Strachwitz raised new Panzerjagdverbände (hybrid mini-Panzer divisions) and participated in the last ditch defense of his Silesian homeland before making his way to the west to enter American captivity in May 1945.

Left: During the refitting of the Division after the battles around Kharkov, officers of the newly-raised Panzerregiment Grossdeutschland pose outside for group photographs at their camp at Poltava in Southern Russia. They wear Panzer field jackets with both piped and unpiped collars, and all the "Schiffchen" have the pink Waffenfarbe soutache. Only the bare-headed Oberleutnant is out of uniform with his felt winter boots and newly-issued M43 Einheitsfeldmütze (field service cap) with aluminum braid denoting officers' rank. Some authors have suggested that, just as it had with other uniform items, GD was selected to field test this new cap — apparently not yet available in Panzer black uniform cloth.

Above right and left: Crewmen of an Auto-Union Horch "Einheitsfahrzeug" (standard vehicle) are assisted out of the spring mud by local Russian peasants. The Horch was in production from 1937 to 1943. Most models had 3.8 liter V8 engines. Some models had four wheel drive while others were powered only by the front wheels. The Horch was produced in very large numbers and saw service as a passenger car, radio-communications vehicle, and propaganda vehicle. Panzer divisions used great numbers of Horches, and GD's Panzerfüsilier Regiment rode in it, as well as using other light trucks in this range.

Right: The crew of a 6x6 "Einheitsdiesel" of Sanitätsstaffel GD sit down on piles of army blankets for a leisurely round of the German soldier's inevitable game of "Skat." In the background is a pup tent assembled from Model 31 Zeltbahnen (shelter quarters).

Facing page: In the spring of 1943, OKH planned to form a powerful central armored reserve corps for the Eastern Front, built around I.D.(mot.) Grossdeutschland. Command of the corps was to be given to General Hermann Balck, one of the Army's master operational tacticians. In order to familiarize him with his new command, Balck was placed in temporary command of GD. As a result of his visit, General Balck submitted a proposed reorganization of GD to General Guderian. Balck felt that the Division as it was currently structured was far too large to be effectively controlled by one man. Indeed, it would be possible to make two average-strength Panzer divisions out of it. GD's size and scale of equipment reflected more the OKH's desire to possess a powerful counterweight to the growing prestige of the Waffen-SS than any critical, clearly defined, tactical requirements. The core elements of Balck's recommendations were the formation of three combined-arms battlegroups, a full Panzer regiment and increasing the integral Tiger I company to battalion strength. The latter two recommendations were eventually carried out, but GD always remained an unwieldy though powerful instrument for its commanders. In this photograph, General Balck is accompanied by Major Walter Pössl of I/P.R. GD. Partially visible behind Balck is Hauptmann Walter von Wietersheim of 5./P.R. GD.

Below: A Pz.Kpfw. III Ausf. M. of 2. or 3./Pz.Rgt. GD moves along at its top road speed (25mph) on the training ground at Akhtyrka, spring 1943. 250 Ausf. Ms were built between October 1942 and February 1943. The Ausf. M was the last main battle tank version of the Pz.Kpfw. III, first produced in 1937. By 1943 it had passed its peak as a battle tank but its chassis continued to serve the Army until 1945. The Pz.Kpfw. III used a new suspension system of six road wheels, individually supported by torsion bars. The vehicle had a well-laid out interior for its five-man crew. Weighing nearly 23 tons, the Ausf. M was powered by a Maybach HL120TRM engine coupled to a transmission with six forward and six reverse gears. The hand-operated turret traversed 360°; elevation of the 5cm KwK 39 L/60 gun was from -10° to +20°. Close-in defense was provided by two 7.92mm MG 34s. The Pz.Kpfw. III had benefitted from successive up-armoring of earlier versions, but could no longer stand up to powerful new Soviet AT rounds. The Ausf. M was the first tank in this series to have a built-in deep wading system installed. When fitted with the "Ostketten" (Eastern Front tracks), width was increased to 3.72m, giving it much improved flotation in deep snow. Inter-tank communications were maintained by the radioman/hull machine gunner using the standard FuG 5 radio set. The 5cm KwK39 L/60 fired HE and AP rounds, 92 of which were carried in the vehicle. It could penetrate 48mm armor at 1,000 yards. The gunner leaning out of the side access hatch of the turret in this photograph is holding a "scissors periscope." To aim the gun he used the Tzf5e sight. Dischargers for firing smoke candles are visible at the front corner of the turret. The camouflage appears to be red-brown or olive-green hand-painted on overall dark yellow.

Along with 14 other officers and men, Hauptmann Peter Frantz was ordered home in early April 1943 to receive the Eichenlaub to his Ritterkreuz, the higher grades of which were always personally presented by Adolf Hitler. Frantz received his award in the Reich Chancellery on April 14, 1943 and after a brief spell of home leave, returned to the Division's camp at Akhtyrka. Upon his return to his battalion, he was the object of a day-long celebration highlighted by a parade in his honor presided over by divisional Ia Oberst i.G. Oldwig von Natzmer, representing Generalleutnant Hoernlein, who was enjoying a month's leave.

Right: Hauptmann Frantz stands at the head of his Stabsbatterie (HQ Battery) StuG.Abt. GD, during the parade and review in his honor.

Below: Jubilant NCOs and men hoist the battalion commander on their shoulders to carry him to his command vehicle for the start of the parade in his honor. At the far left, looking up at Frantz, is Oberwachmeister (Sergeant-Major) Bruno Kliche, a former Spiess.

Above left: The heavily-garlanded battalion commander gratefully accepts a keg of beer from one of his gunners. Behind Hauptmann Frantz is his radioman, Gefreiter Lämmers.

Below left and above: With the keg safely stowed away and Master of Ceremonies Oberst i.G. von Natzmer standing behind him on the engine deck, Hauptmann Frantz proudly salutes his battalion of StuG IIIs as they pass in review. Note the railings for external stowage, made necessary by the need to cram as much ammunition as possible in the fighting compartment. These railings were always made up by unit workshops and followed no particular standard pattern.

Below: A StuG. III Ausf. G from the battalion. Note the railings for the Schürzen (Aprons) and the spare track links bolted on as additional armor protection. The tactical sign for self-propelled anti-tank weapons was painted in white on the upper nose plate.

The following sequence of photographs was taken in the spring of 1943 at the camp at Akhtyrka, north of Poltava. At this time, Grossdeutschland was undergoing its transformation into an all-volunteer Panzergrenadier Division. Regularly during the intense training, there were breaks for award ceremonies, sports competitions, and organized recreation. The warm, late spring weather permitted some respite for veterans of the brutal winter fighting and for the newly-arrived replacements alike. Physical training and sports had been a very important part of the routine of the old Reichsheer, building physical strength and coordination as well as a team spirit and mutual respect and confidence among all ranks. In the World War Two German Army, with its egalitarian ideal and cult of physical perfection, it reached its height. Nowhere was this more apparent than with the near-perfect physical specimens who served in the Grossdeutschland Division.

Above: The company mascot stands watch over carefully folded and arranged blouses, cuff-titles upwards, laid out on the banks of the Vorskla River at Akhtyrka during a swimming break.

Right: "Zum Schwimmen angetreten!" – "Fall in for a swim!" Standing somewhat self-consciously in their swimming trunks in a typical display of German orderliness, a platoon awaits the order to plunge into the water. The pre-war Army had required all its soldiers to learn how to swim in full equipment, and many soldiers would owe their lives to their ability to swim fast-flowing Russian rivers during the retreats and encirclements of 1944.

Below: Into the water!

Soldiers of the newly-renamed Pz. Aufklärungsabteilung GD drive their Volkswagen Schwimmwagen, one of several in the reconnaissance battalion, into the river for some outboard motoring. The VW typ 166 Schwimmwagen was a reliable, capable amphibious vehicle highly prized for reconnaissance duties because of its excellent cross-country performance. It had four-wheel drive and an extra "low-low" gear which allowed the car to climb up steep river banks. Over 16,000 were built, though not nearly enough to meet the demand.

Major Otto-Ernst Remer

Major Otto-Ernst Remer was born on August 18, 1912 in Neubrandenburg and joined the Reichsheer in 1932. Remer joined GD in April 1942 as commander of IV(schw.)/G.R. GD 1. In mid-February 1943, Remer was in command of I (gep.)/G.R. GD at Kharkov. His grenadier battalion, mounted in Sd.Kfz. 251 armored personnel carriers, successfully covered the withdrawal of SS-Obergruppenführer Paul Hausser's SS-Panzerkorps through the last escape route from the nearly surrounded city. Remer's battalion further distinguished itself in the German counterattack which retook Kharkov and pursued the beaten Soviets as far as Belgorod, thereby reversing many of the gains of the Soviet winter offensive, and giving back to Germany the initiative for the spring and summer campaign season. For his leadership of the battalion, Otto-Ernst Remer was awarded the Ritterkreuz on May 18, 1943.

Major Remer led his battalion capably during the failed Operation "Zitadelle" and its aftermath which resulted in desperate retrograde movements back to the Dnieper River and beyond. The SPW battalion's achievements near Krivoi Rog earned its commander the Eichenlaub on November 12, 1943. In March 1944, during the retreat to the Bug River, Remer turned over command to his replacement, the veteran Major Harald Krieg, and proceeded to Berlin to assume command of Wachbataillon GD from Oberstleutnant Kurt Gehrke.

Wach-Btl. GD, the only large body of combat troops in Berlin, played a vital role in crushing the July 20th plot to assassinate Adolf Hitler and replace his regime with a military-backed provisional government. Not convinced of the conspirators' claims that Hitler was dead, a reluctant Remer led a detachment to the Propaganda Ministry to secure it and arrest Dr. Goebbels. Thinking quickly, Goebbels cleverly persuaded Remer to let him telephone Hitler's headquarters. Coming to the telephone, Hitler immediately promoted Remer to Oberst with full authorization to brutally suppress the plot. Largely thanks to Remer, Ersatzheer (Replacement Army) HQ in the Bendleblock was in government control by that evening with the chief conspirators rounded up and hastily executed by an army firing squad.

Oberst Remer was slated to assume command of Pz.Füs.Rgt. GD in early September 1944. Visiting Führer HQ on the way to his new posting, Remer, a fanatical supporter of Adolf Hitler who had been lionized by Nazi propaganda in the wake of the failed coup, was given command of the Führerbegleitbrigade (Führer Escort Brigade, a GD "Sister Unit"). The rapidly-raised brigade was rushed into action in East Prussia where its inexperience and Remer's inadequate leadership caused it to suffer heavy casualties. Transferred to the west for the Ardennes Offensive, Remer's brigade again made meager gains in return for very high losses. By now a full division (though numerically weak) the FBD was in action during the recapture of Lauban in Upper Silesia in March 1945 where Generalmajor Remer's noticeable lack of skill in handling his division earned the severe criticism of 1. Pz. Armee's Commander, General Walter Nehring. A very brave and able company and battalion commander, Otto-Ernest Remer had no proper training for higher command and owed his meteoric promotion entirely to his proven loyalty to Adolf Hitler.

Above right: The proud "fresh-baked" Ritterkreuzträger, photographed by the Kriegsberichter shortly after the award ceremony. He wears the German Cross, War Service Cross, Wound Badge, General Assault Badge, and the Iron Cross I Class. German soldiers commonly wore all their decorations even in combat, even when there were orders to the contrary.

Below right: Major Otto-Ernst Remer, commander of I (SPW)/Pz.Gr.Rgt. Grossdeutschland, poses in mid-January 1944, wearing the Eichenlaub to his Ritterkreuz. Major Remer was awarded the Eichenlaub personally by Adolf Hitler on November 12, 1943, in Rastenburg, East Prussia, in recognition of his leadership and his SPW Battalion's achievements in the fluid defensive fighting around Krivoi Rog in Southern Russia. All Grossdeutschland infantry, whether Panzergrenadier or Panzerfüsilier, wore the traditional white Waffenfarbe of the infantry. Beneath his German Cross in Gold, Remer wears the Bulgarian award "For Bravery in War," IV Grade, I Class.

Right: Major Otto-Ernst Remer receives his Ritterkreuz from his regimental commander, Oberst Karl Lorenz, at the camp at Akhtyrka, west of Belgorod, on May 18, 1943.

Below: Major Remer passes his battalion in review after receiving his award.

Above: General Hermann Balck visits a training area at GD's camp at Akhtyrka during his brief tenure as Divisional Commander while Walter Hoernlein was on leave. The vehicle is a rather vividly camouflaged Mercedes-Benz 1500A 4x4 command car. The new dark yellow color has been sprayed in lines over the original dark gray.

Below, right and sequence on facing page: An infantry squad, with the standard Flammenwerfer 41, puts on a demonstration of street fighting for General Balck. Each infantry company in GD had two Flammenwerfers, a hallmark of the Division. The Soviets were extremely adept at street fighting, particularly during the withdrawals of the first half of the war, when they would leave parties of snipers and engineers behind, long after their main body had withdrawn. Specialist detachments of the infantry Pionier companies — well-provided with flamethrowers, satchel-charges, wire cutters, and automatic weapons — were the best troops to clear out villages and city blocks quickly and efficiently.

Left: Members of the battalion MG company's mortar platoon lay their 8cm medium mortar prior to firing. These indispensable weapons were known in the German Army as the "Little Man's Artillery." Each mortar platoon had six three-man sections with one mortar apiece. The Model 34 mortar was a smoothbore, muzzle-loading weapon designed for high angle fire. The round was fired by contact with a firing pin situated on the inside of the breech at the lower end of the barrel. The 7 3/4 lb HE round's effective range varied from a minimum of 437 yards to a maximum of 1,312 yards. A trained three-man crew could fire six rounds in nine seconds. In this photograph the gun commander, an Obergefreiter, is using the Model 35 panoramic sight for fine adjustments (a line was painted on the tube for rough aiming) while simultaneously using his right hand to turn the traversing handwheel. The loader grips the cross-leveling handwheel while the ammunition carrier steadies the bipod of the 125 lb mortar.

Right: The Gewehr Sprenggranate (rifle grenade launcher) attached to the muzzle of a Kar 98k rifle. The discharger cup was rifled, 3cm in bore diameter, and came with a special sight which clamped behind the rifle's rear sight. 9 types of grenades firing at least 15 types of ammunition were supplied as general issue. The standard HE rifle grenade had a 4.5-second delay fuse. The grenade launcher was simple to operate — the grenade was withdrawn from a canvas pouch and inserted into the discharger cup with a twisting motion. Each grenade was packed with a bulletless blank cartridge which was chambered immediately after loading the discharger cup. Firing the weapon was quite conventional.

Left: A sniper equipped with a Zielfernrohr 41 scope on his Kar 98k rifle. The most common of all scopes, the Zf41 was a 1.5-power scope with a base assembly. By 1942 6% of all 98ks were to be fitted with a short dovetailed rail, machined on the left side of the rear sight band. This scope gave riflemen thus equipped a local sniping capability while the 4-power scope was issued to specialist sniper-trained personnel. The Zf41 came with a special metal carrying case worn on the waistbelt. The case contained a "Klarinol" cleaning cloth and lens brush. Each scope also was furnished with front and rear rain shields. With its low magnification (1.5x), the Zf41 was more of an enhanced sighting device than a true sniper's telescopic sight.

Right: A Feldwebel of G.R. GD 1, wearing the reed-green drill material summer uniform, stands in a shallow hole holding a short-barreled 27mm flare pistol. This model, 24.5cm in length, and the long-barreled model adopted in 1935, fired a variety of over forty different rounds. The pistol was carried in a black leather holster which came furnished with a cleaning rod and shoulder strap. The flares themselves were carried in either a small flare pouch containing 12 short flares or a large pouch containing 18 long flares. The pouches were produced in standard black leather or pressed cardboard as well as in canvas (for the larger model only) for tropical use. Both the holster and pouches could also be worn on the waistbelt.

Below: s.MG 42 gunners of a heavy machine gun section sight in the mount and test their weapon by firing a 50-round belt of ammunition. In the hands of a skilled crew, the MG 42 proved to be the finest light machine gun in the world.

I(PZ.HAUBITZE)/PZ.ARTILLERIEREGIMENT GD

As befitted the Panzer division, it in fact was Grossdeutschland's TO & E (Table of Organization and Equipment) to include a Panzer Artillery Regiment of four Abteilungen (battalions) plus a headquarters and an observation battery. The latter, according to Oberst i.G. Cord von Hobe of the divisional staff, did not live up to expectations. Its usefulness (particularly in the defense) did not justify its cost in men, equipment, and motor vehicles.

I/Pz.A.R. GD consisted of a Stabs (HQ) batterie in modified Pz.Kpfw. III command tanks; two self-propelled batteries of Sd.Kfz. 124 Wespes mounting 10.5cm howitzers, six vehicles per battery, and one battery of six Sd.Kfz.165 Hummels with 15cm howitzers. In total, the battalion of 538 officers and men had 28 other vehicles plus two motorcycles/Kettenkrads.

II/Pz.A.R. GD consisted of a Stabsbatterie in 4-wheeled light trucks, two batteries of four 10.5cm le.FH 18 howitzers apiece drawn by halftrack prime movers, and one four-gun battery of 15cm heavy howitzers also drawn by halftrack prime movers. With an additional 29 motor vehicles and motorcycles, the battalion had a total authorized strength of 488 officers and men. III/Pz.A.R. GD was a mixed light artillery battalion with two four-gun batteries of 10.5cm light field howitzers and one four-gun battery of 10cm FK18 field guns, all drawn by halftrack prime movers. With an additional 29 vehicles, the battalion had an authorized strength of 480 officers and men. IV/Pz.A.R. GD was another mixed light medium battery, organized the same as II/Pz.A.R. GD.

Battery commander Major Süssmann in his Sd.Kfz. 143 armored artillery observation tank. Süssmann's battery was one of two "Wespe" (Wasp) batteries of I/Pz.A.R. GD. The anti-tank Schürzen (skirts) on the turret were permanently attached, while those on the hull slipped onto frames and could be removed if they or the running gear were damaged.

Above: The same vehicle as on the facing page, seen from the front. Note both the dummy main gun and the sealed-up bow machine gun port. Major Süssmann conducts a briefing for officers and men of Pz.A.R. GD, using his observation tank as a handy podium.

Right: A Sd.Kfz. 143 Artillerie-Panzerbeobachtungswagen (Pz.Kpfw. III) of the Stabsbatterie of I/Pz.A.R. GD. Two hundred sixty-two of these observation tanks were produced from February 1943 to April 1944, by converting older Pz.Kpfw. III Ausf. Es through Hs. They were introduced with the first Hummel and Wespe batteries. The basic specifications were the same as for the Pz.Kpfw. III described elsewhere in this volume apart from the following: extra armor plate was added to the hull front and rear and to the rear of the superstructure. The machine gun in the superstructure was removed and the hole plugged. The original gun mantlet was replaced by a thicker mantlet with a dummy gun and an MG 34 mounted in the center of the mantlet. Two types of radio, the FuG 4 medium wave receiver "C" which operated in the 835-3000 KC range and functioned solely as a receiver, and the FuG 8 30 watt transmitter "A" and medium wave receiver "C," operating in the 1120-3000 and 835-3000 KC ranges respectively. This latter radio had a range of 31 miles using a key code and 9.3 miles by voice when stationary. On the move it could transmit by key code 24.8 miles and by voice 6.2 miles using its roof-aerial. Using an 8 meter wind mast and star aerial (visible in this photograph on the rear of the engine deck) the range was increased to approximately 93 miles (key) and 31 miles (voice).

Right: A Sd.Kfz.165 Hummel (Bumblebee) self-propelled armored 15cm field howitzer of 3./Pz.A.R. GD moves at its top speed of 25mph down a road behind the lines. The Hummel was designed to provide the Panzer and Panzergrenadier divisions with artillery support on an armored, fully-tracked chassis. The hybrid Pz.Kpfw. III/IV chassis was selected for what Army Ordnance meant to be merely an interim solution until a chassis designed specifically as a self-propelled gun platform could be produced. GD had a full six-gun battery by the start of Unternehmen "Zitadelle" in July 1943, together with two of the complementary Munitionsfahrzeuge (ammunition carriers) Hummels with the 15cm gun removed to carry spare rounds (18 rounds were carried on the Hummel itself). The 15cm s.FH 18/1 L/30 had 15° left, 15° right (hand operated) traverse and could be elevated from -3° to +42°. Sighting was via the Rblf 36 panoramic telescope gun sight. The gun's range was 14,630 yards. The shell's projectile weight was 95.7 lbs with eight increments of propellant charges for the HE, anti-concrete, AP and smoke rounds. Although built on a medium tank chassis, the Hummel, at 24 tons, was thinly armored, especially the very high walls around the fighting compartment, necessitated by mounting the s.FH 18/1 above the engine. Master tactician General Hermann Balck would have preferred that no such vehicles be used, as they were large targets which were difficult to conceal. Also, when the vehicle broke down, the gun too was put out of action — something that rarely happened with guns pulled by prime movers, which had nearly equal cross-country mobility. All SP batteries consisted of six guns rather than the four in a towed battery, as two of the SPs were usually "in the shop" at any one time.

Facing page, above: Hummels of 3./Pz.A.R. GD move into position. The very high silhouette of the vehicle is evident in this photograph. Note the ventilation flaps for the centrally located HL120TRM engine. The Hummel's normal crew consisted of a driver, a radioman, and four gunners for the 15cm s.FH 18/1 L/30. Modest anti-aircraft protection was provided by an MG 34 or 42 mounted on the fighting compartment. Occasionally the situation was so desperate that these highly-skilled gunners had to be employed as infantry. Hauptmann Hans-Friedrich Graf zu Rantzau received the Ritterkreuz for leading his gunners in an infantry counterattack on March 15, 1944, at Kwitka in the Ukraine, retaking the town in fierce fighting and preventing the German front from being ripped open.

Facing page, below: Sd.Kfz. 124 le. Feldhaubitze 18/2 auf Fahrgestell Pz.Kpfw. II(SF) Wespes of either 1. or 2./Pz.A.R. GD ford a shallow stream in Southern Russia, summer 1943. The Alkett-designed and FAMO-built Wespe was chosen as the most practical mounting for the le.FH 18 light howitzer and the best use of the Pz.Kpfw. II chassis. 676 were built between February 1943 and July 1944. Another 159 Munitions-SF auf Pz.Kpfw. II (ammunition carriers), each holding 90 rounds, were built simultaneously and issued two per six-gun battery. The highly successful Wespe had a slightly lengthened hull with the engine relocated to the center of the chassis. The glacis was also extended and the cooling louvers completely redesigned. The suspension was modified by adding one extra road wheel on each side and reducing the return rollers from four to three. In order to absorb the recoil loadings, spring bumper stops were added to the road wheels. The driver sat isolated from the rest of the crew in a small forward compartment. The gun crew themselves were located in the rear fighting compartment, built up from angled plates. The ammunition carrier's design permitted maintenance units to install the le.FH 18/2 as a replacement for actual Wespes taken out of service. The HL62TR engine permitted a maximum speed of 25mph. 32 rounds of HE, smoke, incendiary, and hollow-charge shells weighing 32.1 lbs were stored in bins inside the fighting compartment. The gun had a maximum range of 13,480 yards. Hand traverse was 17° left, 17° right. Elevation was -5° to +42°. The gunner used the standard Rblf 36 panoramic telescope to aim the howitzer.

FELDKAMPFSCHULE

rom June 1939 until April 1942, Infanterie Regiment (mot.) GD and its successor division drew its enlisted personnel from the general armed forces replacement pool of eligible recruits — in GD's case from throughout the Reich. Up to the start of the war, many of its original personnel had been assigned on rotation to the Regiment for a six-month period, and then returned to their parent units. Officers and NCOs served a year-long tour with the Regiment. The outbreak of war hardly affected this arrangement, with the obvious exception that the personnel on duty on September 1, 1939 stayed with the Regiment.

In April 1942, the Regiment was enlarged to divisional strength, and with this expansion went a new charter. As the "Lifeguards Regiment of the German People" GD was to present "the ideal picture of the German soldier." From this point on all recruits were to be volunteers (officers and key specialists would continue to be assigned as required by the Division) in good health and a minimum of 5'7" (1.70m) in height. The maximum age was 23 years old on enlistment and no wearers of eyeglasses were to be accepted (this requirement, to judge by photographic evidence, was not strictly enforced). Recruits were also required to be of "sound political conviction." In practice this usually meant expressing a love of country and the will to win the war.

Simultaneously with the expansion to divisional strength, the Ersatz-Bataillon GD grew to regimental strength and moved its headquarters within Brandenburg from Neuruppin to Cottbus. This

barracks was the future Grossdeutschland soldier's first taste of life in the Division until the end of the war. Recruits were assigned to one of the Training Regiment's three battalions, organized like a normal four-company field battalion.

As exceptionally fit young men who had already received paramilitary training in the Hitler Youth and the Labor Service (RAD), until 1944 the recruits were given the full 16 week basic training course, which was divided into three broad parts: individual training; individual training within the squad; and squad training within the platoon. This was followed by a period of advanced training at company and sometimes even at battalion level. While basic training focused on the military basics and personal weapons, the period of advanced training included heavy weapons and cooperation with artillery and armor. Close-order drill, including the famous "Paradeschritt," or goose-step, lapsed as the war situation grew more urgent. By late 1944, basic training had been cut to eight weeks and recruits were then being

harangued by so-called "National Socialist Leadership Officers."

As 1944 approached, the commanders and staff of Pz.Gr. Ersatz und Ausbildungs Brigade (replacement and training brigade) GD realized that more would need to be done to provide the field division with properly trained replacements and qualified NCOs. From early 1944 all recruits lived and trained in a "Russendorf" ("Russian Village") specially constructed on the depot grounds. An NCO school was instituted in May 1944 to train sergeants selected from among recruits and convalescents. These measures would be of some help when GD expanded to corps-level and created numerous "sister" units.

When basic and advanced training had been completed, the recruits were formed into Marschkompanien (transfer companies) for transfer to the parent unit. Once with Grossdeutschland, the newly-arrived replacements were assigned to the Field-Replacement Battalion for varying periods at the Divisional Battle School. Here, instructors with even more recent combat experience than those at the Depot instructed the replacements in current fighting methods. Officer candidates had schools of their own as did Panzer, artillery, and other specialist personnel.

Facing page, top: One of the veteran instructors who helped the young recruits become useful replacements. This Oberfeldwebel is a holder of the German Cross in Gold as well as both classes of the Iron Cross. The NCO wears a custom-made M43 field cap.

Facing page, middle: Crossing a hip-deep river occasionally called for disrobing entirely and carrying uniform, gear and weapons on one's head. In this case wearing the steel helmet was not a tactical necessity. Needless to say, this hardly ever occurred in action.

Facing page, bottom: A recruit in the reed-green fatigue uniform crawls from a dug-out during training. These exercises were as realistic as possible, on the theory that the better the training, the fewer the casualties in action.

Above: Recruits, some showing the strain of training, double time across an open field. Hard physical conditioning was an integral part of German military life.

Right: Recruits take the hurdles in fighting order. This demonstrates the German military's emphasis on physical fitness.

Recruits during a pause in the training. Although the monogrammed shoulder straps are worn, no cuff titles are present, as they were awarded upon completion of training.

Right: A thirsty recruit drinks from his Feldflasche (felt-covered canteen).

Below: Two recruits light up after the exercise. Each German soldier was issued two cigarettes or cigars as part of his daily ration. Soldiers could purchase cigarettes from unit stores or from private canteens.

At the end of the exercise, tired but happy and increasingly fit and self-confident, recruits of a training squad allow themselves a moment of satisfaction before their instructors bring them back to earth. Three different models of fatigue jackets are worn in this photograph: the first (white, unpocketed); second (reed-green, unpocketed) and third (reed-green, pocketed).

K U R S K ,   J U L Y   4 - 1 8 ,   1 9 4 3

ield-Marshal Erich von Manstein's brilliant series of counterattacks between February and March 1943 succeeded in restoring much of the old German frontline and caused heavy losses in Soviet manpower and materiel. The spring thaw found the defeated Soviets still holding a large salient projecting westwards between the junctions of German Army Groups Center and South. As the spring wore on, debate raged in both the German High Command and on the Eastern Front as to when, where, how, and indeed, if to attack at all in 1943. By April 1943, over the strong objections of newly-appointed Inspector General of the Panzer Troops Generaloberst Heinz Guderian, Hitler and his commanders had chosen to use the carefully built-up Panzer reserves to eliminate the Soviet salient at Kursk as soon as possible. The operation, known as Unternehmen "Zitadelle," was beset by delays — above all, were Hitler's wishes to

wait until the new Pz.Kpfw. V Panther tanks were available in sufficient numbers. Very early on, the Soviets were aware of the German plans and massed considerable forces in, behind, and on both sides of the salient. They elected to wait for the enemy and then mount their counterattack once the Germans' blows had been absorbed.

The terrain in the salient consisted of low hills and open, undulating country in the basin of the confluence of the Upper Don and Dnieper Rivers. It was ideal tank country and the Soviets began extensive preparations to fortify the salient with lines of trenches, belts of minefields and so-called Pakfronts — several batteries of anti-tank guns carefully dug in and sighted on every likely approach to Kursk.

After much discussion, the Germans decided that von Manstein's Army Group would be allocated the major part of German resources in tanks, guns, and men, while Luftflotte 6 would provide air cover for both attacking forces. Walter Model's 9. Armee, much weaker in numbers, would attack from the north toward Kursk to link up with

Manstein's forces, primarily Hermann Hoth's 4. Pz.Armee moving north via Oboyan to Kursk.

After spending the spring at the camp at Akhtyrka completing its transformation into a Panzergrenadier division, Grossdeutschland was fully-manned and equipped, and was assigned to General Otto von Knobelsdorff's XXXXVIII Pz.Korps. GD was now a de-facto Panzer Division itself with its own Panzer regiment and a company of Tiger I heavy tanks (two more Tiger companies were training in Germany).

The long-delayed assault began for GD on July 4, 1943 when Pz.Füs.Rgt. GD and 3. Pz.Div. attacked and seized some hills near Gerzovka north of the main sector of the attack. Resistance was ominously heavy, revealing the loss of surprise, and heavy casualties continued until the divisional engineers cleared the minefields for 3. Pz.Div. During this attack, while leading his Füsiliers, Oberst Erich Kahsnitz was fatally wounded and was awarded a posthumous Ritterkreuz. Early on July 5, having withstood a preemptive Soviet barrage — yet more proof that surprise had been lost — the main attack began, with Pz.Gr.Rgt. GD moving north of Belgorod toward its immediate objective of Oboyan on a direct line to Kursk and the

anticipated link-up with 9. Armee. The Division again took heavy casualties but did make some progress. The Panther tanks suffered numerous breakdowns before they even reached the battlefield. Pz.A.A. GD successfully thrust to the Pena in the direction of Verchopenye on July 7.

Pz.Stu.Pi.Btl. GD came up rapidly to seize and repair a bridge over the Pena and soon the tanks of "Gruppe Strachwitz" were heading northeast. GD was stalled within sight of Oboyan for the next three days and the focus of the attack shifted to SS-Obergruppenführer Paul Hausser's SS-Panzerkorps at Belgorod. GD was a spectator of the greatest clash of armor in history. Three hundred tanks on either side were destroyed by the evening of July 12.

With the Soviets pouring in reinforcements, and news of Allied landings in Sicily, Hitler ordered the end of Unternehmen Zitadelle. At the same moment, the Soviets mounted a massive offensive of their own on the German salient at Orel, north of Kursk. The Germans could only attempt to avert a looming disaster with their badly depleted forces. On July 18, Grossdeutschland was sent back to Tomarovka, prior to moving into HG Mitte's sector at Karachev.

Gefreiter Paul Schmid, a radioman in Oberst Lorenz's command SPW, receives a message from Gefreiter Alois Rippl. This photo was taken near Belgorod, July 1943, during the Kursk offensive.

The MG42. The MG 34 was the world's first general-purpose machine gun and was a formidable factor on the battlefields of the first half of the Second World War. By late 1941 its defects, such as its overly complex manufacturing process and susceptibility to jamming, led to developing something much simpler. As far back as 1937, Grossfuss of Dobeln had came up with a design for new fast-firing machine gun which combined the basic layout of the MG 34 with some contemporary Polish and Czech features.

With Mauser in charge of the program, the MG 42 entered production in early 1942. As had been the case with the MP 40, traditional gun-making methods were discarded in favor of easily-manufactured spot welds, drop forgings and stampings. With Germany facing a desperate production crisis, the MG 42 was easier and much cheaper to produce than the MG 34. In contrast to the MG 34, the MG 42 had a quick and much simplified barrel change. The gun was easy to maintain and had an extremely high (1,500rpm cyclic; 500rpm normal) rate of fire which gave it a unique signature. It also leveled the playing field somewhat for German soldiers facing hordes of Soviet soldiers armed with automatic weapons of all types. Few existing accessory components of the MG 34 were adaptable to the MG 42 and new ones had to be designed. On its 42 lb Lafette 42 carriage, the all-up weight of the s.MG 42 heavy machine gun was about 68 lbs. 50-round metallic non-disintegrating link belts of 7.92mm rounds could be linked to feed the gun which had a high muzzle velocity of 820 m/sec. Sustained and indirect fire was possible using the Zf40 telescopic sight but, unlike the MG 34, no selective fire was possible. GD was one of the first units provided with the MG 42 and had an allotment double that of other formations.

Left and above: GD infantry train on the s.MG 42 heavy machine gun at the camp at Akhtyrka. Note the 250-round ammunition boxes hanging from the Lafette 42 carriage and the starter tab for the ammunition belt. Interestingly the Zf40 telescopic sight was not fitted for sustained or indirect fire. The Unteroffizier crew-chief has used shelter-quarter material to fashion a camouflage cover for his steel helmet.

Below: The gunners relax with an alfresco lunch after the day's practice.

Above and below: Team sports being played on a soccer field at the Akhtyrka encampment — more for pure enjoyment than for competition.

Top: Soldiers from all sub-units of the Division, including some convalescents, cheer on their side in a match.

By the spring of 1942, German divisions on the Eastern Front which had been in constant action and suffered heavy losses were transferred to France to rest, refit and train replacements. Here they enjoyed a close approximation of peacetime garrison life while simultaneously guarding the inactive Western Front from any Allied incursions. In addition, a generous leave policy was instituted for individual soldiers. By mid-war, Grossdeutschland had become the "Fire Brigade" of the Eastern Front and could not be removed from the theatre of operations. Consequently, apart from individual sub-units who went to the West to train on new weapons and vehicles, GD remained in the East throughout the war. Between battles, when the front had stabilized, the Division would be withdrawn into OKH Reserve — the Army High Command being solely responsible under Adolf Hitler for the Eastern Front — to rest, train, reequip and absorb replacements and soldiers returning from convalescent leave. At such times, every effort was made to give the troops as much relaxation and recreation as possible. GD enjoyed these rest periods from April-June 1942; August 1942; April - July 1943 and from mid-June to late July 1944. By summer 1944 the situation in the East had worsened so much that Grossdeutschland was constantly in action until the last day of the war.

Above: A desperate sprint to the finish line in a relay race. Minefield safe-lane tape and flags have been whimsically used to mark off the track.

Left: Soldiers suit up to take part in one of the German Army's favorite athletic pasttimes — running a race and doing gymnastics in full marching order.

Oberleutnant Hanns Magold

Herbert Karl Johann "Hanns" Magold was born five days after the Armistice ending World War I on November 16, 1918 in Unteressfeld in the community of Bad Königshofen im Grabfeld of Lower Franconia, Bavaria. After a conventional education, Hanns Magold joined the German Army as a Fahnenjunker in 1.Batterie of the Bavarian Artillerieregiment 74. on November 3, 1937. Promoted Fahnenjunkergefreiter on April 1, 1938 during his basic training and Unteroffizier on August 1 of the same year, Magold was assigned as a Fähnrich for officer's training at the Kriegsschule in Dresden between November 15, 1938 and August 14, 1939, graduating as a Leutnant in I/Pz.Art.Rgt. 74 of the Viennese 2. Pz.Division. Leutnant Magold served throughout the Polish and French Campaigns with his battalion and was appointed Battalion Adjutant on August 14, 1940. Oberleutnant Magold held his appointment throughout the Balkans Campaign and the first year of the war in the Soviet Union before being placed in temporary command of 5./Pz.A.R. 74 on April 17, 1942.

Oberleutnant Magold attended a course for battery commanders between July 1-26, 1942 and then took up his duties as commander of 3./Pz.A.R. 74 and Adjutant of I. Abteilung. Ten days later, on August 5, 1942, Magold was seriously wounded in the left thigh by enemy MG fire and was sent back to Germany for a five-month convalescence. Returning to duty in the desperate second half of January 1943, Oberleutnant Magold served for eleven days on temporary duty as a training officer with the newly-raised XIII Fliegerkorps before being posted as battery commander of 1./StuG.Abt. GD on January 25, 1943, his appointment as Chef being confirmed on February 1, 1943.

Oberleutnant Magold led his battery throughout the see-saw fighting around Kharkov in February 1943. During Manstein's counteroffensive to re-take Kharkov, which began on March 7, 1943, Magold's battery passed through Grigorovka and destroyed numerous enemy sled-columns packed with troops and supplies on Hill 188 and reached Alexandrovka. Here the battery was halted by an enemy anti-tank gun line and shortly thereafter Soviet tanks appeared. In this fighting 1. Batterie destroyed seven T-34s, four 12.2cm anti-tank guns, 21 7.62cm

anti-tank guns and 16 light (4.5cm) anti-tank guns. Magold accounted personally for five of the seven T-34s. As a result of his successes Oberleutnant Magold was recommended for the award of the Ritterkreuz, which was bestowed on him on April 3, 1943. Soon afterwards, Magold was promoted to the rank of Hauptmann. In the meantime, Magold achieved the singular success of destroying 14 out of 15 Soviet tanks during the break-in to Stanovoye on March 14.

Hauptmann Magold commanded 1. Batterie throughout 1943 before succeeding Major Peter Frantz in command of StuG.Abt. GD on January 16, 1944. Magold led the battalion through most of the heavy rearguard and defensive fighting from the Bug to the Dniester and Prut Rivers. On July 26, 1944 Hanns Magold assumed his new post as Kommandeur of Sturmgeschützbrigade 311 in Heeresgruppe Mitte's sector. On September 15, 1944 the OKH Heerespersonalamt (Army Personnel Office) announced that Hauptmann Hanns Magold had fallen in action at the head of his brigade at Luzagora near the Dukla Pass in Poland. Shortly thereafter his brigade buried him with full military honors at the German World War I cemetery at Gorlice outside of Warsaw.

1944

GERMAN PANZER TACTICS

The basic principle of German tank tactics was to use concentrated formations of combined arms (armor, armored infantry, artillery, and engineers) to strike a crippling blow at a section of the enemy's frontline to effect a breakthrough of sufficient size and depth to disrupt and then destroy the enemy's ability to organize and carry out an effective defense. Cut-off enemy units were to be mopped up and reduced by the infantry as the tanks and forward supporting elements advanced into the enemy rear areas.

The Germans knew the value of reconnaissance, and every Panzer and Panzergrenadier division had a reconnaissance battalion. In addition, information was gathered by forward observers and also by the Luftwaffe reconnaissance and army cooperation squadrons. When the lay of the land and the positions of enemy troops and fortifications were determined, the attack was then laid out in some detail. German units were allowed considerable latitude in their tactics and movement so long as the combat objectives were met. This allowed the armor units to adapt to conditions on the battlefield and take the initiative in exploiting unexpected opportunities.

The basic armor formation in 1942 and 1943 was the blunt wedge, involving a Panzer battalion advancing with the tanks spread out wider in the rear echelons; typically two companies abreast, followed by the battalion staff company, and the third company in train. The self-propelled artillery was generally behind, and the Panzergrenadiers in armored halftracks (SPWs) were behind the lead elements of the tank formation.

When attacking the enemy front, the tanks broke through while the armored infantry and self-propelled anti-tank guns dealt with enemy strongpoints and armor. The tanks generally attempted to reach and destroy the enemy's artillery before they could begin counter fire to break up the German assault. The pioneers, in SPWs, blew up anti-tank obstacles and aided the tanks in crossing natural features such as rivers or anti-tank ditches. Motorized infantry would then be brought in as reinforcements. At the same time, the lighter tanks in the formation formed screens at the sides to protect the flanks and provide covering fire for the infantry. The assault gun batteries, when attached to a unit or when part of a formation, often supplemented or replaced the lighter tanks as the screening force.

Tanks in the assault used the terrain for cover as much as possible and usually advanced in a leapfrog maneuver which allowed forward tanks to lay down support and suppressing fire while rear echelons advanced forward to new firing positions. These vehicles then laid down fire while the original line of tanks advanced through the new positions and drove on until they set up firing positions to bring up the other line of tanks. Similar tactics were employed for the supporting infantry. The armored infantry took enemy infantry-held positions and, just as important, warned the tanks of the presence of enemy anti-tank guns. They also protected the tanks from Russian tank-killing teams, which were very aggressive in pressing their attacks.

With the introduction of the Panther, each division now had a breakthrough tank in the same way the corps level commander had Tiger tanks at his disposal. The attack formation was changed to the

Left: The Richtschütze (Gunner) of a Pz.Kpfw. IV Ausf. H of II/Pz.Rgt. GD lights a cigarette during a pause in his platoon's standing patrol in the Ukraine. Over his ears is a Kopfschutzer (Toque).

Right: By mid-January 1944, the Soviet offensives launched by the 1st and 2nd Ukranian Fronts had been halted behind the Dnieper and the Eastern Front temporarily stabilized. Tiger I crewmen of 9./Pz.Rgt. GD put the respite in the fighting to good use to rest and clean and repair their gear. Tiger tanks were unheated, and wearing heavy winter clothing and using woolen blankets was indispensable in the bitter cold of a Ukranian winter. Apart from the markings on the sides of the turrets no other identification is present on the tank. An interesting detail is the fitting of later production tracks on this early Tiger I. This could have resulted from the tracks being switched during transport preparations, or simply that the original tracks had worn out and had to be replaced.

"Panzerglocke" (Armor Bell), with the Panthers forming the crown of the "bell" in a blunt wedge formation, and the PzKpfw.IVs and assault guns forming the skirts (sides). In this way, the center of the bell formation was well-protected, allowing the infantry, artillery, and reserve formations to be close enough that they could reinforce any weak spots or counteract any enemy counterthrusts. It also allowed the formation commander much better control over the conduct of the assault.

In the defense, the Germans preferred to use terrain where possible to provide good basic cover supplemented by defensive positions. The basic principle was to counterstrike in a concentrated effort away from the main point of the enemy's attack. Breaking through at such a weak point would often halt an attack almost immediately as the attacking forces would have to reinforce the weak area in the line. At the same time, artillery would attempt to break up enemy positions and concentrations of troops, tanks, or artillery. In enemy breakthroughs, artillery was used to destroy as many enemy troops as possible and reserves were brought up to mount a counter-attack or sudden assault. At any time, should the enemy attack fail, the Germans would then go over to the attack immediately to exploit the changing situation. Panthers, and Tigers when available, were used to destroy enemy tanks and guns at long range to support the defense, as this reduced the wear and tear on their chassis. Such tactics worked superbly, even in the face of superior enemy forces, until the difference was so great that tactics alone could not overcome it.

Tiger Tank

The Henschel VK4501(H) was selected to equip almost all the heavy tank companies from late 1942 until the spring of 1944, when the first Tiger II Ausf. B heavy tanks were issued. The Henschel design, designated "Tiger Ausf. E, Sd.Kfz. 181," was a massive boxy vehicle, a product of prewar German automotive and armor design. Front armor was 100mm, side superstructure armor was 80mm, lower side armor was 60mm, the rear plate was 80mm, and the formed horseshoe turret of 82mm, with a roof of 25mm plate. The hull roof plate was also 25mm. With this great amount of armor, the tank weighed a massive 57 tons.

Power was by a 690 hp Maybach V-12 engine, the HL210P45, later replaced by the 700 hp HL230P30. The final drive was a fully regenerative steering unit developed from the British Merritt-Brown design, and gave the Tiger excellent maneuverability. Though the turret had to be removed to replace any of the transmission assemblies, this was simple to do, requiring only a gantry crane to lift the turret. Road speed was 23 mph, but normal range was short, 75 miles on roads, even less cross-country.

The Tiger's main armament, the 8.8cm KwK 36, L/56, was built by Krupp, and was capable of destroying virtually all Allied tanks at maximum range. Armor penetration with the Pzgr. 39 standard APC ammunition was 100mm at 1,000 yards, enough to stop all of the existing enemy tanks of the period. 1,354 Tiger Ausf. Es were built from July 1942 to August 1944. Most Tigers were assigned to corps-level independent heavy tank battalions, where they were used as strategic armored units.

Production improvements came steadily. An improved lower cast cupola appeared in July 1943. New steel-rimmed "silent bloc" roadwheels were introduced in January 1944, and the outermost row of wheels was eliminated. Very late production vehicles had a smaller muzzle brake and simplified loader's hatch. The gunner's binocular

JS II or the 8.8cm KwK 36 of the Tiger. The KwK 42 could penetrate 111mm at 1,000 yards, and 124mm at 500 yards, using Pzgr. 39 APC ammunition, 10% more than the 8.8cm. KwK 36.

The Panther Ausf. G appeared in 1944, and featured single piece side plates, deletion of the driver's visor to strengthen the glacis, and various detail improvements. There were 850 Ausf. Ds, 2,000 Ausf. As, and 3,126 Ausf. Gs built from January 1943 to April 1945. In spite of the mechanical weaknesses, the Panther was one of the most effective combat tanks of the war and was usually the dominant force on the battlefield until overwhelmed by superior enemy forces.

Panzerkampfgruppen

German Army divisions were ideally suited, by virtue of their organization, allotment of weapons, and organic logistical elements, for the formation of combined arms teams within the divisions. As early as the summer of 1941, I.R.(mot.) GD assembled Regimentsgruppen (Regimental Groups — mixed arms combat teams) during the battles in the Desna Bend. When the race to the Lower Don threatened to stall due to lack of fuel, Divisional HQ formed a Kampfgruppe of the Division's tracked elements, with extra infantry riding on the tanks and assault guns. By spring 1943, when it was reorganized as a Panzergrenadier division, GD had grown so large and was so well provided with weapons and vehicles that it had the strength of two ordinary Panzer divisions. This allowed the Division to be subdivided as required into task-tailored battle groups such as Panzergruppe Strachwitz at Kursk.

By summer 1944, the Division had completed its growth cycle and established a basic method of forming armored battle groups within the Division. Such an armored battlegroup might consist of the Begleitkompanie of the Division in its Sd.Kfz. 251 SPWs, one of the two tank battalions (usually I(Panther)/Pz.Rgt. 26), the organic Pz.Gr.Pionierkompanie in SPWs, I(SPW)/Pz.Gr.Rgt. GD, part or all of I/Pz.A.R. GD with its "Wespe" and "Hummel" SPs and the required communications and medical echelons, also being fully tracked. Reconnaissance units would come from the tracked element of Pz.A.A. GD. The Division's unique size and supply of tanks and tracked

sight was replaced with a monocular sight in early 1944. In spite of shortages, design problems, and the development of effective Allied countermeasures, the Tiger Ausf. E. retained its reputation as a superbly effective fighting vehicle to the end of the war.

Panther

The Panther's combat debut during the battle of Kursk in July 1943 was a mixed blessing: the promise of tremendous power on the battlefield marred by an epidemic of mechanical failures caused by rushed development and incomplete training. By the time the initial Panther Ausf. D had been replaced by the Ausf. A, many of these defects had been identified and corrected. However, through its entire service life, the promise of the Panther's design was compromised by mechanical unreliability, the result of a shortage of high strength alloy steels and a tank industry that could not produce a reliable powertrain.

The Panther Ausf. A, designated Pz.Kpfw. V Ausf. A, was not, by Allied standards, a medium tank. It weighed 43 tons, was 8.86 meters long, 3.4 meters wide, and 2.95 meters high. Following the practice of the Soviet T-34, the hull armor was well sloped, but this was the T-34's only contribution. The engineering layout, typically German, placed a 700 hp Maybach HL230P30 engine in the rear, with the transmission and final drives up front. The suspension used double torsion bars on each axle to allow greater speeds cross country, and a more comfortable ride. The Panther could reach a top speed of 29 mph.

The Panther's armor layout provided good protection, especially in the front. The glacis was 80mm, lower nose was 60mm, sides were 40mm, the rear was 45mm, and the turret had a 100mm front plate with 45mm sides and rear. The Panther's major advantage on the battlefield was its superb main gun. The 7.5cm KwK 42 L/70 was a more effective anti-tank weapon than either the Soviet 122mm gun of the

vehicles permitted it to raise a second armored battle group around the new SPW battalion of Pz.Füs.Rgt. GD, the second tank battalion (II(Pz.IV)/Pz.Rgt. GD), the Pz.Füs.Pionierkompanie and of the Sd.Kfz. 250 SPW squadrons of Pz.A.A. GD. Occasionally, the reconnaissance SPWs formed the basis of a third, weaker battlegroup. As these were not permanently constituted formations, the above can serve only as a guide to normal practice. Artillery towed by prime movers was assigned to the second armored battle group and, if the situation required it, heavy 17cm guns towed by prime movers could be attached to either battle group. Self-propelled light and medium Flak were allocated equally to both battle-groups. Command functions were exercised, as the situation warranted, by either the divisional commander, the Panzer regimental commander, or one of the two

infantry regimental commanders. This flexibility and mobility was a powerful weapon in the hands of the divisional commander and it was used time and again to mount strong counterthrusts and raids on Soviet forces who possessed nothing remotely comparable. It did, however, possess a number of unavoidable drawbacks. First, with the Division's entire mechanized (i.e. tracked) element serving in the armored battlegroup(s) and the Division's logistical elements fully absorbed in supplying these formations, the Division's remaining assets were largely relegated to positional warfare. This particularly applied to the Division's four truck-borne infantry battalions, who could not maneuver if suddenly confronted with a Soviet attack on their positions. Secondly, command of the entire extra-large division was made even more difficult when the divisional commander was fully involved with directing the armored battlegroup at whose head he had placed himself. Nevertheless, the armored battlegroup must be seen as the most advanced method of employing armor in the Second World War and was a generation ahead of anything yet thought of or practiced in the Allied camps.

Facing page, top left: Operating conditions on the Eastern Front were brutal in the winter, and this was made worse by the fact that most maintenance and repairs had to be performed outside. Crews commonly had to transfer fuel and lubricating oil and grease from shipping drums using hand operated pumps.

Facing page, below right: The Pz.Kpfw. IV Ausf. G was the second version of this tank to mount a long-barreled 7.5cm KwK 40, L/43 gun. It was in service by the summer of 1942, and surviving examples served to the end of the war. The external smoke dischargers were deleted on later models.

Above: This Pz.Kpfw. IV Ausf. H of II/Pz.Rgt. GD shows the poor wearing qualities of the temporary winter white camouflage paint. In spite of the good front armor of 80mm, most Pz.Kpfw. IV crews added extra armor to improve their chances. Spare track links were by far the most common form of added protection.

Below right: A view of a StuG. III Ausf. G of Sturmgeschützabteilung GD with the full Schürzen, mounted to cover areas too thinly armored to resist hollow charge anti-tank weapons. These thin shields made incoming hollow charge rounds detonate before making contact with the vehicle's armor.

Below left: Another view of a Sturmgeschütz III Ausf. G. The sheet metal spaced "skirts" to protect against against hollow charge anti-tank rounds have been attached only on the fighting compartment sides.

6 . / H E E R E S F L A K A B T E I L U N G   G D

By 1942 the German High Command realized that relying on the Luftwaffe to furnish Army formations with anti-aircraft protection was no longer sufficient. Consequently, Army divisions were to have their own organic Flak groups. The Heeresflakabteilung GD consisted of a Stabs-Batterie, the 1.-3. (heavy) Batteries equipped with 8.8cm Flak guns towed by 8-ton prime movers, the 4.-5. (medium) Batteries equipped with 3.7cm Flak guns on 8-ton prime movers and the 6. (light) Battery with 2cm Flakvierlings on 8-ton prime movers. In June 1943, the Battalion was restructured as follows: 1. and 2. Batteries with 3.7cm SP mounts; 3.-5. (heavy) Batteries with 8.8cm guns; and 6. Battery with Flakvierling SPs. The Battalion saw constant service in both ground

and anti-aircraft roles for the remainder of the war.

Originally developed for the Kriegsmarine, the 2cm Flakvierling 38 was quickly adopted by the Luftwaffe and the Army as well, Weighing 1509kg in action, the 4-barreled gun had a 360° traverse and elevation from -10° to +100°. The ammunition feed was supplied by four 20-round box magazines. Muzzle velocity was 830m/second firing AP/HE rounds and 900m/second firing HE. The maximum effective ceiling was 2200m and the practical rate of fire was 720-800rpm. Regulations stated that only two barrels be fired at one time but, in the stress of combat, all four barrels were frequently fired simultaneously. The Flakvierling was lethal when used in batteries against low-flying aircraft and was equally effective against "soft" ground targets.

A Flakvierling 38 set up in firing position. While often mounted on 8-ton prime movers, the Flakvierling 38 could be mounted on its triangular base mount for stationary employment. Behind the gun is its special two-wheel Sonderanhänger 52 trailer.

Left: With the barrels elevated 60°, a gunner scans the horizon for incoming low-level aircraft. The gunner had two foot pedals to fire the guns. The left pedal fired the upper left and lower right weapons and the right pedal fired the upper right and lower left guns. This balanced the recoil forces and kept the mount from being forced off target. Normally only two guns were fired at one time. For continuous engagement, the guns were fired until the magazines emptied. Then the gunner opened fire with the other two guns and the loaders inserted new magazines into the empty weapons. In this way, a steady stream of fire could be maintained as long as the ammunition held out.

Below: A Flakvierling 38, elevated to about 70°. Kanonier I uses the electrically operated Flakvisier 40 range-rate sight to track his target. In tracking the approaching target, the reticles of the sight head were displaced by the battery voltage, calibrated in hundreds of meters, and by the tachometer generator voltage in such a way that the gun was trained automatically on the desired position. The use of electrical current eliminated the normal mechanical time lag, thus making the Flakvierling even more deadly to enemy aircraft.

Major i.G. Helmut Beck Broichsitter

Helmut Beck-Broichsitter was one of GD's most illustrious and long-serving soldiers. Born in the port city of Kiel on August 30, 1914, the 20 year old Beck-Broichsitter graduated from Hamburg's Humanistische Gymnasium and joined the Reichsheer in 1934. By 1937 he had been commissioned as a Leutnant in the Infanterie-Lehrregiment at the Infantry School at Döberitz, serving successively with the grenadier, MG, mortar and anti-tank platoons. The invasion of France on May 10, 1940 found Oberleutnant Beck-Broichsitter in command of 14.(Pz. Jäger)/I.R.(mot.) GD. Near Stonne, on the Meuse River, between May 14-17, Beck-Broichsitter's company successfully halted a divisional-scale attack on the vulnerable German bridgeheads by the French 3.e Division Legere Mechanique, the company's 3.7cm PaKs destroying 83 enemy tanks in the process. Beck-Broichsitter's feat of arms was rewarded by the first award of the Ritterkreuz to a member of GD on September 4, 1940.

Beck-Broichsitter served as Battalion Adjutant of I/I.R.(mot.) GD during the opening months of Unternehmen Barbarossa. The dreadful winter battles outside Moscow found him commanding I./I.R.(mot.) GD where he suffered from frostbite and jaundice. After convalescent leave, Hauptmann Beck-Broichsitter spent the summer of 1942 at OKH serving as an expert on grenadier companies, his concerns being training, equipment and weaponry, before being posted for general staff training to the Württemberg 23. Pz. Division in the Caucasus. In the attempt to relieve the encircled 6.Armee in Stalingrad from December 1942 to January 1943, Hauptmann Beck-Broichsitter was twice wounded. The first time was only slightly, the second was a more serious injury. During these operations, Beck-Broichsitter was mentioned in the Wehrmacht Communique and enrolled in the Honor Roll of the German Army. 1944 was spent in General Staff training and in attending the Kriegsakademie (War College) in Hirschberg where he graduated with an "exemplary" commendation. The by-now Major i.G. Beck-Broichsitter was assigned to the newly-formed Pz.Korps GD where in mid-January 1945 he was again wounded outside Lodz, Poland, while single-handedly destroying a Soviet "Joseph Stalin" tank. Major i.G. Beck-Broichsitter was sent back to Germany to recover from his wounds. It was during his convalescence in the Army Hospital in Dresden that he witnessed and survived the Allied air raids which resulted in the destruction of Dresden in February 1945. Due to his still unhealed wounds, Major i.G. Beck-Broichsitter would see no further action in the war.

Above: Major i.G. Helmut Beck-Broichsitter lectures a group of Hitlerjugend and BDM Mädel (Hitler Youths and BDM Girls) at the Waldstadion (Forest Stadium) in Berlin, late spring of 1944.

part from the general-issue Model 31 shelter quarter, the German Army never made a deliberate attempt to issue camouflage pattern clothing to its soldiers in the Second World War. Besides the helmet cover and the smock shown in these photographs, only the camouflaged side of the reversible-to-white winter combat suit was available in large, regularly-issued numbers. Individual soldiers and sometimes entire units made up their own camouflage clothing from both German and Italian shelter-quarter material. Some were as crude as loose aprons while others were close copies of the normal field-gray uniform. Even armored personnel had camouflaged versions of their special field uniforms. From 1943, Grossdeutschland was fortunate enough to receive large supplies of the newly issued smock — both with and without the integral hood and trousers — as well as the helmet cover with its loops for attaching foliage. The camouflage came in three distinct patterns: the sharply splintered type; the "blurred edge" splinter type and the so-called "water" pattern — the first of which usually had a gray-green base color while the latter two had a tan base color.

As is evident from the man firing the Kar 98k, the three components of the Army's camouflage clothing were rarely issued and worn simultaneously.

A machine gunner wearing a belt of 50 7.92mm rounds for the squad's MG 42 light machine gun. These belts were metallic and non-disintegrating and in an emergency could be filled by inserting loose rounds from the riflemen's 5-round clips. Six of these belts could be linked together to fill an ammunition box for the machine gun.

Right: An Offizieranwärter (officer candidate) checks Model 39 "egg" grenades from a member of his squad. Both Offizieranwärter and Offizierbewerber (officer aspirants) wore two loops of NCO Tresse at the base of their shoulder straps. The M 39 grenade contained 112 grams of TNT surrounded by thin sheet metal. A blue-capped assembly with a friction igniter screwed into the top. The grenade was armed like the M 43 stick grenade. This M 39 is the later pattern, which was manufactured with a ring at the bottom to permit the grenade to be secured to the uniform buttons or to the soldier's personal equipment.

Below: The MG 42 section crouches along a shallow trench. The MG 42's Schütze II also has a belt of 7.92mm rounds draped around his neck.

PANZERFÜSILIERREGIMENT GD

On April 1, 1942, I.R.(mot.) GD was officially constituted as Infantriedivision (mot.) Grossdeutschland. As part of the upgrading to Divisional status a second infantry regiment was raised. At first known as I.R.(mot.) GD 2, it was later renamed on October 1, 1942, as Füsilierregiment (mot.) GD.

The designation "Füsilier" had several different meanings in German Army history. In the 17th century füsiliers were the first troops to be armed with flintlocks, as their mission was to guard the artillery in battle and flintlocks were far safer around open powder barrels than the usual matchlock muskets. Frederick the Great preferred tall men for his infantry and chose to place men of shorter stature in the new füsilier regiments. Late in the 18th century füsilier battalions of infantry regiments were trained, uniformed and equipped for skirmishing and open-order fighting. By the 19th century, the title was purely honorary as all infantry were trained and armed to the same standard. In the German Army of the Second World War, the term "Füsilier" had three distinct sets of meanings. It could be, as before, a purely honorary term, serving to remind members of the particular units of their regimental heritage. Beginning in 1943, the term distinguished ordinary infantrymen (Grenadiere, itself a term as ancient and formerly exclusive as Füsilier) from those infantrymen who manned divisional reconnaissance (Füsilier) battalions. Finally, in the case of two divisions — Pz.Gr.Div. GD and Pz.Div."Feldherrnhalle" — the terms were employed to distinguish between these divisions' two otherwise similar infantry regiments.

A few selected officers and NCOs from the old regiment as well as from other units within the German Army at large supplied the cadre around which the "Kriegsfreiwillige" from the depot at Cottbus were assembled. The new regiment was organized and equipped similarly to I.R. GD except that the motor transport of its 18 companies consisted exclusively of 1 1/4-ton Horch-type light trucks. After training in the Orel and Faetsch areas, the new regiment participated in the advance to Voronezh and the Lower Don, taking part in all subsequent operations until May 1943, when, as part of the

redesignation of the Division, it was again renamed as Panzerfüsilierregiment GD. As such, it bore its full share of the various actions until May 31, 1944, when I/Pz.Füs.Rgt. GD returned to Germany to be reequipped with some 50 Sd.Kfz. 251 SPWs (the Stabskompanie was already mounted in SPWs). As with Pz.Gr.Rgt. GD, the Regiment saw its strength reduced from four 5-company battalions to three 4-company battalions. The final TO & E of the Regiment as of June 1, 1944, was as follows: a Stabskompanie mounted in Sd.Kfz. 251 SPWs; I/Pz.Füs.Rgt. GD had a battalion HQ company in Sd.Kfz. 251s, four companies also in SPWs, and a truck-borne maintenance company.* II/Pz.Füs.Rgt .GD had a headquarters company and its füsilier companies in Horch-type trucks, a heavy weapons company towed by 1 ton halftrack prime movers, and a truck-borne maintenance company. III/Pz.Füs.Rgt. GD was quite a bit larger, having a HQ and four companies mounted in trucks like II/Pz.Füs.Rgt. GD. In addition, it too had a truck-borne maintenance company as well as an SP infantry gun company, a motorized engineer company, and four Pz. Jäger companies towed by halftrack prime movers. As with Pz.Gr.Rgt. GD, the SPW components of the Regiment frequently served apart from the motorized element in armored battlegroups.

One of the very few cases of conflict within GD, and one which had very serious consequences, was the very poor relationship between Pz.Gr.Rgt. GD and Pz.Füs.Rgt. GD. The cause of this ill-will goes back to April 1942, when I.R.(mot.) GD 2 was raised from outside the original I.R. GD with no cadre personnel of the latter. Over the following two years, the regiments functioned apart with little or no contact between them and referred to each other by derogatory nicknames. When Karl Lorenz became divisional commander in 1944 this bad situation took a turn decidedly for the worse. Lorenz had won great renown as commander of Pz.Gr.Rgt. GD and as Divisional Commander hardly bothered with the füsiliers. In February, 1945, the distinguished commander of the Füsilier Regiment, Oberst Heinz Wittchow von Brese-Winiary, protested to General Lorenz over the misuse of his II Battalion. He and long-time Adjutant Hauptmann Dr. Boldt were immediately relieved of their posts, regimental command being assumed by I.L.R. and GD veteran Major Max Fabich.

* The exact composition of the SPW element is the same except in minor details to that described for Pz.Gr.Rgt. GD.

Right: Oberst Horst Niemack visits forward positions of Pz.Füs.Rgt. GD in Romania. The sign in the background instructs anyone reporting to RHQ to report first to the Adjutant. Oberst Niemack wears a very well-cut camouflage jacket and officer's mounted breeches.

Generalmajor Horst Niemack

Horst Niemack, one of Grossdeutschland's most distinguished regimental commanders, was born on March 10, 1909 in Hannover. After graduating from the Cavalry School in Hannover, Leutnant Niemack joined 18.(Baden-Württemberg) Reiter-Regiment in Bad Canstatt, Württemberg. After a spell of regimental duty, Oberleutnant Niemack returned to the Cavalry School as an instructor where his superb equestrian skills were allowed full play in some of the finest horse country in Germany. Although an Olympic-caliber horsemen in the most tradition-conscious branch of the Army, Horst Niemack had a very modern, forward-thinking turn of mind, perfectly adaptable to the mobile combined-arms doctrine which the pre-war Army had evolved. Rittmeister Niemack went to war in 1939 with Aufklärungsabteilung 5 of the Baden-Württemberg 5. Infanteriedivision (later Jägerdivision). His leadership of his squadron in the French Campaign earned him the Ritterkreuz on July 13, 1940. While still in command of A.A. 5, Rittmeister Niemack became the 30th recipient of the Eichenlaub while leading A.A. 5 in the advance on Moscow on August 10, 1941.

Major Niemack spent the first half of 1942 at the Kavallerie/Panzerschule in Potsdam before serving in the attempt to capture Stalingrad with I/Pz.Gr. Rgt. 26 of the East Prussian 24. Pz.Div. — the former 1. Kavalleriedivision. Assuming command of Pz.Füs.Rgt. GD in late 1943, Oberst Niemack led the regiment through the heavy defensive battles around Iasi and Targul Frumos in the spring of 1944. For his regiment's achievements and for his own gallantry, Oberst Niemack became the 69th recipient of the Schwerter (Swords) to the Ritterkreuz on June 4, 1944. Seriously wounded in late August 1944, Horst Niemack spent some time convalescing before becoming Panzerlehrdivision's last commander in the West in the spring of 1945.

Facing page, above: Oberst Niemack and Leutnant Felix Pahl, commander of the RHQ Security Detachment, visit a frontline observation post.

Facing page, below and this page, right: The regimental commander inspects the firing position of a 12cm Granatwerfer 42 of the Schwere (Heavy) Kompanie of II/Pz.Füs.Rgt. GD. The heavy company had a battery of these powerful weapons, copied from the Soviet 120mm PM-38 mortar, which the Germans also used in large numbers. The Granatwerfer 42 weighed 616 lbs., had a maximum traverse of 16°, elevation from 45° to 85°, and a maximum range for its 35 lb. shell of 6,600 yards. On its integral wheeled carriage and with its bipod clamped to the barrel, the Granatwerfer 42 could be quickly brought into action and towed or manhandled to a new firing position. The mortar round itself and the weapon's long range allowed for the same type of support fire given by the le.FH 18 field howitzer.

Below: Oberst Niemack and his driver and "Bursche" (orderly — personal assistant), Obergefreiter Hüttenrauch, climb back into the commander's Schwimmwagen after inspecting the remains of a totally demolished Soviet tank.

On March 8, 1944, the 1st, 2nd, and 3rd Ukrainian Fronts (a Front, the Soviet equivalent of an army group, had the strength of a German army, a Soviet army being equal in size to a German army corps) attacked along a broad front west of Kirovograd in the Western Ukraine. The Soviets had planned to use their overwhelming superiority in artillery to destroy GD in a box barrage and overrun the remnants in a massed tank and infantry attack. Using previously worked-out tactics, GD destroyed large numbers of Soviet tanks before successfully disengaging and rapidly withdrawing to the hoped-for refuge of the Bug River. During this fighting, GD received valuable and timely assistance from its left-hand neighbor, 3. SS-Panzerdivision "Totenkopf". The Bug, however, was now little more than a temporary delay to the onrushing Soviets. GD's brilliant defensive tactics and the employment of the Division piecemeal as a "Fire Brigade" (the first use of the term), were largely unsuccessful. Uman, site of a brilliant encirclement victory in 1941, fell on March 10. Grossdeutschland conducted a series of cleverly executed delaying actions, for which it was ideally suited as an armored division, to cover the withdrawal of Heeresgruppe Nordukraine before itself withdrawing. At one point on its march to the Bug, GD was actually retreating parallel to the Soviet advance. While mercilessly harried by Soviet Il-2 Shturmovik ground attack aircraft, ominously known by the Germans as "Der Schwarzer Tod" (Black Death), GD managed to disengage from the enemy. Grossdeutschland then withdrew to its new concentration area behind the Dnestr near Kishinev, Bessarabia, where it remained until March 30.

When the Division reentered the line on the Dnestr at the end of March, it was confronted with the chaos resulting from the Soviet breakthrough. Its first task was to buy some time for the retreating German units to reorganize. At first only Pz.Gr.Rgt. GD was available, but Oberst Lorenz's men managed to hold off two successive attacks. Gradually, other GD units arrived to extend and deepen the line. The Soviet's objective was to cut the Germans' main supply road. This was averted through stubborn rearguard actions by Pz.Gr.Rgt. GD, which counterattacked so successfully at Parliti Sat that the Soviets remained inactive for several days thereafter. Thwarted at Parliti Sat, the Soviets resumed their advance on April 9 by moving around GD past Iasi and on to Targul Frumos in the foothills of the Carpathian Mountains. During this advance the Soviets were repeatedly counterattacked by Pz.Füsilierregiment GD, reinforced by Pz.Gr.Rgt. GD. The Germans retook Targul Frumos and dug in on the heights north and northwest of the town. After heavy fighting the Soviets broke through, driving GD back on Bala. At this point GD's right-hand neighbor, the East Prussian 24. Pz.Div., attacked the enemy in the left flank with a strong armored thrust. This and a second armored counter thrust so disrupted the Soviets that GD had time to dig in and lay a defensive belt of minefields in front of its new positions.

Led by over 400 tanks, the Soviets launched a major assault on Targul Frumos on April 26, attempting to get into the Sereth Valley. Over a four day period 150 Soviet tanks were destroyed by GD's infantry. On April 30, Divisional Commander Hasso von Manteuffel personally lead a counter thrust by III(Tiger)/ Pz.Rgt. GD, with no preliminary artillery barrage — a Manteuffel hallmark which he used again at Vilkovishken and in the Ardennes. 56 Soviet tanks were blazing on the battlefield as the enemy withdrew. On May 2, the Soviets launched a renewed onslaught against GD's lines. After an hour-long "fire strike" by massed artillery, wedges of tanks and infantry advanced with more infantry masses in reserve. GD's lines were rapidly penetrated in fierce fighting, and in the ensuing chaos indi-

vidual tank-hunting teams stalked the Soviet armor with Panzerfausts and Teller mines. The Division's infantry lured the Soviet tanks into a line of 8.8cm Flak guns of Heeresflakabteilung GD. Using the tested "shield and sword" technique the Flak first shot up 25 superheavy JS II tanks. At this point of maximum uncertainty and vulnerability the Soviets were then hit by the Tigers of III/Pz.Rgt. GD. Simultaneously, a battlegroup of I/Pz.A.R. GD and infantry advanced to scatter the enemy's follow-on infantry.

A Soviet thrust towards Ruginoasa on the northwestern (left) flank of GD was halted by I(SPW) and III/Pz.Gr.Rgt. GD. By May 7, the Soviet assault had largely spent its strength and General von Manteuffel felt the time was right for a counterattack. An important hill to the north of Targul Frumos was chosen and supported by Panther tanks of I/Pz.Rgt. 26 of the Brandenburg 26. Pz.Div., which was temporarily assigned to GD while its own I/Pz.Rgt. GD was in France converting to Panthers, Pz.Füsilier-Rgt. GD advanced to clear Point 256 in particularly ferocious fighting. A short rest followed the operation. During this time, G.R.(mot.) 1029 GD, formed from the Replacement Battalions and previously on occupation duty in Hungary, arrived to reinforce the badly depleted division. GD's losses had been so severe that both infantry regiments were reduced from four to three battalions and their battalions reduced from five to four companies. Soon G.R.(mot)1029 GD was broken up to bring the two infantry regiments up to a level closer to their authorized strength. More SPWs were added, I/Pz.Füs.Rgt. GD and Pz.A.A. GD receiving Sd.Kfz. 251s and Sd.Kfz. 250s respectively.

On June 2, 1944, the partly replenished division attacked from Podul to take hills on either side of Orsoaeria near Iasi. GD surged forward in bitter hand-to-hand fighting and by June 3, Orsoaeria had fallen. The Division remained in the line until June 8, when it was withdrawn to rest and regroup about 62 miles south of Iasi. Here it remained in theatre reserve until the catastrophic situation on the Baltic coast demanded the transfer of the "Führer's Fire Brigade" to its new theatre of operations.

Many Grossdeutschland soldiers had distinguished themselves in this savage series of battles, most notably Hauptmann Diddo Diddens of 1./StuG.Bde. GD who received the Eichenlaub for his part in storming the heights on the Sereth on April 25, and Oberst Horst Niemack who received the Schwerter on June 5 for his leadership of the Panzerfüsiliers throughout the battle.

Facing page, above: The crew of a Sd.Kfz. 251 command vehicle during a lull in the fighting which swirled around Targul Frumos. The SPW battalion of Pz.Gr.Rgt. GD bore a particularly heavy burden at this time, as its vehicles were hurried from one crisis to the next over the 13 week period from March 7 to June 5, 1944.

Facing page, below: Soldiers of I(SPW)/Pz.Gr.Rgt. GD deploy from their Sd.Kfz. 251 Ausf. C armored personnel carriers during the fighting around Targul Frumos, May 1944. One man in the background is carrying one of the newly issued Panzerfaust 30 anti-tank grenade launchers. Panzergrenadiers normally stored their gear in the SPWs and thus were often seen in light fighting order without the belt support straps and battle pack.

Right: Weary Panzergrenadiers trudge past an SPW on their way back from the fighting. All of the soldiers are wearing the Army Tarnjacke (camouflage smock). The second man in line has a Red Army waistbelt to carry additional equipment.

Left: A very dapper-looking Obergefreiter during the May fighting. The method of attaching the later pattern Model 39 egg-shaped hand grenades is shown very well in this photograph.

Left: A Hauptmann takes a gulp from his canteen. He appears to have seen little previous active service since the Russian winter campaign of 1941-42. Perhaps he is one of the former training staff at the Depot in Cottbus, hastily mobilized for frontline duty with G.R.(mot.) 1029 GD. Suspended from his enlisted man's waistbelt — often worn by officers in the field — are the officer's pattern belt support straps. Attached to a button on his blouse is a standard Army flashlight.

Below: A Feldgendarme wearing the unique GD gorget and some Romanian soldiers examine the wreckage of a Soviet aircraft shot down over Iasi, May 1944. The aircraft appears to be a lend-lease item as evidenced by the stenciling visible in the center of the photo. Soviet aircraft harassed GD relentlessly throughout the battle but the Division managed to inflict heavy losses in return, the Flakabteilung shooting down 19 Soviet aircraft during the last days of fighting in early June.

Weary grenadiers of Pz.Gr.Rgt. GD dig in to consolidate their gains during the fighting outside Targul Frumos, Romania, May 1944.

Panzergrenadiers advance through the rubble of a village which lay in the path of the Soviet advance towards Targul Frumos.

Left: Young replacements, twin brothers, read their first letter from home in the shelter of a very hastily dug trench.

Below: Machine gunners refill 50-round 7.92mm belts for the MG 34 and MG 42. These guns were fed using non-disintegrating metallic link belts, six of which could be joined together with a starter tab and inserted in the standard Model 41 ammunition box.

Above: A veteran Feldwebel wearing the Panzervernichtungsabzeichen (tank destruction badge) explains to a young replacement the operation of a Panzerfaust 30 anti-tank grenade launcher. The Pzf. 30 one-shot launcher fired a hollow charge grenade with an impact fuse. The end-tube extension held the propellant and had fold-back, spring-operated stabilizing fins at the rear. The tube of the grenade was inserted into the steel launching tube with its firing mechanism. The tube had a simple vertical rear sight with the border of the warhead itself serving as the front sight. Simple to operate and effective against all Allied armor at a range of 30 yards, the Panzerfaust was manufactured in the millions from early 1944 until the end of the war. GD made its first widespread use of the Panzerfaust at Targul Frumos and had great success with it.

neralleutnant
sso von Manteuffel

eneralleutnant Hasso Eccard Freiherr von
Manteuffel was descended from a line of Junkers
and generals who had served Prussia for centuries.
n January 14, 1897, in the "Soldatenstadt" Potsdam,
Hasso von Manteuffel attended the
adettenanstalt (Chief Cadet School) at Gross-
elde, afterwards being appointed a Leutnant in
n-Regiment von Zieten (Brandenbürgische) Nr. 3.
uffel served with his regiment at the Front, being
ed in the Somme in October, 1916. After convalesc-
was transferred as orderly officer to the Ia of the 6.
ie-Division, where he finished the war. Between the
eutnant Hasso von Manteuffel served with Reiter-
nt 3 (six years as adjutant) and became a celebrat-
nament horseman. Manteuffel was one of those cav-
icers who came to embrace the mechanization of the
s the best path for preserving the cavalry's tradition-
His assignment as Chef of an Eskadron of R.R. 17.
erg" — two of whose squadrons had converted to
hützen — allowed Manteuffel his first personal expe-
of mechanized tactics. The last years before the out-
of the Second World War saw Major von Manteuffel
recting courses for NCO candidates of the Vienna 2.
and serving in the Panzer Inspectorate.
rving in the early campaigns of the Second World
berstleutnant von Manteuffel, the old "Zietenhusar,"
d command of Schützenregiment 6 of the Thuringian
erdivision just after the invasion of the Soviet Union in
. Pz.Div., the famous "Ghost Division" of 1940, had
od fortune of nurturing some of Germany's finest
soldiers — men such as Erwin Rommel, Karl
urg, Adalbert Schulz, Dr. Karl Mauss and Hasso von
uffel. Manteuffel led his regiment to the Moskva-Volga
earning the Ritterkreuz on October 27, 1941. Serving
Central Front and on occupation duty throughout
1942, 7. Pz.Div. returned to the East at the end of

1942 (Manteuffel was briefly in command of an ad hoc division in
Tunisia in early 1943), and saw continuous service there for the remainder of the war. 7. Panzerdivision was prominent during Unternehmen
"Zitadelle" and in November of that year retook Zhitomir in a brilliant
counter thrust planned by General Hermann Balck. His division's success
won Hasso von Manteuffel the Eichenlaub to his Ritterkreuz — the 332nd
soldier of the Wehrmacht to be so honored, on November 19, 1943.

Assuming command of the Army's premier division, Pz.Gr.Div.
Grossdeutschland in early 1944, Generalleutnant von Manteuffel earned
the Schwerter to his Ritterkreuz, the 50th awarded thus far, on February 22,
1944, for his old command's success at Radomshil in the Kiev Salient. Under
his command Grossdeutschland became the "Fire Brigade" of the Eastern
Front, restoring some stability to the crumbling Romanian Front before moving to its deadliest challenge in East Prussia.

Above: Divisional commander Hasso Eccard Freiherr von Manteuffel confers
with his Ia, Oberst Oldwig von Natzmer. Manteuffel's uniform in this view is a
DAK tropical model, possibly first worn during his service in the African campaign in early 1943.

Left: Hasso von Manteuffel in a Kfz. 15 Horch medium car, the most common
field car used by many divisional commanders. Over his uniform he wears a
rabbit fur vest. The Germans adopted a number of standard, non-standard, and
captured items of clothing to cope with the extremely varied climactic conditions
on the Eastern Front.

Major Harald Krieg

Harald Krieg was very typical of the many battle-proven officers assigned to GD in the second half of the war. Born on July 2, 1910 in Waldenburg in Silesia, Krieg was commissioned in the German Army in the early 1930s. Serving in the Thuringian 1. Panzerdivision through the war's early campaigns, Oberleutnant Krieg was commander of 4(MG)/Schützenregiment 1 when he was awarded the Ritterkreuz during the advance on Leningrad (St. Petersburg) on July 15, 1941. During the winter fighting in 1941-42, Krieg commanded all of the Division's remaining SPWs while serving in S.R. 113. Hauptmann Krieg was promoted to Major on February 1, 1943, and a year later replaced Major Otto-Ernst Remer as commander of I(SPW)/Pz.Gr.Rgt. GD when Remer was made commander of the Wachbataillon GD in Berlin. Major Krieg, one of the army's most experienced SPW commanders, was an ideal choice to lead GD's armored infantry in the ferocious fighting on the Romanian border from April to June, 1944. Krieg was temporarily in command of Panzerfüsilierregiment GD while Oberst Horst Niemack was receiving the Schwerter to his Ritterkreuz at Rastenburg in early June 1944. He led the Regiment in the successful counter thrust to retake Vilkovishken. Shortly after, he was posted to the Pz.Gr.Ersatz und Ausbildungsbrigade GD at Guben, and accompanied the Brigade in its last actions against the British 2nd Army in Emsland on the Dutch frontier.

Right: Generalleutnant von Manteuffel, his aide, Lt. Schröder, and Major Harald Krieg of I(SPW)/Pz.Gr.Rgt. GD crouch in a slit trench outside Targul Frumos on May 6, 1944 while U.S.A.A.F. B-17s carpet bomb GD's lines in support of the Soviet offensive in Romania. Major Krieg wears a ribbon on his right sleeve for the single-handed destruction of an enemy tank.

Below: Major Krieg, Commander of I(SPW)/Pz.Gr.Rgt. GD, confers with two junior officers in Romania, early spring 1944. Major Krieg wears a very well tailored privately purchased sheepskin coat while the Oberleutnant to his right wears the standard-issue rubberized coat.

Right: A young Panzer crewman assists a wounded Romanian mountain infantryman to a dressing station during the fighting around Iasi. Romania had mobilized its entire army for service on the Eastern Front and had suffered considerable losses due to outmoded equipment. Its morale, never very high, had sunk dangerously low by the time the Soviets reached the frontier. Germany made great belated efforts to rearm the Romanians and some units were reasonably reliable and efficient. Lack of enthusiasm, however, for continuing the war together with the semi-feudal relationship between officers and men, common throughout Central and Eastern Europe, ensured that the Romanians would remain a burden to their ally.

Below: Wounded GD soldiers and Romanian mountain troops are loaded into an ambulance of one of GD's three ambulance platoons at the regimental aid station some 200 to 500 yards behind the front line. The main dressing station handled stretcher cases while the walking wounded were sent to a collecting point for the slightly wounded. Both facilities were controlled by the Chief Medical Officer of the Division and were co-located as often as possible. The main dressing station took care of serious cases such as surgery, amputations, hemorrhages, etc. and then sent the casualties on to the rear. The slightly wounded remained at the collection point until returned to their units. The seriously wounded were sent on by ambulance to a series of hospitals located mostly at railheads. These handled only cases who could be moved. Those who could not be moved remained at mobile field hospitals until fit enough to travel. Any hospital could pronounce a soldier fit for duty. If in a forward hospital, he would be returned immediately to his unit. If in a general hospital for more than eight weeks, he would return to the Replacement Army for reassignment (many GD convalescents in Germany would serve as instructors at the Depot until returned to the front). German military medical care was excellent and the overwhelming majority of wounded recovered and returned to duty. The wound tags around the soldier's necks were filled out at the battalion aid station to show the next aid station what treatment had been administered and the nature of the wound. GD's medical arrangements were essentially the same as for other units. Direct access, however, to the Army Hospital Inspectorate in Berlin permitted GD to maintain perhaps a better personnel and supply situation throughout the war.

Facing page, above: An officer of Pz.A.A. GD chats with a wounded platoon commander during the fighting in Romania.

Facing page, below: A young wounded grenadier of the Stabskompanie of II/Pz.Gr.Rgt. GD receives a light from his company commander, Hauptmann Hans Weizenbeck. Note the bronze version of the tank battle badge on Weizenbeck's left breast pocket.

This page: Divisional commander Hasso von Manteuffel is briefed by a young, probably German-speaking Romanian soldier — possibly an ethnic German, of which Romania had a sizeable minority — on the Iasi Front, spring 1944. Romania mobilized her entire remaining forces with the 25 divisions of 3. and 4. Armies — 500,000 men to defend her eastern borders. This soldier wears the khaki woolen field uniform (only officers wore collar patches) and the "Dutch" steel helmet — so called because it was manufactured by the Dutch firm Verblifa for the Romanian Army. The waistbelt buckle is painted black. Only the guards regiments wore polished brass buckles embossed with a crown.

Facing page, above: A young Fahnenjunkergefreiter (Officer Cadet) of the Fernsprech-Kompanie (Telephone Company) mans a Model 33 field telephone and attached switchboard. Panzernachrichtenabteilung GD had three motorized companies: a telephone company, a Funk (radio) company and a maintenance company. Armored units, with their emphasis on speed and maneuverability, relied far more on radio during mobile operations but telephones, with their greater reliability and lesser vulnerability to enemy eavesdropping, came back into their own during static warfare. The great disadvantage of telephones was their cables' vulnerability to enemy artillery fire.

Left: A Leutnant observes the enemy lines while a signaler calls in information to headquarters over a field telephone. The Scherenfernrohr (scissors telescope) could be fully extended horizontally to give a wide panoramic view of the terrain.

Above: While an Obergefreiter of one GD's infantry battalions keep watch on the Soviet lines through a scissors tele-scope mounted on a tripod, a soldier moves to the rear past a knocked out T-34 tank. The T-34 is the "D-5T" type. Introduced by the Soviets in 1943, it was the first T-34 to mount the 85mm gun, selected as an antidote to the Tiger and Panther.

Oberfeldwebel
Karl Schwappacher

Oberfeldwebel Karl Schwappacher, was a Zugführer (Platoon Commander) in 17.(IG)/Pz.Gr.Rgt. GD during the fighting in Romania, spring 1944. "Schwapp," as he was known to one and all in the Regiment, was another of those indispensable veterans of the Infanterielehrregiment Döberitz, where he had been a top gunnery instructor on the s.IG 33, joining I.R.(mot.) GD in late 1939. A native of Bavaria, Karl Schwappacher served throughout the war with GD, participated in every campaign and was decorated with the German Cross in Gold, the Honor Roll Clasp of the German Army and the General Assault Badge with bar for 25 engagements. In spite of all the action he saw in Russia, Karl Schwappacher recalls the crossing of the Meuse at Sedan and the intense fighting at Stonne in May 1940 as the most memorable of his experiences with GD. At the base of his shoulderstraps, OFW Schwappacher wears the white cloth slip-ons which distinguished Pz.Gr.Rgt. GD from Pz.Füs.Rgt. GD who wore red slip-ons.

Oberleutnant Bruno Kikillus

Oberleutnant Bruno Kikillus, an East Prussian of Lithuanian extraction, was born on September 1, 1914, in Sensburg in the Masurian Lakes region. At the time this photograph was taken in April 1944, Kikillus was (from early June 1944) Kompaniechef of 17./Pz.Füs.Rgt. GD, the Regiment's Bison-equipped self-propelled 15cm heavy infantry gun company. Bruno Kikillus wears the cloth version of the German Cross in Gold he was awarded on January 25, 1944 for his personal gallantry during the winter fighting southwest of Kirovograd. The infantry guns rarely operated as complete companies usually being assigned as platoons or sections among the infantry battalions, and were frequently caught up in close combat, explaining the Nahkampfspange (Close Combat Clasp) on Kikillus's left breast. As commander of what was in effect a howitzer battery, Oberleutnant Kikillus holds an artillery map board and wears powerful Voigtländer 10x50 artillery binoculars around his neck. Already awarded the Wound Badge in Silver, Bruno Kikillus suffered what proved to be a fatal wound outside Targul Frumos in early June 1944, while his company was in close support of the Panzerfüsiliers. Evacuated to the dressing station, he was transferred to the Division's field hospital at Roman where he died on June 12, 1944. He was buried in the adjacent German military cemetery.

Major
Heinrich Gerbener

Heinrich "Hed" Gerbener was born in Düsseldorf, Rhenish Prussia, in the heart of the Ruhr industrial basin, on May 2, 1914. Gerbener's father was an officer in the German Army, killed on the Aisne in September, 1914. After leaving school young Heinrich applied for admission into the Reichsheer. As the son of a regular soldier, Gerbener received preferential consideration and was accepted into the 16.(Oldenburg) Infanterie-Regiment in May 1932. An exceptional recruit in a superbly trained professional army, Heinrich Gerbener rapidly progressed from Schütze to Unteroffizier by 1934. Unteroffizier Gerbener, although not an Abiturient (Gymnasium graduate), was accepted for officer's training at the Kriegsschule in Potsdam. Two years later Leutnant Gerbener received his commission signed by his instructor, Oberstleutnant Erwin Rommel.

After a brief return to I.R. 16 in Oldenburg, Leutnant Gerbener was posted to the prestigious Infanterielehrregiment in its new barracks in the Olympic Village at Döberitz. Gerbener's company commander was the later Ritterkreuzträger Major Alfred Bruno Eduard Greim.

In June 1939 the Infanterielehrregiment was called upon to provide a battalion under the command of the East Prussian Oberstleutnant Eugen Garski together with a battalion from the Pomeranian I.R. 92. Simultaneously, a IV (Heavy) Battalion was formed, with Leutnant Gerbener and other old hands from the I.L.R. joining its 15.(s.IG) Kompanie. Marrying in October, 1939 (and fathering a son the next summer), Heinrich Gerbener served in the Mosel region during the winter and spring of 1940, being promoted to Oberleutnant on April 20, 1940.

Oberleutnant Gerbener served with his company during the invasion of France in May 1940, taking part in the crossing of the Meuse at Sedan, the race to the Channel near Dunkirk, and the breakthrough of the Weygand Line.

Gerbener's company participated in the German campaign in the Balkans in April-May, 1941, and in the invasion of the Soviet Union in June, 1941, advancing as far as Tula, southwest of Moscow, before the drive collapsed in the face of a brutal winter and fierce Soviet resistance. Until 1942, Gerbener's company had been where all of GD's "hard cases" were sent. Heinrich Gerbener, as a self-admitted rough-hewn man who had grown up among miners, steelworkers and ferry-boat men, was the ideal commander for these reluctant soldiers. He molded them into first-class troops by a mixture of stern discipline and generously applied praise. For men who had never been praised in their army careers, this was a revelation and Gerbener's company became an elite within the Regiment.

"Kompanie Gerbener" [17.(IG)/I.R.(mot.) GD 1] advanced to the Don in July, 1942. It endured and barely survived the atrocious conditions in the Rzhev Salient from September to December, 1942. Hauptmann Gerbener was in temporary command of II/Pz.Gr.Rgt. GD at one time or another he commanded II, III and IV Battalions) in

With Gerbener in the lead and his grenadiers shouting "Iwan Scheisse!," the counterattack succeeded and Hauptmann Gerbener received the German Cross in Gold on December 18, 1943.

On May 2, 1944, Gerbener and best friends Diddo Diddens and "Olhans" Wentzke celebrated "Hed's" 30th birthday in Gerbener's bunker in Romania. Four days later Battalion HQ was flattened in a memorable raid by the U.S. 15th Air Force and Gerbener and Wentzke were dug out of the ruins of the command bunker with severe concussions after having been buried alive (the third time this happened to Gerbener during the war). After convalescing in Roman Romania, Gerbener was ordered back to the Depot at Cottbus in late July, 1944.

Major Gerbener spent the remainder of 1944 with Pz.Gr.Ersatz und Ausbildungsbrigade GD before accompanying it to its new location in the Ems district in Northwest Germany. By the spring of 1945 Gerbener commanded a battalion of convalescents and young, barely trained recruits in Regiment Wackernagel GD. On May 8, 1945 Heinrich Gerbener's long and tumultuous war finally ended when he

Hauptmann Diddo Diddens

Diddo Siebels Diddens was born on his family's farm in Bunderhammrich in the Leer District of Ostfriesland (East Frisia) on April 22, 1917. After serving as a Hitler Youth leader in his hometown, Diddo Diddens completed his compulsory six month's service in the Reichsarbeitsdienst before reporting for army duty. Commissioned as a Leutnant der Reserve in 1940 after the French Campaign, Diddens played a decisive part in 18. Armee's advance along the Baltic coast as commander of the 2. Zug, 2./Sturmgeschützabteilung 185 (Major Lickfeld). Leutnant Diddens so distinguished himself during the terrible winter fighting of 1941-42, knocking out 35 Soviet tanks, that Oberst Otto Lasch, commander of I.R.43 of the East Prussian 1.Infanteriedivision, recommended him for the Ritterkreuz, which was awarded on March 18, 1942. During this period, platoon commanders did not possess Sturmgeschütze of their own and rode in 3-ton SPWs. Diddens, like most other conscientious platoon commanders however, elected to command his platoon from one of his assault guns.

Diddo Diddens reluctantly left StuG.Abt. 185 to take over a platoon of Major Hans-Joachim Schipers' new StuG.Abt. GD in the spring of 1942. Diddens fought his way to Voronezh in July, 1942, and down the Don to Manytsch before leading his platoon through the grueling defensive fighting in the Rzhev Salient. During a patrol in December 1942, near Bolkhov, Diddens and his crew miraculously escaped death at the hands of a 3.7cm PaK 35 crew of 19. Pz.Div., when the gun fired on them in error, seriously damaging Diddens' vehicle.

Serving throughout the various campaigns of 1943 from Kharkov through Kursk and back to the Dnieper by the autumn of 1943, Oberleutnant Diddens continued to build his reputation as a daredevil tank killer. By April 1944, GD was attempting to keep the Soviets out of Romania and its vital oil fields. On April 25, 1944, Oberleutnant Diddens, now in command of 1./StuG.Abt. GD — the battery Peter Frantz and Hans Magold had previously commanded — supported an attack by II and III/Pz.Gr.Rgt. GD in a woods between Barbatesti and Vascani, north of Targul Frumos. The enemy was driven back from the well-defended position and Diddens noticed further anti-tank gun positions which needed to be eliminated. 1.Batterie knocked out a further 23 anti-tank guns and then itself confronted a large Soviet tank assembly area. Diddens knocked out three Soviet tanks and two anti-tank guns on his way back to the German lines. This achievement was acknowledged in the Wehrmacht Communique of April 27, 1944. Between May 2 and 10, 1944, Diddens continued to distinguish himself but characteristically insisted that every soldier present had an equal share in the achievement and had their names published in an Order of the Day.

The Soviets renewed their attacks on May 23, 1944 north of Zahorna with heavy air support and penetrated into the town. An

immediate counter thrust by StuG.Bde. GD, led by Hauptmann Diddens with Rittmeister Gerhard Schroedter's Pz.A.A. GD in support, retook Zahorna but was then halted by overwhelming enemy forces. With both Diddens and Schroedter seriously wounded, the attack on Point 181 was called off and a new defensive line set up.

Diddo Diddens lay near death in an Army hospital on June 15, 1944, after having his right leg amputated. Generaloberst Ferdinand Schörner, Hitler's ferocious "Generalfeldgendarme," personally visited Diddens to bestow on him the Eichenlaub to his Ritterkreuz which his grave wounds prevented him from receiving personally from Adolf Hitler. Schörner did everything possible to ensure that Diddens made a good recovery and letters wishing him well poured in from everyone of Diddens superiors in GD. Eventually, Diddens emerged from the hospital near the end of the war to resume light duties with local defense forces in his home district.

Above: Standing in the cupola of his command Panther, Panzerregiment GD commander Oberst Willi Langkeit watches with amusement as Oberst Karl Lorenz of Pz.Gr.Rgt. GD chats with Leutnant Wentzke (in the camouflage smock) and Hauptmann Gerbener outside Targul Frumos, May 1944.

Left: Oberst Lorenz and the crew of his Sd.Kfz. 251 Ausf. C SPW watch with some satisfaction as Hans-Ulrich Rudel's Stukas fly overhead in support of the Division in Romania, May 1944. Grossdeutschland enjoyed at this time some rare effective close-support from the Luftwaffe, particularly the Stuka dive bombers and tank-destroyer aircraft. On this occasion, Lorenz had assembled a scratch force of rear area troops to support the threatened I/Pz.Gr.Rgt. GD, and had transported them to the front lines using his RHQ command SPWs. In the SPW, from right to left, are Oberst Lorenz, Ogefr. Bergmann, Uffz. Alfred Ebel, Ogefr. Paul Schmid, and (far left) the NSFO, the regiment's political officer, an arrogant man disliked by the RHQ staff. As Paul Schmid put it, "We had no need for the likes of him keeping an eye on us!"

Top: Oberst Lorenz talks to Hauptmann Diddo Diddens (right) as Oberleutnant Kurt Göldel (behind Diddens) watches. Oberleutnant Göldel was an officer in the Regimental Stabskompanie. He was born in 1897 in East Prussia, a veteran of World War I, and was considerably older than most others of his rank. He was a high-ranking official in the Reich sports organization, and was respected by his comrades as he had not used his party connections to avoid frontline combat service. In the summer of 1944, Göldel assumed command of the Regimental Stabskompanie.

Middle: Hauptmann Heinrich Gerbener (right) confers with Oberst Lorenz (left) on May 6, 1944, during the fighting around Targul Frumos, Romania.

Below: Three veteran officers of GD, photographed by Kriegsberichter Hans Scheerer of Generaloberst Schörner's staff on the Upper Moldau River in Romania. From left to right are Hauptmann Heinrich Gerbener (III/Pz.Gr.Rgt. GD), Hauptmann Diddo Diddens (1./StuG.Bde. GD) and Oberleutnant Hans Wentzke (16(Fla.)/Pz.Gr.Rgt. GD). Hauptmann Diddens was one of the Division's most decorated assault gun leaders. On April 25, 1944, while storming heights east of the Sereth River lined with enemy anti-tank guns, Hauptmann Diddens used his own initiative to penetrate deep into the Soviet rear, destroying three tanks and 31 anti-tank guns and successfully returning to the German lines. In recognition of this feat, Diddens became the 501 recipient of the Eichenlaub on June 15, 1944, shortly after this photograph was taken.

Left: Oberst Lorenz and Oberleutnant Wentzke review troop dispositions on a situation map. Hans "Olhans" Wentzke, one of GD's most popular and talented soldiers, was born on November 27, 1922 in Berlin. Commissioned from Oberfeldwebel, Wentzke was the long-time company commander of 16.(Fla.)/Pz.Gr.Rgt. GD. His outlook on life was summed up by his motto "It's a joy to be alive" which he had painted and hung on the wall of his company HQ. Diddo Diddens, along with one of his best friends Heinrich Gerbener, remembered Hans Wentzke as "the type of Berliner one reads about in books — clever, refined, amusing; all good things." Wentzke explained to Diddens that since reason told him it was useless to worry he might as well be as cheerful as possible. This optimism was often reflected in Wentzke's encouragement of his comrades in even the direst of circumstances.

Below: Oberst Lorenz and Oberleutnant Wentzke, company commander of 16.(Fla)/Pz.Gr.Rgt. GD, chat with some of Wentzke's men, Romania, spring 1944. Wentzke has hung his P-38 automatic by its lanyard rather than holstering it, not a common practice.

The regimental commander cheers up one of his wounded grenadiers. A wound like this was known in the Wehrmacht as a "Heimatschuss" (home shot) — a serious, but not life-threatening or incapacitating injury, guaranteed to send the wounded man back to a base hospital in Germany. As was common during the close-quarter fighting in the foothills of the Carpathians, both grenadiers are well-stocked with M 24 stick grenades and late-version M 39 egg grenades.

T A R G U L   F R U M O S

On May 2, 1944 the Red Army began its offensive southwards to break through to Targul Frumos and then drive onward to the oil fields. I.(SPW)/Pz.Gr.Rgt. GD and its Romanian allies occupied a well wired-in and T-Mine-strewn line running to the right of 3. SS-Pz.Div. "Totenkopf's" positions. The Soviets advanced in great waves, their tanks and infantry mixed together. Moving much faster then the Germans had anticipated, they overwhelmed Leutnant Dieter Bernhagen's 1. Kompanie, wiping it out to the last man. While temporary battalion commander Major Udo Schwarzrock attempted to halt and repulse the Soviets with what was left of his battalion, the Romanians to the left of 2. Kompanie cowered in their trenches like "herrings," as company commander Oberleutnant Hans-Karl Richter later recounted. Indeed, the Romanians seemed to have reached an unofficial cease fire with the enemy. That night the Luftwaffe succeeded in mounting an air strike in the enemy rear area, to no avail. The next morning the Soviets resumed their attack, preceding it with a bombardment of phosphorous shells. Over 100 enemy tanks and assault guns advanced against Richter's 3. Zug. With his Romanian artillery remaining inactive, Richter could count only on the support of three of Oberleutnant Diddo Diddens' Sturmgeschütze and the four 15cm Nebelwerfer multiple rocket launchers of 10./Pz.A.R. GD. Richter's company was soon back to the Nebelwerfers' position where it formed a "hedgehog" defense. Richter and a handful of his men then managed to gain the temporary safety of the railway embankment in their rear. His battalion scattered, Major Schwarzrock sent Oberleutnant Richter with four SPWs to cover the wide-open left flank, completely vulnerable when the Romanians abandoned their positions. Although the enemy had not made any deep penetrations, the tension of the past two days had exhausted the Panzergrenadiers. "Suddenly," Hans-Karl Richter wrote, "four T-34s were in among the SPWs when, as if by magic, tanks and assault guns of the SS-Division "Totenkopf" appeared. Before a single T-34 could train its gun, all had received direct hits." Immediately thereafter Oberst Hans-Ulrich Rudel's Ju87 Stukas led off a counter thrust by "Totenkopf's" Panzerregiment, accompanied by Richter's four SPWs. The Panzergrenadiers took a measure of revenge for what they had endured over the past 48 hours, and for their murdered comrades in 1.Kompanie, before being pulled out of the line to regroup and refit.

Facing page: Oberleutnant Hans-Karl Richter, Kompanieführer of 2.(SPW)/Pz.Gr.Rgt. GD, briefs his opposite number, an SS-Hauptsturmführer of SS-Pz.Gr.Rgt. 6 "Theodore Eicke" when the latter relieved Richter's exhausted command near Targul Frumos on May 3, 1944. Richter recalls that after a perfunctory conversation when maps and documents were turned over to the SS, he and his men boarded their SPWs and went back to the rear to rest. Richter never learned the Hauptsturmführer's name and never saw him again.

Left: While Oberleutnant Richter and the SS-Hauptsturmführer confer, Richter's men pack their equipment for removal to the rear.

Large shot: Feldwebel Carl Gerber, a platoon leader in 2.(SPW)/Pz.Gr.Rgt. GD gets a light from an SS-Scharführer of Regiment "Eicke." GD and "Totenkopf" had previously served together in the Kremenchug bridgehead and at Kirovograd and the GD soldiers regarded the SS men as thoroughly reliable comrades — a sentiment "Totenkopf" fully reciprocated. The mutual respect born of such shared frontline experiences could at best, however, only cover over but not resolve the profound philosophical and professional differences which existed between the German Army and the Nazi Party's own military elite.

Top: Another photo of Gerber and an SS-Unterscharführer with Feldwebel Weiss in the background.

Right: An SS-Scharführer enters the company HQ bunker to be greeted by Feldwebel Gerber.

Hauptmann Ernst-Günther Lehnhoff coordinates a fire mission with an SS-Oberscharführer of SS-Pz.A.R. 3 near near Targul Frumos, early May 1944.

Facing page: Generalleutnant von Manteuffel with Pz.Füs.Rgt. GD Commander Oberst Horst Niemack at the latter's RHQ shortly after his return from the Führerhauptquartier where he received the Schwerter to his Ritterkreuz.

Left: Oberst Niemack (left) and his staff watch an air strike by Major Hans-Ulrich Rudel's Stukageschwader 2 "Immelmann" in Romania, June 1944. To Oberst Neimack's left are Leutnant Fritz Coenen, Rgt. Nachrichtenoffizier/NO (Regimental Signals Officer), killed later in Latvia, and Leutnant Kurt Bensinger, Orderly Officer in RHQ.

Below: Oberst Niemack, Leutnant Fritz Coenen, an unidentified officer (at right), and Obergefreiter Otto Hüttenrauch (at far left).

Left: A particularly fine study of the type of young man that Grossdeutschland appealed to and whom the Army felt was an ideal role model for German youth of military age. GD was made up of Kriegsfreiwilliger (War-Service Volunteers), and a good public image meant everything when competing with other elite voluntarily recruited services such as the U-Boats and the Luftwaffe's flying and airborne troops.

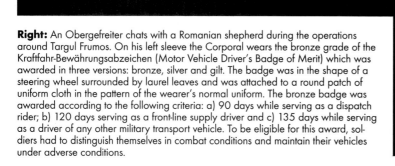

Right: An Obergefreiter chats with a Romanian shepherd during the operations around Targul Frumos. On his left sleeve the Corporal wears the bronze grade of the Kraftfahr-Bewährungsabzeichen (Motor Vehicle Driver's Badge of Merit) which was awarded in three versions: bronze, silver and gilt. The badge was in the shape of a steering wheel surrounded by laurel leaves and was attached to a round patch of uniform cloth in the pattern of the wearer's normal uniform. The bronze badge was awarded according to the following criteria: a) 90 days while serving as a dispatch rider; b) 120 days serving as a front-line supply driver and c) 135 days while serving as a driver of any other military transport vehicle. To be eligible for this award, soldiers had to distinguish themselves in combat conditions and maintain their vehicles under adverse conditions.

Left: A young VW Schwimmwagen driver proudly displays his just-awarded Iron Cross II Class. Recipients of the EK II traditionally wore the full medal and ribbon on the day of its award. Afterward, the ribbon alone was worn, sewn into the second buttonhole of the blouse. Late in the war the Soviets, in a wry commentary on the German's widespread awarding of the Iron Cross and their own overwhelming firepower, made propaganda broadcasts to the Germans which said, "Every second German soldier has the Iron Cross; every second Red Army man has a mortar!"

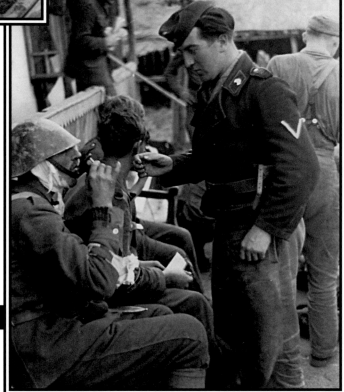

Right: A Gefreiter of Pz.Rgt. GD offers a sip from his canteen to a wounded ally at a Romanian dressing station on the Iasi Front, June 1944. Relations between the Division and its allies were generally very good on a personal level, but the Germans were all too aware that the Romanians were war-weary and likely to collapse entirely when the Soviets penetrated the frontier.

Facing page: In addition to the special dangers of combat, ordinary road hazards resulted in other repair tasks, such as repairing damaged drive axles. This Horch Kfz. 15 E.Pkw. blocks a narrow road and such breakdowns could delay other vehicles for some time. Mechanics were well-equipped with tools and equipment to perform many tasks, and each vehicle had its own basic tool kit. The officer at the right is Werkmeister Zimmermann (commander of the workshop detachment). He wears the field-gray Sturmgeschütz uniform and was awarded the War Merit Cross First Class, seen on the left breast of the tunic. The expanded folding tool kit in front of him was one of a number of efficiently packaged containers for tools and equipment that folded or collapsed for easy stowage in small places.

Right: The typical German armored vehicle required far more maintenance than a civilian car or truck and the majority of such vehicles were of pre-war design. This SdKfz. 251 Ausf. C has suffered a problem with the steering linkage to the front wheels. Operating in muddy, rough conditions placed extra stress on the entire front axle and the steering linkage, which could be bent or broken when pushed beyond its limits. Here the crewman lying down is moving the external linkage by hand while the men on the engine deck observe the internal portion of the steering link assembly for free movement and proper adjustment.

Below right: A Kompanieschneider (company tailor) makes up new uniform items in the field. German uniforms remained reasonably well-made throughout the war, though there was a noticeable loss of prewar smartness and sturdiness. Tailors frequently produced personal or unit-wide field clothing such as camouflage garments made from tent cloth, as well as winter garments. Soldiers were issued "Housewives" (sewing kits) to repair their own clothing wherever possible in a time-honored ritual known as the "Putz und Flickstunde," a type of squad-level sewing bee.

Below: The Kompanieschuster (company cobbler) at work putting a new heel on a pair of Knobelbecher (dice shakers), the soldier's name for the traditional marching boots. Specialists like this man had usually pursued the same trade in civilian life and were valued members of their companies.

anzergrenadier-Division Grossdeutschland was actually considerably larger and stronger than most full Panzer Divisions, and was one of only two Army formations to receive an organic battalion of Tigers (the other was Panzerlehr). Well before the Kursk offensive ("Unternehmen Zitadelle") in 1943, Grossdeutschland received its first Tiger tanks, which were incorporated as 13. Company in the Panzer Regiment. The company marking was an "S" (for "schwerer," heavy) as the unit symbol with platoon and vehicle numbers as per the normal number system.

13. Company went into action for the first time in early March 1943, during the drive to retake Kharkov. At this time, the Tigers proved to be excellent weapons and 13. Company was credited with a considerable portion of the 300 Soviet tanks destroyed during the Kharkov offensive by GD.

The Kursk offensive, though ultimately a failure, provided an excellent opportunity to demonstrate the combat superiority of the Tiger, and GD's 13. Company was quite successful in destroying Russian armor, far beyond the limited strength of one heavy tank company. The Tiger had proved a very valuable weapon.

Following the failure of the Kursk offensive and the withdrawal from the area, GD was strengthened by the formation of a full battalion of Tiger Ausf. E tanks as III/Pz.Rgt. GD, consisting of 9., 10., and 11. Companies. 9. Company was formed from GD's old 13. Company, 10. was organized from 3./Pz.Abt. 501, and 11. Company was raised from crews from 3./Pz.Abt. 504. Each company had a complement of 14 Tigers, including two command tanks. In addition, three Tigers were assigned to battalion headquarters, for a total of 45 Tigers. Most of the crews were experienced veterans familiar with the Tiger.

The markings were somewhat unusual in that the companies were designated by letters rather than numbers. "A" denoted tanks of the 9. Company; "B," 10. Company; and "C," 11. Company. "S" denoted the battalion staff command tanks. The platoon and vehicle numbers were assigned according to the usual numbering system, platoon number in the middle followed by the vehicle number last. This system appears to have been used the whole time GD possessed a Tiger battalion.

In late July, 1943, III/Pz.Rgt. GD was commanded by Major Herbert Gomille (S01-S03). 9. Company (A01-A02, A11-A14, A21-A24, A31-A34) was commanded by Leutnant Folke. 10. Company (B01-B02, B11-B14, B21-B24, B31-B34) was commanded by Hauptmann von Villebois. 11.Company (C01-C02, C11-C14, C21-C24, C31-C34) was commanded by Oberleutnant Bayer.

The battalion first went into action in August 1943, during the Soviet offensive after Kursk. The over stretched German forces were driven back from Kharkov toward the Dneiper River. The initiative on the Eastern Front had passed to the Red Army and the majority of German battles would be defensive, though there were always opportunities for decisive counter strikes. III/Pz.Rgt. GD took part in most of these actions and lost a number of Tigers. Nonetheless, the unit was responsible for halting several Soviet attacks and knocking out dozens of enemy tanks and guns. This was the auspicious beginning of exemplary service of the Tigers of Grossdeutschland, which would last until March 1945, when the last vehicles were lost in the Königsberg area during the fighting in East Prussia. The last two Tigers were destroyed on March 20, only weeks before the end of the war in Europe.

III/Pz.Rgt. GD originally was equipped with early production Tigers having the rubber tired roadwheels and Feifel air cleaners for tropical service. In 1944, the unit began to receive Tigers with the new lower cast cupola, steel rimmed roadwheels, and Zimmerit antimagnetic cement coating. Many of these Tigers were adapted by their crews, extra armor protection in the form of attached extra track links being a favorite method. In November 1944, GD was designated as a Panzerkorps. III/Pz.Rgt. GD was redesignated as s.Pz.Abt. Grossdeutschland, a fully reorganized Tiger battalion. Because of heavy losses, it was partially re-equipped. The companies were now referred to as 1. Company, 2. Company and 3. Company. 1. Company received the new Tiger II Ausf. B ("Königstiger," King Tiger), but 2. and 3. Companies retained the Tiger I Ausf. E. The vehicle marking system remained the same: "S" for battalion headquarters Tigers, "A," 1. Company, "B," 2. Company, "C," 3. Company.

As was the case with many other Tiger units, the Tigers and crews of GD proved the great value of the Tiger as an operational weapon in both offense and defense. Their courage and combat record stand as a testament to the morale of their unit and their value to Grossdeutschland as a whole.

Facing page: The Oberfeldwebel in the center wears a field blouse made from "splinter" pattern camouflage cloth, made up by a unit tailor earning some extra income. "Zeltbahns" (shelter quarters) and camouflage cloth were the most common sources of the material, and a skillfully made camouflage uniform could be almost identical in cut to the standard issue uniform. The man at left wears a green work shirt and the black trousers of the standard Panzer uniform, while the man at right wears the green denim work uniform.

PANZER TRANSPORTATION

Because of their limited mechanical reliability, tanks generally were not driven any great distances other than in combat. Travel to and from the theater of operations was normally done by train, and there were also several types of towed trailers for transporting these vehicles by road, usually towed by the Sd.Kfz. 9 18-ton tractor.

There were two types of trains which carried tanks and self-propelled artillery: the "Sonderpanzerzüge" for medium tanks and the "Sonderzüge" for heavy tanks. The Sonderpanzerzüge train normally consisted of 33 cars and carried up to 20 PzKpfw. III or IV tanks, and also carried medium SP artillery. Additionally, this train would carry support vehicles and crews, as well as maintenance equipment. The Sonderzüge were originally intended to transport the Tiger heavy tank, but were also used to carry the Panther medium tank, as its transport requirements were essentially the same as the Tiger's. The Sonderzüge consisted of between 30-35 cars and carried 4-6 Tigers or 6-8 Panthers. The cars carrying the tanks were interspersed with lighter cars to balance the train and minimize damage to the tracks. The Panther could be transported without preparation, but the Tiger was too wide for standard railway clearances and had to be converted with narrow tracks and removal of the side mudguards to meet the clearance limits. In open areas of Russia, clearances were not a concern and Tigers were often shipped within Russia in combat configuration, with the wide tracks and mudguards fitted. The tanks were blocked into position to prevent shifting.

Standard practice was to use a high platform to match the height of the cars carrying the tanks to make loading and unloading easier. If this was not available, then a ramp was usually built at the end of a track, and the tanks were driven up the ramp and over the connected flatcars until reaching the cars assigned. Entire trains were loaded this way. A special problem in Russia was that the Russian rail system was a wider gauge than the European standard, and in many areas trains had to be off loaded and reloaded onto Russian rolling stock until standard gauge tracks could be laid.

The materiel demands of a Panzer division were staggering, and dozens of trains were required just for carrying the basic equipment and personnel. Resupply was an additional task requiring many trains and careful logistical planning.

At the end of July 1944, GD was withdrawn from Romania after the battles around Targul Frumos and sent to Courland (East Prussia and Lithuania). At this time the Tiger battalion was at full strength — 45 Tiger Is. They were off loaded in Trakehnen, East Prussia, the heart of German horse country, from July 30 to August 1, and were the first unit of GD to enter action in the Gumbinnen-Wisballen-Vilkovishken sector of the East Prussian-Lithuanian front. After a successful first engagement which destroyed dozens of Russian tanks and tank destroyers, s.Pz.Abt. GD was withdrawn to take part in the counterattack mounted to recapture Vilkovishken and relieve Generaloberst Ferdinand Schörner's Heeresgruppe Nord (Army Group North), cut off by a major Soviet offensive.

Below: This overall view shows the whole procedure involved in unloading a Tiger Ausf. E and preparing it for action. In the foreground is the Tiger's special flatcar with the wooden beams fastened to the bed with bolts and metal straps and angles. Whenever possible, raised platforms were used so the Tigers could be driven directly off the flatcars without the need for special ramps. In some situations, a ramp was constructed at the end of the track, and the Tigers were driven up the ramp and then across several flatcars until they reached their assigned car. In the background, the Tiger I "A23" has had the left combat track installed, and the outer set of roadwheels has been attached on the right side. The combat track has been laid out in a straight run behind the Tiger, and the left hand transport track at the right illustrates how these narrow tracks were rolled up for storage. With practice, it took less than an hour to prepare a Tiger either for transport or action.

Moving the combat or transport tracks for the Tiger was an immense task, as each full track run weighed several tons. Typically the tracks were rolled up into a coil after the change out was complete and were then lifted onto the Tiger's special flatcar by crane. The track runs then had to be uncoiled and laid out on the car so the Tiger could be driven over them, in the case of the combat tracks as shown here. The narrow transport tracks could be left rolled up as normally they were on the Tiger when it was shipped by rail. Here the crane on a Famo 18-ton Sd.Kfz. 9/1 tractor pulls the combat tracks out onto the flatcar. The long wooden beams guided the driver of the Tiger when driving the vehicle onto the flatcar.

Above: Crewmen from Pz.Rgt. GD enjoy a meal of canned meat spread and "Kommissbrot" (Army bread) on reaching the East Prussian border, July 1944. They wear the green denim summer uniforms with standard insignia and shoulder straps. The man in the center wears a numbered tank battle badge.

Left: The transportation requirements for a Panzer formation the size of Grossdeutschland were enormous. Hundreds of individual trains were required to move and resupply just one unit. The standard train for transporting Tiger tanks was designated as an "S" train, and typically carried six Tiger tanks plus other vehicles, at least two Flak cars, and several freight cars. Each "S" train was normally loaded to provide initial support for the six Tigers carried on the train. Here, the crew of this late production Tiger Ausf. E has erected a shelter using their individual Zeltbahn shelter quarters. The Tiger has been prepared for shipping by fitting the narrow transport tacks and removing the side mudguards.

Below: "A22" is another later-production Tiger Ausf. E, featuring the steel rim "silent bloc" roadwheels. An advantage of this later suspension design was that the outer-most roadwheels of the original design had been deleted and so did not have to be removed for transport and reinstalled for combat. This made it easier and faster to prepare the later Tigers for shipping or action. This special 50-ton capacity flatcar was designed for use with the Tiger, and most Tigers were shipped on this type of car. At the right is a Panther Ausf. A of I/Pz.Rgt. 26.

Left: This view illustrates how the tracks were changed. The wide combat track has been laid out behind the tank. The next step was to unlink the narrow-track after positioning the tank so that it would roll off the narrow track directly onto the wide track. The small track-laying cable carried on the hull side was then hooked to the rear end of the combat track and pulled forward, up and over the roadwheels, using the drive sprocket as a capstan winch. The track was then connected, and then the process was repeated for the other side. Though the need to switch tracks was time-consuming, careful planning could eliminate lost time.

Below: Tigers of III/Pz.Rgt. GD were marked with "S" for the battalion command Tigers, and "A," "B," and "C" for the three companies. "A12" thus is the second tank of the first platoon of "A" company. The Tiger battalion was the third battalion in the regiment and its companies were numbered 9., 10., and 11. The outer panels of the front and rear mudguards folded up to match the width of the hull superstructure, the maximum width allowable for rail transport.

V I L K O V I S H K E N

By the beginning of August 1944, the Soviet offensive which had destroyed Heeresgruppe Mitte had begun to lose strength as it approached the Vistula River in Poland. In order to keep the German High Command off balance, the Soviets began to launch attacks on many other sectors, especially that of Heeresgruppe Nord along the Baltic Coast and the border of East Prussia. Grossdeutschland arrived at its concentration area south of Wisballen to bolster a front held by the remains of various divisions and detachments of "Volkssturm" (home guards) made up of old men, invalids, and young boys. Initial efforts on August 3 by III(Tiger)/Pz.Rgt. GD to keep the Soviets from cutting the highway from Vilkovishken just over the border in Lithuania to Gumbinnen in East Prussia were unsuccessful. As more GD units arrived, a Panzerkampfgruppe was sent in but was halted by fierce Soviet resistance, losing four Tigers. Grossdeutschland was then withdrawn from the line to regroup for a new assault on Vilkovishken.

In the foggy early morning of August 9, a battlegroup of tanks and Panzergrenadiers jumped off to a surprise attack with no preliminary barrage. As the sun began to dissipate the fog, the attackers were exposed to heavy artillery fire. The advance went forward in two columns, the Panzergrenadiers on the left moving due north on Vilkovishken while the Panzer and the Panzerfüsilier Regiments on the right advanced in broad outflanking maneuvers to attack the enemy in the rear. The Soviets had entrenched themselves in front of the town and had turned Vilkovishken itself into a small fortress. The Panzers and Füsiliers were soon halted just beyond the town by minefields and swampy ground while subjected to the merciless attention of Soviet artillery, Katyushas and Shturmovik ground attack aircraft.

The Grenadiers on the left, however, with I/Pz.Gr.Rgt. GD in the lead, fought their way through a maize field and into the town, where savage house-to-house fighting raged late into the night, until the town was finally cleared. In the meantime, II/Pz.Füs.Rgt. GD had crushed a Soviet attempt to break out to the east and relief attacks from the west above the Seimena River.

The counter-thrust which retook Vilkovishken offers a useful example of the many variations on tank/infantry cooperation practiced by the German Army. In this attack, the Panzers avoided a direct attack on the fortified village and instead conducted a wide flanking attack on the right while covered by the Panzerfüsiliers, who rode up in their new Sd.Kfz. 251s, dismounting to fight on foot. The Panzergrenadierregiment conducted a simultaneous frontal attack working with I/Pz.Gr.Rgt. GD's SPWs to battle their way into the village. When the tanks could advance no further, the Füsiliers proceeded on alone with the outflanking maneuver, smashing break-out and relief attacks in the process.

Facing page: Tiger B01 of Hauptmann von Villebois of 10./Pz.Rgt. GD rumbles down the road to Vilkovishken, August 10, 1944, past a collection point for captured Soviet ordnance. Extra track links are bolted on to the front of the hull and turret sides. This is a late-model Tiger with all-steel road wheels.

Left: While Tiger B12 of 10./s.Pz.Abt. GD rumbles behind them, two Panzergrenadiers anxiously scan the skies over Vilkovishken for signs of increasingly uncontested Soviet air activity. Several of the excellent Soviet 7.62cm anti-tank guns have been collected for removal to the rear for reboring to standard German 7.5cm anti-tank rounds. Due to its peculiarly high velocity, the detonation of the shell was audible before the report of the 7.62's firing was heard, thus giving the gun its German nickname of "Ratsch-Bumm" (crash-boom) An obsolete but still widely issued 14.2mm anti-tank rifle can be seen beneath the 7.62cm gun at the left.

Below: An Obergefreiter squad leader and two machine gunners on the way to mopping-up Soviet resistance in recaptured Vilkovishken. In the background is an amphibious Schwimmwagen jeep of Regimental HQ of Pz.Gr.Rgt. GD.

Below, inset: A Sd.Kfz. 2 half-track motorcycle (NSU Kettenkrad) of Pz.Gr.Rgt. GD headquarters drives past two abandoned Soviet 7.62cm anti-tank guns on the outskirts of Vilkovishken, Lithuania. The Sd.Kfz. 2 entered service in 1940 and by 1945 8,733 had been produced. The Kettenkrad was powered by a 1.5 liter Opel engine and could attain a top road speed of 70kmh. The Kettenkrad was a very useful and versatile vehicle, but suffered from a serious defect: the vehicle could easily tip over, with the driver having no quick means of escape.

Above: Generalleutnant Hasso von Manteuffel, the old "Zietenhusar," takes a short pause during the recapture of Vilkovishken on August 10, 1944. Around his neck is a pair of powerful Zeiss 10x50 binoculars.

Above: An MG 42 light machine gun team takes up its position under the signpost at the edge of Vilkovishken.

Left: A few minutes later the machine gunners have been replaced by a Raketenpanzerbüchse 43 (Panzerschreck or Ofenrohr – "Stovepipe") team. At very close range, this 8.8cm rocket launcher was able to destroy any Allied armor then in service. Unlike other infantrymen who had to drag their powerful new weapons around on foot, Grossdeutschland was largely mechanized by 1944 – only Panzerlehrdivision was fully mechanized, and then only for a few months prior to the Normandy Invasion.

Below: Generalleutnant von Manteuffel rides a Sd.Kfz. 251 Ausf. D late-model SPW into Vilkovishken. The division sign is painted in outline on the left of the rear door.

Left: "Manteuffel am Apparat!" (Manteuffel on the line!) The Division Commander checks in with his sub-ordinates on the outskirts of Vilkovishken. The Fernsprecher 33 came with a hand-set and casing of Bakelite. A hand generator and bell were provided with the telephone, but no buzzer. The 12 1/2 lb. phone's current was supplied by one cell.

Below: Two communications specialists test the circuits on a Model 33 field telephone. Panzer units, with their need for mobility, relied far more heavily on radio communications than hard telephone lines, and generally had twice as many radio units as telephones in their Panzernachrichtenabteilung and all divisional operational units.

Major Hugo Schimmel

Major Hugo Schimmel was yet another of the highly-qualified officers routinely assigned to GD throughout the war. Joining the Reichsheer's 20. I.R. in 1933, Schimmel spent the next several years with the Bavarian 10. I.D.(mot.). He was badly wounded outside Moscow during "Barbarossa" and received the Ritterkreuz in January 1942. After a lengthy convalescence, Major Schimmel was assigned to OKH in Berlin to verify recommendations for the Ritterkreuz. Despite repeated requests for frontline duty, Major Schimmel remained in OKH until August 1944 when he was assigned to take over Pz.Gr.Rgt. GD after its commander, Oberst Karl Lorenz, was given command of a Kampfgruppe for the Vilkovishken operation in Lithuania. Hastily joining the Division in East Prussia, Major Schimmel successfully led his new command through the August fighting before being wounded when his SPW was knocked out. After a short medical leave, Major (from October 1944, Oberstleutnant) Schimmel assumed command of Gren.Rgt. 19 "Infanterieregiment List" of the Bavarian 7. I.D. When he was wounded for the last time in March 1945 outside Danzig, Hugo Schimmel had been promoted to the rank of Oberst. After recovering yet again, Oberst Schimmel was ordered late in April 1945 to report to the army personnel office in Hitler's bunker in Berlin for new orders. Fortunately, his orders took him to Bavaria as part of the army's reserve of temporarily unattached officers. On the way to Bavaria, he was captured by American troops and was released from captivity in 1946.

General von Manteuffel confers with Major Hugo Schimmel, commander of Pz.Gren.Rgt. GD, outside Vilkovishken. In the background, a disabled Sd.Kfz. 251 Ausf. D awaits recovery. As was often the case in Grossdeutschland, Manteuffel's aide, Leutnant Schröder (right), wears field-gray cloth slip-ons on his shoulder boards.

Oberfeldwebel Hans Röger

Hans Röger, one of Grossdeutschland's best scouts and "Panzerknackers," was born in Lauingen an der Donau (Danube) on July 13, 1920. After completing his schooling and his six months compulsory RAD service, Röger volunteered for the duration as a Kriegsfreiwilliger on February 14, 1940 and was assigned to the Austrian 45. Infanterie Division. Gefreiter (from June 1, 1940) Röger took part in the entire French Campaign before being transferred in early 1941 to 11./I.R. 227 of the newly raised Austrian 100. Jägerdivision. As an Obergefreiter (from May 1, 1941) Hans Röger was to be engaged in ceaseless combat from the invasion of the Soviet Union until being wounded in February 1942. Although he was awarded the Iron Cross II Class on October 31, 1941, the Infantry Assault Badge on December 1, 1941, and the Medal for the Winter Campaign in Russia on March 15, 1942, Röger would not receive the Wound Badge in Black until September 27, 1943.

Fighting with few pauses from Kursk, where he was promoted to Unteroffizier on July 16, 1943, through the retreat to the Dnieper and into Romania and on into Kurland and East Prussia, Röger steadily built a reputation as one of battalion commander Major Hans-Dieter von Basse's most reliable NCOs. Near Jassy, Romania, in April 1944, Unteroffizier Röger successfully carried out a reconnaissance mission unique in the annals of his division and of the German Army itself. Wearing Romanian shepherd's clothing over their uniforms, Röger and a comrade drove a flock of sheep through the enemy lines. While Röger smiled and constantly mumbled "Good Morning" to the amused Frontovniks (Soviet frontline soldiers), he and his comrade surreptitiously glanced from side to side carefully noting enemy positions and reserves. After splitting up to return separately to the German lines, Röger was able to cap off his mission by blowing up a railway overpass used by Soviet tanks. Hans Röger's daring was rewarded on April 30, 1944 with the Iron Cross I Class.

Assigned to the spearhead of his battalion during von Manteuffel's counterattack at Vilkovishken, Lithuania in August 1944, Unteroffizier Röger's SPW came under fire from well concealed Soviet infantry, causing several casualties among the crew. Rallying the survivors, Röger dashed forward firing his MP 40 machine pistol and overran the Soviets, capturing a 15.2cm howitzer together with its prime mover. He then held his position against a determined enemy attempt to retake the gun. For his initiative and courage, Hans Röger was awarded the

Ritterkreuz on August 21, 1944. The award of the Nahkampfspange (Close Combat Clasp) in Bronze followed a week later, with his promotion to Feldwebel following on August 30, 1944.

The desperate fighting in East Prussia which followed the opening of the Soviets' grand offensive on January 12, 1945 saw Oberfeldwebel (from January 15, 1945) Röger begin his career as a legendary "tank buster." Having already destroyed three T-34s, Röger on February 2, 1945 was about to tackle a fourth when another Feldwebel snatched the Panzerfaust from his hands saying: "You've already got three. Give someone else a chance!" and then roared off on a BMW 750 motorcycle/sidecar to successfully attack a JS II tank. Röger nonetheless managed his fourth kill that same day. He also became an ace in knocking out emplaced enemy machine guns and mortars by using his Panzerfaust as a mortar to deliver plunging fire into buildings and bunkers.

The day before being admitted to the Honor Roll of the German Army on March 15, 1945, Oberfeldwebel Röger was seriously wounded in the right foot and evacuated from East Prussia to the base hospital at Bad Elster in Saxony where he received the Wound Badge in Silver on April 18, 1945. Early in May 1945, Hans Röger fled the advancing Red Army and reached the US lines at Hof, Bavaria where he remained a prisoner of war until his release on July 12, 1945.

Left: Newly-decorated Ritterkreuzträger Unteroffizier Röger accompanies various high-ranking officers of the Division to a reception following the award ceremony. In the front row from the left are Oberst Heinz Wittchow von Brese-Winiary, commander of Pz.Füs.Rgt. GD, Oberst Karl Lorenz (wearing the Demyansk Shield on his left sleeve), Unteroffizier Röger and Major Hans-Dieter von Basse. In the second row are Oberst Willi Langkeit, commander of Pz.Rgt. GD (partially obscured), longtime adjutant of Pz.Füs.Rgt. GD Hauptmann Dr. Bernhard Boll and Hauptmann H.S. Graf Rothkirch und Trach, commander of I (Panther)/Pz.Rgt. 26. At the right rear are Hauptmann Fritz Meissner, Technical Officer of Pz.Füs.Rgt. GD and der Spiess of Röger's company, Hauptfeldwebel Thilo John.

D O B L E N · M I T A U · M E M E L

After the recapture of Vilkovishken, Grossdeutschland proceeded to march north towards Stauliai (Schaulen) in Lithuania on August 12, 1944. Generaloberst Ferdinand Schörner's Heeresgruppe Nord (Army Group North) was threatened by having its direct land link with East Prussia cut off and this would have consequences equally as disastrous as the destruction of Heeresgruppe Mitte (Army Group Center) the previous month. Grossdeutschland formed part of the second wave of the counterattack which began on August 18. This attack was not as immediately successful as the fighting at Vilkovishken. The initial objective, Kursenai, resisted GD's first attempts to take it and the Division was forced to engage in a night attack — a Soviet specialty which the Germans never mastered to the same degree — which was a surprising success. Although the attack continued forward, it resulted in an untenable salient, which forced GD to withdraw to another sector.

GD now redeployed to reanimate the attack towards Tukkums and Mitau and eventually Riga, the Latvian capital, which other Panzer divisions had already begun and had stalled some 22 miles from Heeresgruppe Nord's outposts. Graf Strachwitz's Panzerkampfgruppe of GD's tracked units attacked on August 22 and penetrated the Soviet encirclement, reaching Tukkums and continuing its advance towards Riga. GD now began to run into much heavier opposition and casualties grew so high, with some platoons being commanded by corporals, that after reaching Doblen on the Latvian-Lithuanian border on August 25, OKH was forced to order an end to any further attempts to reestablish a land link with Schörner's army group.

For the next five weeks, GD dug in and held the line which had been reached around Doblen. During this time, on September 1, Generalleutnant von Manteuffel handed over command of the Division to Oberst Karl Lorenz. On October 3, a new Panzerkampfgruppe was formed within GD and pulled back west of Stauliai (Schaulen). The next day, the entire Division passed into OKH Reserve. On October 5, the Soviets launched a major offensive westward in the direction of Memel. Sweeping westwards across the Venta River, the Soviets easily brushed aside GD's hastily mounted counter thrusts. So great was the Soviet's numerical advantage that they did not bother to deploy properly but rather rushed on in a great mass of armor and tank-riding submachine gunners. Ably supported by Generalmajor Dr. Karl Mauss's Thuringian 7. Pz.Div., GD's armor and Panzerjägers accounted for large numbers of Soviet tanks but by October 7, Luoke, west of Stauliai, was threatened and OKH ordered GD to hold the town at all costs. The Soviets met this challenge by simply flooding around Luoke. GD had no option but to withdraw farther west toward Gaduvannas. To

avoid a costly frontal engagement with Grossdeutschland, the Soviet forces altered the direction of their attack towards Memel on the coast. Memel was vital to German hopes of maintaining a coherent line of defense for East Prussia and GD was now ordered to fight its way into the besieged city and bolster its defenses. By October 10, GD had reached Memel, whose garrison, in addition to GD, consisted of 7. Pz.Div. and G.R. 220 of the Lower Saxon 58. Infanteriedivision. By the end of October 14, when the Soviet attack on Memel began, GD had accounted for 36 of the 66 Soviet tanks knocked out. GD remained in Memel until November 28, 1944, when the Soviet threat to East Prussia had assumed so ominous a character that OKH could no longer leave two elite armored divisions tied down in positional warfare in a besieged city at the fringe of the main front. Accordingly, GD and 7. Pz.Div. were evacuated by sea to Königsberg, East Prussia. Once in East Prussia, Grossdeutschland settled down to complete its transformation into a full Panzerkorps, together with Pz.Gr.Div. "Brandenburg," a change which had been ordered on November 1, 1944.

The planned Panzerkorps, however, never served in combat. After the Korps-level HQ units had been set up, and "Brandenburg" transferred to East Prussia, the Panzerkorps HQ and the "Brandenburg" Division were hurriedly transferred to protect the vital Silesian industrial basin from the massive Soviet attack which erupted on January 12, 1945 from bridgeheads on the Vistula River. Thus, GD was left to fight on alone in East Prussia. Unable to stem the advance of vastly larger Soviet forces, GD was forced back to the coast near Königsberg, suffering frightful casualties in the process. The Division lost 17,000 men (killed, wounded, and missing) in just the month of March 1945. Much of the Division's remaining complement was evacuated from Samland by ferry to Denmark, arriving in Copenhagen in April 1945. From there, most of the Division marched south into Schleswig-Holstein in northern Germany, where they eventually surrendered to British forces. The units trapped in East Prussia were overrun by Soviet troops, entering a captivity from which few would emerge many years later.

This page and facing page: Pz.Füs.Rgt. GD commander Oberst Horst Niemack (left foreground), Generalleutnant Hasso Freiherr von Manteuffel (center foreground) and Oberst Willi Langkeit (right foreground) confer during the advance into Lithuania to relieve Generaloberst Ferdinand Schörner's army group in Courland, mid-August 1944. Just behind Oberst Niemack is his regimental adjutant, Hauptmann Dr. Bernhard Boll. To the rear of the staff officers the 7.5cm "Stummel" ("Stump") of one of the Panzerfüsiliers' "Kanonenwagen" SPWs can be seen hidden in the foliage.

Warmly clad against the early morning chill of late August in Lithuania, Hauptmann Otto Friedrich Emminghaus (center, in greatcoat) confers with Hauptmann Gerlach (in motorcyclist's coat), Batteriechef of 6./HeFlakAbt. GD, prior to an advance by II/Pz.Füs.Rgt. GD. One of I(SPW)/Pz.Füs.Rgt. GD's Sd.Kfz.251/9 "Kanonenwagens" has moved up for close support of Emminghaus's truck-mounted II Battalion. While his orderly officer Leutnant Klaus Noak (back to camera) takes an animated part in the conversation, Emminghaus's longtime dispatch runner Obergefreiter Otto Häntzschel, stands by for orders. Very unusual for the Eastern Front, Häntzschel is armed with a 9mm Beretta MP739(i) machine pistol.

Below: Hauptmann Emminghaus hastily scribbles orders using the back of one of his füsiliers as a writing table while men of I(SPW)Btl. and a StuG.III stand by.

Sd.Kfz.251/7s of I(SPW)/Pz.FAs.Rgt. GD gather prior to advancing towards Stauliai (Schaulen), Lithuania, late August 1944. Their presence indicates that both unfordable watercourses and anti-tank ditches are to be reckoned with. Both the Divisional Pz.Stu.Pi.Btl. and the Regiment's own Pz.Füs.Pi.Kp. had such vehicles at their disposal for just such purposes.

Left: Obergefreiter Hans Sachs of 5./Pz.Füs.Rgt. GD is congratulated by his former company commander Hauptmann "Ottfried" Emminghaus on his receiving the Ritterkreuz on September 10, 1944 — an event set in motion by Emminghaus when he recommended Sachs for the award. Named after the famous "Meistersinger of Nürnberg" in Wagner's opera of the same name, Hans Sachs took some good-natured teasing from his comrades. "Ottfried" Emminghaus recalls having also had a Richard Wagner and a Martin Luther in 5. Kompanie.

B I B L I O G R A P H Y

GROSSDEUTSCHLAND DIVISION UNIT HISTORIES

Anonymous, "Vom Wachregiment Berlin," In Deutsches Soldaten Jahrbuch, 1966, Schild-Verlag, München-Lochhausen, 1966.

Durian, Wolf, Regiment Grossdeutschland Greift An, serialized in "Die Woche," Nos. 5-9, 29 January - 26 February 1941, Scherl Verlag, Berlin, 1941.

Fillies, Oberleutnant Fritz, Grossdeutsche Grenadiere im Kampf, Zeitgeschichte Verlag, Berlin, 1941.

Lucas, James, Germany's Elite Panzer Force: Grossdeutschland, MacDonald and Jane's, London, 1978.

Quarrie, Bruce, Panzer-Grenadier Division "Grossdeutschland," Vanguard No. 2, Osprey, London, 1977.

Scheibert, Horst, Panzer Grenadier Division Grossdeutschland, Squadron/Signal Publications, Carrollton, 1987.

Spaeter, Helmuth, Die Geschichte des Panzerkorps Grossdeutschland, 3 Volumes, Selbstverlag Hilfswerk Ehemalige Soldaten für Kriegsopfer und Hinterbliebene e.V., Duisburg, Ruhrort, 1958.

Spaeter, Helmuth, Panzerkorps Grossdeutschland Bildokumentation, Podzun-Pallas Verlag, Friedberg, 1984.

Spaeter, Helmuth, Die Einsätze der Panzergrenadier-Division "Grossdeutschland," Podzun-Pallas Verlag, Friedberg, 1986.

Spaeter, Helmuth, Panzerkorps Grossdeutschland, Berichte und Bilder über das Erleben, Einsätze, die Männer und Kampfraüme, Podzun-Pallas Verlag, Friedberg, 1988.

UNPUBLISHED GROSSDEUTSCHLAND DOCUMENTS

Büttner, Hauptfeldwebel a.D. Hans, Autobiography

Burchardi, Hauptmann a.D. Joachim, Autobiography and history of Pz.A.R.GD

Diddens, Hauptmann d.R. a.D. Diddo S., Autobiography and documents concerning Sturmgeschützbrigade Grossdeutschland

Dürre, Obergefreiter a.D. Gerhard, Autobiography

Frantz, Oberst (BW) d.R. a.D. Peter, Autobiography

Gerbener, Oberstleutnant (BW) a.D. Heinrich, Autobiography, documents Haarhaus, Oberleutnant a.D. Ernst-Günther, Autobiography

Jung, Oberstleutnant (BW) a.D. Hans-Joachim, Geschichte des Panzerregiments "Grossdeutschland"

Konopka, Major d.R. a.D. Gerhard, Autobiography and account of the tank destruction course at Akhtyrka, April 1943.

Rahn, Oberfeldwebel a.D. Eberhard, Autobiography

Richter, Oberleutnant a.D. Hans-Karl, Autobiography

Roger, Hauptmann (BW) a.D. Hans, Autobiography and account of "tank busting" in East Prussia, Nov. 1944

Schimmel, Oberst a.D. Hugo, Autobiography

Schwarz, Oberleutnant a.D. Kurt, Autobiography

Spaeter, Major i.G. a.D. Helmuth, Autobiography

Weiss, Hauptfeldwebel (BW) a.D. Anton, Autobiography

GENERAL

Angolia, LTC. John R., For Führer and Fatherland, Military Awards of the Third Reich, R. James Bender Publishing, San Jose, 1976.

Angolia, John R. And Adolf Schlicht, Uniforms and Traditions of the German Army, 1933-1945, 3 Volumes, Bender Publishing, San Jose, 1984-1987.

Anonymous, Das Reichsheer und Seine Tradition, Haus Neuerburg, 1933.

Author's Collective, Wörterbuch zur Deutschen Militärgeschichte, 2 Volumes, Militärverlag der Deutschen Demokratischen Republik, Berlin, 1987.

Benary, Oberstleutnant, a.D. Albert, Unsere Reichswehr, Verlag Neufeld und Henius, Berlin 1932.

Bergschicker, Heinz, Der zweite Weltkrieg, Eine Chronik in Bildern, Deutscher Militärverlag, Berlin, 1963.

Brownlow, Donald, Panzer Baron: The Military Exploits of General Hasso von Manteuffel, Christopher Publishing House, North Quincy, 1975.

Carell, Paul, Hitler Moves East, 1941-1943, Little Brown, Boston,1964.

Carell, Paul, Scorched Earth, Harrap, London, 1970

Cron, Hermann, Geschichte des Deutschen Heeres im Weltkrieg 1914- 1918, Reprint of 1937 Edition, Biblio-Verlag, Osnabruck,1990.

Culver, Bruce, Panzer Colors, 3 Volumes, Squadron/Signal Press, Carrollton, 1976-1983.

Die Geschichte des deutschen Unteroffiziers, Published by the Reichstreuebund, Ehemalige Berufssoldaten, Berlin, 1939.

Doyle, Hilary, Peter Chamberlain and Thomas Jentz, Encyclopedia of German Tanks of World War Two, Arco Publishing, Inc., New York, 1978.

Erickson, John, The Road to Stalingrad, Harper and Row, New York,1975.

Forster, G. and N. Paulus, Abriss der Geschichte der Panzerwaffe, Militärverlag der Deutschen Demokratischen Republik, Berlin, 1977.

Gander, Terry and Peter Chamberlain, Weapons of the Third Reich, Doubleday and Company, Inc., Garden City, New York, 1979.

Gerlach, Major i.G., "Artillerie im Gefecht," in Jahrbuch des Deutschen Heeres, 1938, Verlag von Breitkopf und Härtel, Leipzig, 1938.

Grosse, Generalmajor a.D. Dr. rer. pol. Walther, "Aus dem Werdegang des Deutschen Pioniers," in Deutsches Soldaten Jahrbuch, 1963, Schild-Verlag, München-Lochhausen, 1963.

Grossmann, Horst, Rschew, Eckpfeiler der Ostfront, Podzun Verlag, Bad Nauheim, 1961.

Grundzüge der deutschen Militärgeschichte, Two volumes, commissioned by Militärgesschichtliches Forschungsamt, Freiburg im Breisgau, Rombach Verlag, Freiburg, 1993.

Haupt, Werner, "Der Reichsarbeitsdienst und Sein Einsatz im Krieg 1939-1945," III Concluding Installment in Deutsches Soldatenjahrbuch 1987, Schild-Verlag, München-Lochhausen,1987.

Heeresdienstvorschrift (H.Dv.) 66, Richtlinien für Führung und Einsatz der Panzerdivision vom 3.12.40, Unveränderter Nachdruck (unaltered reprint), 1942, Oberkommando der Wehrmacht, Berlin, 1942.

H.Dv. 470/10, Ausbildungsvorschrift für die Panzertruppe Heft 10: Richtlinien für Führung und Kampf des Panzerregiments und der Panzerabteilung von 1945, Oberkommando der Wehrmacht, Berlin, 1945.

H.Dv. 298/39, Ausbildungsvorschrift für die Panzertruppe. Führung und Kampf der Panzergrenadiere Heft 1: Das Panzergrenadierbataillon (Gp.) vom 5.8.1944, Oberkommando der Wehrmacht, Berlin, 1944.

H.Dv. 300 (T.F.), Truppenführung vom 17.10.1933 mit Deckblatt vom 1.5.1938, Oberkommando des Heeres, Berlin, 1938.

Hermann, Gustav, "Das Königl. Preuss. Lehr-Infanterie- Bataillon zu Potsdam," in Deutsches Soldatenjahrbuch, 1980, Schild Verlag, München-Lochhausen, 1980.

Hohn, Hans, Feuerkraft der Aggressoren. Zur Entwicklung der Artillerie in den Landstreitkräften des deutschen Militarismus von 1935 bis 1960, Militärverlag der Deutschen Demokratischen Republik, Berlin, 1961.

Hoth, Hermann, Panzer Operationen, Kurt Vowinckel Verlag Heidelberg, 1956.

Hube, Major Hans, Der Infanterist, Handbuch fur Selbstunterricht und Ausbildung des jungen Soldaten der Infanterie, 3. Auflage, Verlag Offenes Wort, Berlin, 1932.

Jany, Generalmajor a.D. Curt, Geschichte der Königlich Preussischen Armee, 4 volumes, Revised and expanded edition published by Biblio-Verlag, Osnabruck, 1967.

Keilig, Wolf, Das Deutsche Heer 1939-1945, Three Volumes, Podzun Verlag, Bad Nauheim, no date.

Keubke, Klaus-Ulrich and Manfred Kunz, Uniformen der Nationalen Volksarmee der DDR, 1956-1986, Brandenburgisches Verlagshaus, Berlin, 1990.

Kling, Constantin, Geschichte der Bekleidung, Bewaffnung und Ausrüstung des Königlich Preussischen Heeres, Dritter Teil Die Leichte Infanterie oder Die Fusilier Bataillone 1787- 1809 und Die Jäger 1744-1809, Weimar, 1912; Facsimile reprint by LRT Verlag, Buchholz-Sprötze, 1992.

Kollatz, Karl, General Hasso von Manteuffel, Erich Pabel Verlag,Rastatt, 1964.

Kollatz, Karl, Generalmajor Horst Niemack, vom Reiter zum Panzergeneral—Der Letze Kommandeur der Panzerlehrdivision, Erich Pabel Verlag, Rastatt, 1964.

Kollatz, Karl, Peter Frantz, Das Porträt eines Sturmgeschütz- Kommandeurs, 2nd Edition, Erich Pabel Verlag, Rastatt, 1974.

Kunowski, Johannes von (Editor), Wir Soldaten, Eine Gemeinschaftsarbeit von Jungen und Alten Soldaten, Verlag für Volkstum, Wehr und Wirtschaft Hans Kurzeja, Berlin,1938.

Kurowski, Franz and Gottfried Tornau, Sturmartillerie, Fels in der Brandung, Maximillian Verlag, Herford, 1966.

Lagarde, Jean de, German Soldiers of World War Two, Histoire et Collections, Paris, 1994.

LeFevre, Eric, La Wehrmacht, Uniformes et Insignes de l'Armee de Terre Allemande (Heer), Editions Jacques Grancher, Paris, 1986.

Lewis, S.J., Forgotten Legions: German Infantry Policy, 1918-1941, Praeger, New York, 1985.

McLean, Donald B. (Editor), German Infantry Weapons, Normount Armament Company, Forest Grove, 1966.

McNair, Ronald, Les Panzers 1944, Volume I, les Divisions de Panzers du Heer, Editions Heimdal, Paris, 1991.

McNair, Ronald, Les Panzers 1944, Volume II, les Divisions de Panzers SS et les Bataillons Independants, Editions Heimdal, Paris 1992.

Manstein, Erich von, Lost Victories, Methuen, London, 1958.

Mehner, Kurt and Reinhard Teuber, Abkürzungen der Deutschen Wehrsprache von der Kaiserlichen Armee bis zur Bundeswehr, Militär-Verlag Klaus D. Patzwall, Norderstedt, 1994.

Mellenthin, Friedrich-Wilhelm von, Panzer Battles, University of Oklahoma Press, Norman, 1972.

Middeldorf, Eike, Taktik im Russlandfeldzug, Verlag von E.S. Mittler und Sohn, Berlin, 1956.

Milsom, John, German Military Transport of World War Two, Hippocrene, New York, 1975.

Model, Hansgeorg, Der Deutsche Generalstabsoffizier: Seine Auswahl und Ausbildung in Reichswehr, Wehrmacht und Bundeswehr, Bernard und Graefe Verlag für Wehrwesen, Frankfurt am Main, 1968.

Munzel, Brigadegeneral Oskar, Panzertaktik, Kurt Vowinckel Verlag, Heidelberg, 1959.

Oswald, Werner, Kraftfahrzeuge und Panzer der Reichswehr, Wehrmacht und Bundeswehr, 14. Auflage, Motorbuch Verlag,Stuttgart, 1992.

Pruitt, Michael H. And Robert J. Edwards, Field Uniforms of German Army Panzer Forces in World War Two, J.F. Fedorowicz Publishing Inc., Winnipeg, 1993.

Queckborner, Hauptmann Ludwig, Die Rekrutenausbildung, 2nd Expanded Edition, Verlag von E.S. Mittler und Sohn, Berlin, 1934.

Queckborner, Oberstleutnant Ludwig, Die Schützenkompanie, ein Handbuch für den Dienstunterricht, Verlag von E.S. Mittler und Sohn, Berlin, 1939.

Radke, Hauptmann Dr. Siegfried, "Panzeraufklärung," in Deutsches Soldatenjahrbuch, 1963, Schild-Verlag, München-Lochhausen,1963.

Reibert, Dr. jur., Oberfeldwebel Wilhelm, Der Dienstunterricht im Reichsheer, 5th Revised and Enlarged Edition, Verlag von E.S. Mittler und Sohn, Berlin, 1933.

Reibert, Dr. jur., Oberfeldwebel Wilhelm, Der Dienstunterricht im Heere, Ausgabe für den Kanonier der Beobachtungsabteilung, Verlag von E.S. Mittler und Sohn, Berlin, 1941.

Reibert, Dr. jur., Oberfeldwebel Wilhelm, Der Dienstunterricht im Heere, Ausgabe für den Nachrichtensoldat, Verlag von E.S. Mittler und Sohn, Berlin, 1938.

Reibert, Dr. jur., Oberfeldwebel Wilhelm, Der Dienstunterricht im Heere, Ausgabe für den Schützen der Schützenkompanien, Verlag von E.S. Mittler und Sohn, Berlin, 1943.

Reinecke, Adolf, Das Reichsheer, Biblio-Verlag, Osnabrück, 1986.

Rekers, Karl, Das Kriegsende in unserer Heimat, Speller Schriften, Band 5, Spelle, 1995.

Riemann, Horst, Deutsche Panzergrenadiere, Verlag von E. S. Mittler und Sohn, Herford und Bonn, 1990.

Ruhl, Oberleutnant a.D. Jul. And Anton Sassmann, Major a.D., Die Deutsche Reichswehr in ihrer neuesten Bekleidung, Bewaffnung und Ausrüstung, Verlag Moritz Ruhl, Leipzig,1930.

Scheibert, Brigadegeneral a.D. Horst, Die Träger des Deutschen Kreuzes in Gold, das Heer, Podzun Verlag, Friedberg, 1992.

Schweidnitz, Kurt Graf von, Die Sprache des deutschen Heeres, Biblio-Verlag, Osnabrück, 1989.

Seemen, Gerhard von, Die Ritterkreutzträger, Podzun-Pallas Verlag, Dorheim, 1976.

Senger und Etterlin, Dr. Ferdinand von, Die Panzergrenadiere, J.F. Lehmanns Verlag, München, 1961.

Stoves, Rolf, Die 1. Panzerdivision, Podzun Verlag, Bad Nauheim, 1962.

Tessin, Georg, Deutsche Verbände und Truppen 1919-1939, Biblio- Verlag, Osnabrück, 1974.

Tessin, Georg, Verbände und Truppen der deutschen Wehrmacht und der Waffen-SS 1939-1945, 14 Volumes, Biblio-Verlag, Osnabrück, 1966-1980.

Thomas, Franz and Günther Wegmann, Die Ritterkreuzträger der deutschen Wehrmacht 1939-1945, Teil 1: Sturmartillerie, Biblio-Verlag, Osnabrück, 1985.

Thümen von, Die Uniformen der Preussischen Garden 1704-1836, Verlag von George Gropius, Berlin, 1840; Facsimile reprint by LTR Verlag, Buchholz-Sprötze, 1994.

Toeche-Mittler, Oberleutnant Joachim, Feldartilleristen=ABC, Verlag von E.S. Mittler und Sohn, Berlin, 1933.

Tornau, Gottfried, "Sturmartillerie," in Deutsches Soldaten- jahrbuch, 1964, Schild-Verlag, München-Lochhausen, 1964.

U.S. War Department, TM 30-451, Handbook on German Military Forces, December 17, 1941, Washington, DC, 1941.

U.S. War Department, TME-30-451, Handbook on German Military Forces, 1 September 1943, Washington, DC, 1943.

U.S. War Department, TME-30-451, Handbook on German Military Forces, 1 March 1945, Washington, DC, 1945.

Wedel, Generalmajor a.D. Hasso von, Die Propagandatruppen der Deutschen Wehrmacht, Kurt Vowinckel Verlag, Neckargemünd, 1962.

Zabecki, David, Steel Wind, Colonel Georg Bruchmüller and the Birth of Modern Artillery, Praeger, Westport, 1994.

Ziemcke, Earl, Stalingrad to Berlin, Department of the Army Historical Series, Washington, DC, 1968.

Zobeltitz, H.C. von, with "Peter Purzelbaum," Das Deutsche Heer im bunten und im grauen Rock, Paul Franke Verlag, Berlin, 1935.

G L O S S A R Y

A.: .... Armee (Army)
A.: .... Artillerie (Artillery)
A.A.: .... Aufklärungsabteilung (Reconnaissance Battalion)
Abt.: .... Abteilung (Battalion-sized unit of artillery, tanks, etc.)
a.D.: .... ausser Dienst (Retired)
A.K.: .... Armeekorps (Army Corps)
AOK: .... Armeeoberkommando (Army Headquarters)
A.R.: .... Artillerieregiment (Artillery Regiment)
ARKO: .... Artilleriekommandeur (Artillery Commander at Divisional HQ)
Art.: .... Artillerie (Artillery)
A.u.E.: .... Ausbildung und Ersatz (Training and Replacement)

Brig.: .... Brigade (Brigade)
B-Stelle: .... Beobachtungsstelle (Observation Post)
B-Trupp: .... Beobachtungstrupp (Observation Troop)
Bttr.: .... Batterie (Battery)

D.: .... Division
Div.: .... Division

EK I: .... Eisernes Kreuz I Klasse (Iron Cross, 1st Class)
EK II: .... Eisernes Kreuz II Klasse (Iron Cross, 2nd Class)
E-Messer: .... Entfernungsmesser (Range Finder)

Feldgend.Tr.: .... Feldgendarmerietrupp (Military Police Detachment)
Fla.: .... Flugabwehr (Light Anti-Aircraft, up to 2 cm)
Flak: .... Flugabwehrkanone (Anti-aircraft guns 2 cm and upwards)
Fus.Rgt.: .... Füsilierregiment
Fu.: .... Funker (Radioman/signalman)
Fu.Ger.: .... Funkgerät (Radio Equipment)
Fw.: .... Feldwebel (Staff Sergeant)

GD: .... Grossdeutschland
Gef.: .... Gefreiter (Lance Corporal)
Gen.Kdo.: .... Generalkommando (Army Corps HQ)
Gep.: .... Gepanzert (Armored)
G.F.M.: .... Generalfeldmarschall (Field Marshall)
Gren.Rgt.: .... Grenadierregiment

Hauptfeld.: .... Hauptfeldwebel (Master Sergeant)
Hptm.: .... Hauptmann (Captain)
H.Dv.: .... Heeresdruckvorschrift (Army Manual)
Hgr. .... Heeresgruppe: (Army Group)
Hiwi: .... Hilfswilliger (Russian ex-POW or Civilian Auxilliary of the Wehrmacht)
Hptwm.: ..... Hauptwachtmeister (Artillery, Cavalry or Signals Master Sergeant)

I.D.: .... Infanteriedivision
i.G.: ... im Generalstabsdienst (An Officer serving as a Troop General Staff Officer)
I.R.: .... Infanterieregiment (Infantry Regiment)
I.Truppe: .... Instandsetzungstruppe (Repair Troop)
Ju.: .... Junkers (Aircraft Manufacturer)

K.: .... Kurz (Short)
Kan.: .... Kanonier (Gunner, Basic Rank in the Artillery)
Kar.: .... Karabiner (Carbine)
Kfz.: .... Kraftfahrzeug (Motor Vehicle)
Kp.: .... Kompanie (Company)
Krad: .... Kraftrad (Motorcycle)
Kradsch.Btl.: .... Kradschützen-Bataillon (Motorcycle Rifle Battalion)
KwK: .... Kampfwagenkanone (Tank Gun)

L: .... Lange (Length)
le.FH: .... leichte Feldhaubitze (Light Field Howitzer)
le.IG: .... leichtes Infanteriegeschütz (Light Infantry Gun)
le.MG: .... leichtes Maschinengewehr (Light Machine Gun)
Lkw: .... Lastkraftwagen (Truck)
Lt.: .... Leutnant (2nd Lieutenant)

m: .... Mittlere(r) (Medium)
M.: .... Modell (Model)
Maj.: .... Major
mGrW: .... Mittlere Granatwerfer (Medium Mortar)
(mot.): .... Motorisiert (Motorized, Wheeled Transport)

MP: .... Maschinenpistole (Machine Pistol)
Nachr.Abt.: .... Nachrichtenabteilung (Signal Battalion)
NO: .... Nachrichtenoffizier (Signals Officer)
N.S.F.O.: .... Nationalsozialistischer Fuhrungsoffizier
(National Socialist Leadership Officer,
a type of Political Commissar)

O.: .... Oberst (Colonel)
OA: .... Offizieranwärter (Officer Candidate)
Oberlt.: .... Oberleutnant (1st Lieutenant)
Oberstlt.: .... Oberstleutnant (Lieutenant Colonel)
Obfu.: .... Oberfunker (Signals Private 1st Class)
Ofw.: .... Oberfeldwebel (Sergeant First Class)
Ogefr.: .... Obergefreiter (Corporal)
Ogren.: .... Obergrenadier (Infantry Private First Class from September 1942)
OKH: .... Oberkommando des Heeres (High Command of the Army)
OKW: .... Oberkommando der Wehrmacht (High Command of the Armed Forces)

Pi.Btl.: .... Pionierbataillon (Engineer Battalion)
Pio.: .... Pionier (Engineer Private)
P.K.: .... Propagandakompanie (Propaganda Company)
Pkw.: .... Personenkraftwagen (Passenger Car)
Pz.A.A.: .... Panzeraufklärungsabteilung (Armored Reconnaissance Battalion)
Pz.Abt.: .... Panzerabteilung (Tank Battalion)
Pz.AOK: .... Panzerarmeeoberkommando (Panzer Army HQ)
Pz.A.R.: .... Panzerartillerieregiment (Armored Artillery Regiment)
Pz.Fus.Rgt.: .... Panzerfüsilierregiment
Pz.Gr.Rgt.: .... Panzergrenadierregiment
Pz.Jag.: .... Panzerjäger (Anti-tank)
Pz.Korps: .... Panzerkorps (Tank Corps)
Pz.Kpfw.: .... Panzerkampfwagen (Armored Fighting Vehicle/Tank)
Pz.Nachr.Abt.: ..... Panzernachrichtenabteilung (Armored Signal Battalion)
Pz.Pi.Btl.: .... Panzerpionierbataillon (Armored Engineer Battalion)
Pz.Schtz.: .... Panzerschütze (Tanker, Basic Rank)

R.I.(II): .... Richtkreisunteroffizer (Aiming Circle NCO I or II)
RAD: .... Reichsarbeitsdienst (National Labor Service)
Rgt.: .... Regiment
Rttm.: .... Rittmeister (Captain of Cavalry)

sFH: .... schwere Feldhaubitze (Heavy Field Howitzer)
S.GrW.: .... schwere Granatwerfer (Heavy Mortar)
s.MG: .... schwere Maschinengewehr (Heavy Machine Gun)
Sani: .... Sanitäter (Medic)
Schtz.: .... Schütze (Infantry Private, Pre-September 1942)
Schwdr.: .... Schwadron (Squadron, Company-sized unit of
Cavalry, or Reconnaissance Troops)
Sd.Kfz.: .... Sonderkraftfahrzeug (Special Vehicle)
SFL: .... Selbstfahrlafette (Self-Propelled Carriage)
S.Gefr.: .... Stabsgefreiter (Senior Corporal)
SPW: .... Schützenpanzerwagen (Armored Personnel Carrier)
StuG.: .... Sturmgeschütz (Assault Gun)
StuG.Abt.: .... Sturmgeschützabteilung (Assault Gun Battalion)
StuG.Brig.: .... Sturmgeschützbrigade (Assault Gun Brigade)
StuH.: .... Sturmhaubitze (Assault Howitzer)
StuK.: .... Sturmkanone (Assault Cannon-Flat Trajectory)
Stuka: .... Sturzkampfflugzeug (Dive-Bombing Aircraft)

Uffz.: .... Unteroffizier (Sergeant)

VB: .... Vorgeschobener Beobachter (Forward Observer of the Artillery)

Wachbtl.: .... Wachbataillon (Guard Battalion)
Wach.Rgt.: .... Wachregiment (Guard Regiment)
Wachtm.: .... Wachtmeister (Staff Sergeant of Artillery, Cavalry and Signals)
WH: .... Wehrmacht-Heer (Armed Forces-Army-on License Plates)
W.Kr.: .... Wehrkreis (Military District)
Wkmstr.: .... Werkmeister (Head of a Maintenance or Repair Unit)
W.u.G.: .... Waffen und Gerät (Weapons and Equipment)

Z.F.: .... Zielfernrohr (Telescopic Sight)
Zg.: .... Zug (Platoon)
ZgKw.: .... Zugkraftwagen (Prime Mover)

BA: Bundesarchiv, Koblenz
ECPA: Etablissement Cinématographique er Photographique des Armées, Paris
Top= T, Bottom= B, Center= C

Cover: ECPA
Front Endsheet: ECPA
Back Endsheet: BA
Title Page: BA
Facing Forward Page: BA
Facing Acknowledgements Page: ECPA
Facing Introduction Page: BA
P.11 T & B: BA, P.12 T & B: BA, P.13 T: ECPA, B: BA, P.14 T&B: BA, P.18 ECPA
Title Page 1942: BA
P.19 T&B: BA, P.20 All 3 BA, P.21 All 3 BA, P.22 BA, P.23 All 4 BA, P.24 BA, P.25 T&B: BA, P.26 T&B: BA, P.27 All 3 BA, P.28 BA, P.29 T&B: BA, P.30 T&B: BA, P.31 T&B: BA, P.32 BA, P.33 T&B: BA, P.34 BA, P.35 All 4 BA, P.37 through P.41 Burchardi, P.42 ECPA, P.43 All 4 ECPA, P.44 T&B: ECPA, P.45 T&B: ECPA, P.47 ECPA, P.48 ECPA, P.49 T&B: ECPA, P.50 T&B: ECPA, P.51 ECPA, P.52 T&B: ECPA, P.53 ECPA, P.54 ECPA, P.55 T&B: ECPA, P.56 All 3 ECPA, P.57 T&B: ECPA, P.58 T&B: ECPA, P.59 ECPA, P.60 & 61 ECPA, P.62 ECPA, P.63 ECPA, P.64 & 65 ECPA, P.66 T&B: ECPA, P.67 T&B: ECPA, P.68 ECPA, P.69 ECPA, P.70 T&B: ECPA, P.71 T&B: ECPA, P.72 & 73 ECPA, P.74 All 3 ECPA, P.75 T&B: ECPA, P.76 All 3 ECPA, P.77 T&B: ECPA, P.78 T&B: ECPA, P.79 T&B: ECPA, P.80 T&B: ECPA, P.81 T&B: ECPA, P.82 T&B: ECPA, P.83 ECPA, P.84 T&B: ECPA, P.85 T&B: BA, P.86 BA, P.87 BA, P.88 T&B: ECPA, P.89 ECPA, P.90 ECPA, P.91 T&B: ECPA, P.92 T&B: ECPA, P.93 T&B: ECPA, P.95 BA, P.96 T&B: BA, P.97 T&B: BA, P.98 BA, P.99 BA, P.100 BA, P.101 BA, P.102 T&B: BA, P.103 BA, P.104 T: BA, B: ECPA, P.105 BA
Title Page 1943: BA
P.109 ECPA, P.110 ECPA, P.111 ECPA, P.112 T&B: ECPA, P.113 T&B: ECPA, P.114 T&B: ECPA, P.115 T&B: ECPA, P.116 T&B: ECPA, P.117 T&B: BA, P.118 T&B: BA, P.119 BA, P.120 T&B: ECPA, P.121 T&B: ECPA, P.122 ECPA, P.123 All 3 ECPA, P.124 T&B ECPA, P.125 All 3 ECPA, P.126 T: BA, B: ECPA, P.127 ECPA, P.128 T&B: ECPA, P.129 T&B: ECPA, P.130 T&B: BA, P.131 T&B: BA, P.132 ?, P.133 T: ECPA, C 2&B BA, P.134 BA, P.135 BA, P.136 T&B: BA, P.137 All 4 BA, P.138 All 3 BA, P.139 T&B: BA, P.140 T&B: BA, P.141 T&B: BA, P.142 All 3 BA, P.143 All 4 BA, P.144 All 3 BA, P.145 T&B: BA, P.146 BA, P.147 T&B: BA, P.148 BA, P.149 T&B: BA, P.150 All 3 BA, P.151 T&B: BA, P.152 BA, P.153 All 3 BA, P.154&155 BA, P.156 ECPA, P.157 T&B: ECPA, P.158 T&B: BA, P.158 T&B: BA, P.159 All 3 BA, P.160 T: BA, B: Thomas, P.161 BA, P.162 T&B: BA, P.163 T&B: ECPA
Title Page 1944:BA
P.166 BA, P.167 BA, P.168 T&B: BA, P.169 T&B: BA, P.170 BA, P.171 T&B: BA, P.172 ECPA, P.173 BA, P.174 BA, P.175 T&B: BA, P.177 BA, P.178 All 3 BA, P.179 T&B: BA, P.181 All 3 BA, P.182 T&B: BA, P.183 T&B: BA, P.184 T&B: BA, P.185 All 3 BA, P.186 T: BA, B: Gerbener, P.187 T&B: BA, P.188 T&B: BA, P.189 T&B: BA, P.190 T&B: BA, P.191 All 3 BA, P.192 T&B: BA, P.193 T&B: BA, P.194 BA, P.195 T&B: BA, P.196 All 3 BA, P.197 T&B: BA, P.198 T: Schwarz, B: BA, P.199 BA, P.200 Gerbener, P.201 Diddens, P.202 T&B: BA, P.203 Gerbener, P.204 T&B: BA, P.205 BA, P.206 Richter, P.207 BA, P.208 Richter, C: BA, P.209 BA, P.210 BA, P.211 T&B: BA, P.212 T&B: BA, P.213 T&B: BA, P.214 BA, P.215 All 3 BA, P.217 BA, P.218 BA, P.219 BA, P.220 All 3 BA, P.221 T&B: BA, P.222 BA, P.223 T&B: BA, P.224 All 4 BA, P.225 T&B: BA, P.226 T&B: BA, P.227 through 229 Röger, P.230 & 231 Emminghaus

Special Thanks

The authors would like to give special thanks to the following individuals for their support and encouragement. The staff at RZM Imports, Inc.: Todd Rose, Jeff Conboy, Leslie and Joseph Tavolacci, Masami Minagawa, Garrick Yanosky, and Kaare Numme. Thanks also to Susanne Meusel and Fred and Paul Berger.

C O L O P H O N

The text for "God, Honor, Fatherland" was written using various word processors including MacWrite Pro and Microsoft Word. The text was copy-edited entirely in Microsoft Word. Certain sections were compiled remotely using AOL text and transmitted via America Online.

This book was laid out and designed using QuarkXPress 3.33 on a Power Macintosh 8100/100. All the photographs were scanned using Silverscanner software and edited using Adobe Photoshop 3.0. The GD cipher on the title page was created with Freehand 5.0. The entire book was stored on a Joule removable hard drive for transport to the printing facility. Back-up and archival copies were written to CD ROM. Final film output was done at 1270 dpi. The book is printed on 80 lb. Luna gloss.

The body copy is set in Futura Book, Futura Demi and Futura Bold, with the cover type set in Times New Roman Extra Bold. The history of Futura pre-dates the Second World War and it was commonly seen in German magazines in the thirties and forties, including such wartime publications as "Der Adler" and "Die Wehrmacht."